The Guide to

◆ *FLORIDA WILDFLOWERS* ◆

The Guide to

◆ *FLORIDA WILDFLOWERS* ◆

Walter Kingsley Taylor

TAYLOR TRADE PUBLISHING

Lanham • New York • Oxford

Designed by Deborah Jackson-Jones

Published by Taylor Trade Publishing
An imprint of The Rowman & Littlefield Publishing Group, Inc.
4501 Forbes Boulevard, Suite 200
Lanham, Maryland 20706

Distributed by National Book Network

Library of Congress Cataloging-in-Publication Data

Taylor, Walter Kingsley, 1939–
    The guide to Florida wildflowers / Walter Kingsley Taylor
        p.   cm.
    Includes bibliographical references and index.
    ISBN 0-87833-747-4 : $24.95

    1. Wild flowers—Florida—Identification.   2. Wild flowers—
Florida—Pictorial works.   I. Title.
QK154.T39   1992
582.13′09759—dc20   91-34253
                                                                         CIP

Printed in the United States of America

*To the memory of **Mary Evans Francis Baker** (b. 29 November 1876 Plainfield, Connecticut; d. 23 June 1941 Winter Park, Florida) who with her little book,* Florida Wild Flowers, *opened up a new world to thousands. I also dedicate this book to the honor of **Sam Hopkins** who took a little of his time to show me a few wildflowers.*

◆ C O N T E N T S ◆

ACKNOWLEDGMENTS

There are some special individuals who need to be recognized. Some have helped me more than others. I take pleasure in listing the names of W. E. Adamson, Bruce H. Anderson, Alice Bard, Dr. Budd Berringer, Jim Burney, Dr. J. F. Charba, E. J. Chicardi, Jamie Guseman, Ric Huapalo, Sam Hopkins, Mary Keim, Dr. Robert J. Laird, John Lesman, David Leonard, Steve Myers, Jim Poppleton, Z. A. Prusak, Edward Reed, Kate Reich, Steve Riefler, Anne M. Rodriquez, Allen Shuey, Randy Snyder, Steve Stewart, June Stillman, Eric Stolen, Dr. I. Jack Stout, John Twactman, Tom Ward, and Henry O. Whittier.

Ed Chicardi skillfully prepared the line drawings. Dr. Dan F. Austin, Jim Poppleton, Allen Shuey, and Dr. Richard P. Wunderlin identified or confirmed the identity of some species that were uncertain to me. To them, I am most grateful.

The expert knowledge in the realm of photography was graciously and abundantly shared with me by Richard Spencer and Marjorie Greathouse. Richard has been at my side from the onset of this project. This guide would have never been completed had it not been for Richard and Marjorie.

Holly McGuire, Mary Kelly, and the entire staff at Taylor Publishing Company have been most helpful and encouraging to me throughout the entire publishing process. It is a tremendous pleasure for me to have Taylor Publishing Company on my book.

Most of the photographs are mine. Nonetheless, the following individuals, to whom I am very appreciative, allowed me to use their photographs:

> MARY KEIM—dwarf sundew *(Drosera brevifolia),* floating hearts *(Nymphoides aquatica)*
>
> JACK STOUT—*Clematis reticulata*

Lastly, and by no means the least, I express my sincere thanks and love to my wife, Karin, for putting up with my messes—pressed plants strewn throughout the house, papers, books and boxes here, yon, and there, and the refrigerator with its abundance of plants following a field trip.

P R E F A C E

The Guide to Florida Wildflowers is intended to help those lacking formal training in the botanical sciences to identify many of the wildflowers found in Florida. The majority of species illustrated can be found throughout most areas of the state. A few less common types, such as the scrub lupine *(Lupinus aridorum)* and Florida bonamia *(Bonamia grandiflora)*, are included. Both of these are limited to a few scrub sites in central Florida. The weedy species form an important component of our flora. Many of these have been included as well as the more showy and attractive species of wildflowers. I have, however, excluded for the most part the woody plants, except for some trees, shrubs, and vines that are rather common and produce attractive flowers. In this category I include the lyonias or fetterbushes *(Lyonia)*, blueberries *(Vaccinium)*, greenbriers *(Smilax)*, Virginia willow *(Itea virginica)*, and pepper vine *(Ampelopsis arborea)*. The plants depicted in this guide represent the four growing seasons and 90 families of plants.

Writing a book of this scope is not for the sluggard. It has required countless hours, both in the field and laboratory, and many miles of travel. Despite the time, energy, and cost—and the pesky deerflies, mosquitoes, sandspurs, briers, and snakes—I have had tremendous fun working on this guide. Only once was there a close encounter with a diamondback rattler, and, that is a story in itself! If I can share with some person my joy of finding a new wildflower and the importance of learning some of these beauties growing in Florida, then all of my efforts have been worthwhile. Perhaps some of you might become interested enough to devote your efforts helping to protect some of the species that face extinction.

W.K.T.

◆ *INTRODUCTION* ◆

Wildflowers have captured the interests of people for generations. The broad spectrum of vivid colors, astonishing varieties, sizes and shapes, strange life habits, and medicinal, culinary, and agricultural uses are some of the reasons why so many people have been and continue to be attracted to wildflowers—to their identification, preservation, and propagation. Today, departments of transportation for many states, including Florida, are blanketing acres of highway rights-of-way with wildflowers to reduce the cost of mowing and at the same time to enhance our landscapes. And the interest in wildflower biology still increases: In 1982, former first lady Lady Bird Johnson founded the National Wildflower Research Center, headquartered in Austin, Texas. Support for other wildflower programs is growing—as it should—because these plants are a part of our national heritage.

The early explorers and colonists from Europe were no doubt impressed with the number and variety of wildflowers they found in America. Species often grew in large numbers, forming masses of yellows, purples, or whites. Our pioneer ancestors used wildflowers for making dyes, herbal teas, medicines (such as astringents, linaments, sedatives, laxatives), and wood preservatives. Many of the concoctions developed and used by the early herbalists have been proven effective by modern research methods used in medicines and chemistry. Today, herbalistic botany is a growing field of research.

Then, too, the colonists brought many species of plants, intentionally or accidentally, from the Old World to the New World. Many of these aliens are now well established "weeds" and have wide distributions throughout much of the United States. Often these plants have become more successful than the native species, even to the point of replacing them. Examples of wildflowers within and beyond the boundary of Florida that are native to Europe or Eurasia include the spiny-leaved sow thistle *(Sonchus asper),* common sow thistle *(S. oleraceus),* common dandelion *(Taraxacum officinale),* white sweet clover *(Melilotus alba),* curled dock *(Rumex crispus),* bitter dock *(R. obtusifolius),* and common plantain *(Plantago major).*

Besides Europe, other geographical regions have contributed to our wildflower flora: creeping oxeye *(Wedelia trilobata)* comes from the West Indies, rattle-box *(Crotalaria spectabilis)* from the Old World tropics, hawk's-beard *(Youngia japonica)* from Japan, hairy indigo *(Indigofera hirsuta)* from Africa, and from tropical America the milkweed *(Asclepias curassavica),* sicklepod *(Senna obtusifolia),* and Mexican clover *(Richardia brasiliensis).*

Florida has a dazzling, rich mixture of wildflowers that only a few other states can approach. Three geographical groupings of plants largely comprise this mixture. Many species that are found in Florida also occur north of and beyond the borders of the state. Then, there are the species that are endemic (native). Over 300 endemic flowering species occur in Florida. Most of these are found in the Lake District of central Florida. Lastly, the southern flora, composed of many tropical and subtropical species, is probably more closely related to the flora of the West Indies than to that of the mainland. The majority of plants in Florida are native and not introduced. The Spanish explorer Juan Ponce de Leon aptly named the land he saw in the spring of 1513 as Florida, the "land of flowers."

No other state can claim the diversity and number of species of insectivorous plants that grow in Florida. Florida's unique geographical location, great diversity of soils, and climate all contribute to the vast wealth of wildflowers that can be found here.

♦ **Names of Wildflowers**

The scientific name and its author are given for all species of wildflowers illustrated in this guide. For those plants having an established or fairly widely used common name, this too is given. Not all species of wildflowers have a common name and these names vary from region to region within the United States. Scientific names are more stable than are common names. Often a species of wildflower has more than one scientific name (i.e., a synonym) because specialists differ in their interpretations of relationships. I have included a number of selected synonyms that can be used when cross-referencing to other works. For the most part, I have used Wunderlin's *Guide to the Vascular Plants of Central Florida* for the names of plants, the family names, and the sequence or arrangement of families.

♦ **Geographical Distributions**

The geographical distributions given in the species accounts are from my own field observations and from the regional works of Long and Lakela (1971), Wunderlin (1982), Clewell (1985), Duncan and Foote (1975), and Radford, Ahles, and Bell (1968). (Please see "Suggested References.") No attempt was made to examine distribution records on specimens housed in the various herbaria. Admittedly, the distributions in the species accounts are broadly delineated. We badly need floral analyses detailing the distributions by county for all plant species occurring in Florida.

Flowering Times

For most regions of Florida, there is no time of the year when some species of wildflower is not blooming. The relatively mild, year-round climate for most of the state does not permit the occurrence of distinct seasons so characteristic of our eastern northern neighbors. It is not, therefore, uncommon for species in Florida that characteristically bloom in the winter months of December and January to continue their flowering cycle well into the spring. For instance, violets in central Florida begin blooming in late November, and continue to bloom well into March and April. Spring species overlap the summer species, and the summer forms overlap the fall species. Then, there are those, such as the begger-tick *(Bidens alba)* and greeneyes *(Berlandiera subacaulis),* that bloom year-round.

Despite the continuous growing season in Florida, most wildflowers have their particular time when at least the majority of individuals are blooming. Occasionally individuals of a species may be found blooming at an odd time of the year. Because of the variations that exist in the flowering cycles of our wildflowers, one should visit the same site throughout the year, and preferably, for more than one year. The seasons, as used in the descriptive accounts, are defined as follows: *spring* (March through May), *summer* (June through August), *fall* (September through November), and *winter* (December through February).

Equipment

You need little equipment to make wildflower identifications: a good hand lens, with a magnification of at least 10X, or even better, and access to a dissecting microscope will aid in observing details of structure and the intricate design and beauty of species with small flowers such as sweet broom *(Scoparia dulcis)* and *Cuphea carthagenensis.* Be sure you use your hand lens with ample light and that you hold it close to the eye. It is always good to have a ruler, notepad, and pencil to record structural features, dates of observation, and the habitats where the plants were found.

For serious students who wish to continue their studies, a collection of field guides, technical manuals, and other references is indispensable. A list of suggested books that will be helpful is found at the end of this introduction.

If you must collect a specimen, be selective—insure that there are other individuals in the area. Put the plants in a medium-sized plastic bag while in the field until they can be pressed or put under refrigeration for later observation and analysis. I wrap my plants in a wet newspaper inserted in the plastic bag to delay wilting.

Of course, you cannot pick wildflowers in state parks or preserves, but even outside these parks there are species that are state- or federally protected. Write to the Department of Natural Resources for complete, official lists.

Color Arrangement

The use of color as a visual aid to identify flowers is not new. Color of the bloom is probably the first thing a person sees when looking at a flowering plant. As with most artificial systems, a few problems are encountered. For one, the color scheme crosses genetic or taxonomic lines. Then, there are those species that have flowers of two different colors on the same plant or on separate plants. Perhaps the most troubling plants are those having intermediate or borderline colors, especially of pinks and purples. If a plant looks lavender to you, you should check the plants in both the pink and purple categories. Aside for these shortcomings, the use of color to group wildflowers does work. The color sequence for the plants illustrated in this book is given in the table of contents. For most wildflowers I used the predominant color and for those species, such as asters, that may have two colors, I usually used the color of the ray florets. In the plates, then, the flowers are arranged by color and then by family.

In certain plants with blue flowers (e.g., celestial lily, *Nemastylis floridana;* sky flower, *Hydrolea corymbosa;* and mistflower, *Conoclinium coelestinum),* the camera is insensitive to the blue color and the resulting photo is pinkish or pinkish-purple. Photographers have been aware of this problem and a simple solution does not exist. Using filters does not completely solve this so-called "ageratum effect." For those flowers that should be bluer, I make mention of this under the "Comment" heading of the description.

◆ **Suggested References**
The wildflowers illustrated in this guide were identified using standard technical manuals with keys, herbarium specimens, and other source materials. The following works were especially helpful:

Baker, M. F. 1938. *Florida Wild Flowers.* New Edition. Macmillan Co., New York.

Bell, C. R., and B. J. Taylor. 1982. *Florida Wild Flowers and Roadside Plants.* Laurel Hill Press, Chapel Hill.

Clewell, A. F. 1985. *Guide to the Vascular Plants of the Florida Panhandle.* University Presses of Florida, Tallahassee.

Duncan, W. H., and L. E. Foote. 1975. *Wildflowers of the Southeastern United States.* University of Georgia Press, Athens.

Godfrey, R. K., and J. W. Wooten. 1979. *Aquatic and Wetland Plants of Southeastern United States. Monocotyledons.* University of Georgia Press, Athens.

————. 1981. *Aquatic and Wetland Plants of Southeastern United States. Dicotyledons.* University of Georgia Press, Athens.

Long, W. R. and O. Lakela. 1971. *A Flora of Tropical Florida.* University of Miami Press, Coral Gables.

Myers, R. L., and J. J. Ewel, editors. 1990. *Ecosystems of Florida.* University Presses of Florida, Orlando.

Porter, C. L. 1959. *Taxonomy of Flowering Plants.* W. H. Freeman and Co., San Francisco.

Radford, A. E., H. F. Ahles, and C. R. Bell. 1968. *Manual of the Vascular Flora of the Carolinas.* University of North Carolina Press, Chapel Hill.

Rickett, H. W. 1967. *Wild Flowers of the United States. Volume 2. The Southeastern States.* McGraw-Hill Book Company, New York.

Smith, J. P., Jr. 1977. *Vascular Plant Families.* Mad River Press, Inc., Eureka.

Ward, D. B., editor. 1979. *Rare and Endangered Biota of Florida: Plants.* University Presses of Florida, Gainesville.

Wunderlin, R. P. 1982. *Guide to the Vascular Plants of Central Florida.* University Presses of Florida, Tampa.

Zomlefer, W. B. 1989. *Flowering Plants of Florida. A Guide to Common Families.* Biological Illustrations, Inc., Gainesville.

WHERE TO LOOK FOR WILDFLOWERS

♦

A lthough Florida lacks the rolling hills of Kentucky, Tennessee, and Missouri, and the mountains of the Carolinas and Virginia, it nonetheless has a variety of habitats or ecological communities occurring in its relatively flat terrain. Slight changes in elevation, drainage, climate, and soils are crucial in determining which habitat prevails.

Regretfully, most of the original ecological communities of Florida have been severely modified or obliterated by man for agriculture and residential and commercial developments, often with only small portions remaining in restricted, geographical areas. This tremendous alteration of Florida's communities has by no means ceased, and for many areas of the state the destruction is ever-increasing.

To know the habitat of a wildflower species can aid in locating the plant and in its identification. Knowing the habitat of a wildflower species may be more important than knowing its range. One would not expect, for example, to find the swamp hibiscus *(Hibiscus grandiflorus)* in dry scrub, nor would one expect to find the scrub lupine *(Lupinus aridorum)* of the scrub environs in a swampy area. Common habitats found in Florida with representative wildflowers are given in the brief review below.

Pine Flatwoods. This is perhaps the most common, natural ecological community (past or present) in Florida, although much of it has been modified for grazing cattle or

converted to developments. As implied by the name, the terrain is nearly level land and dominated by one or more species of pine tree. The upper (about 1 meter) soil layer of sand with moderate amounts of organic matter is porous and sandy, but below that level there is usually a "hardpan" of dense organic matter. During the rainy season the hardpan obstructs water drainage and the upper soils, consequently, become waterlogged. Wet flatwoods often contain pond pine *(Pinus serotina)*, and the drier flatwoods are dominated by longleaf pine *(P. palustris)* or slash pine *(P. elliottii)*. Understory, brushy-type plants include saw palmetto *(Serenoa repens)*, fetterbush *(Lyonia lucida)*, gallberry *(Ilex glabra)*, shiny blueberry *(Vaccinium myrsinites)*, and one or more species of runner oaks *(Quercus spp.)* and wiregrasses *(Aristida spp.)*. Common wildflowers include yellow buttons *(Balduina angustifolia)*, vanilla plant *(Carphephorus odoratissimus)*, sensitive briar *(Schrankia microphylla)*, and whitetopped aster *(Aster reticulatus)*.

Sandhills. Well-drained, deep, sandy soils usually with a yellowish appearance and one or more oak species (often turkey oak, *Quercus laevis*), along with longleaf pine,

Pine flatwoods showing the flat terrain, longleaf pines (Pinus palustris) *and saw palmetto* (Serenoa repens). *Photo taken in December.*

Sandhill habitat with longleaf pines (Pinus palustris) *and turkey oaks* (Quercus laevis). *Photo taken in June.*

Sand pine scrub. Plants in this scene are sand pines (Pinus clausa), *rosemary* (Ceratiola ericoides), *and shrubby-types of oaks. Photo taken in December.*

Scrub habitat lacking sand pines observed in the sand pine scrub. Note the spaced rosemary (Ceratiola ericoides) *and white sandy soils. Photo taken in September.*

characterize this community. Because of the presence of these trees, sandhills lack a dense understory of vegetation. A substantial leaf litter, in the absence of fires, accumulates on the forest floor. Wiregrasses dominate the herbaceous layer.

Sandhills have been extensively lumbered for the virgin pines or burned by man-induced fires. With the older pines gone, the oaks often dominate today and an understory of low shrubby oaks and palmetto is present. Much of the area now occupied by citrus groves of central and lower peninsular Florida were former sandhills.

Wildflowers found in sandhills include the butterfly-weed *(Asclepias tuberosa)*, Adam's needle *(Yucca filamentosa)*, alicia *(Chapmannia floridana)*, roseling *(Cuthbertia ornata)*, phoebanthus *(Phoebanthus grandiflora)*, wild buckwheat *(Eriogonum tomentosum)*, and Indian plantain *(Arnoglossum floridanum)*.

Sand Pine Scrub. The scrub community is Florida's oldest and harshest environment. Low nutrients and moisture, loose sandy soils, lack of ground cover of grasses, presence of the dominant sand pine *(Pinus clausa)* and thickets of shrubby-type oaks (such as scrub live oak, *Quercus geminata;* myrtle oak, *Q myrtifolia;* and scrub oak, *Q inopina*), saw palmetto, fetterbush *(Lyonia ferruginea)*, a variety of lichens, and rosemary *(Ceratiola ericoides)* all characterize this community. Periodic fires, caused naturally by lightning, are necessary to maintain this habitat. The Florida scrub is rapidly disappearing or being greatly modified for residential and commercial developments. Many of the rare and endangered plant and animal species (mostly arthropods) are scrub inhabitants.

Wildflowers characteristic of sand pine scrub include the mint *(Calamintha coccinea)*, scrub lupine *(Lupinus aridorum)*, wireweed *(Polygonella gracilis)*, jointweed *(Polygonella polygama)*, and garberia *(Garberia heterophylla)*.

Coastal uplands. Areas along and adjacent to the beaches represent unique, but harsh environments. Plants growing on and along the beach dunes, in the coastal grasslands, marshes, hammocks, and on shell mounds (kitchen middens) tolerate salt in the sandy soils, intense heat from the sun, erosion, and blowing winds that constantly remove the moisture from the improverished soils.

Wildflowers of our coastal habitats include yellowtop *(Flaveria linearis)*, sea daisy *(Borrichia frutescens)*, sea purslane *(Sesuvium portulacastrum)*, railroad-vine *(Ipomoea pes-caprae)*, and seaside bean *(Canavalia rosea)*.

A coastal dune. Coastal habitats, despite harsh environments, support a variety of specialized wildflowers. Photo taken in December.

Rayless sunflowers (Helianthus radula) *in a roadside ditch. Photo taken in November.*

Disturbed sites. Much of Florida's landscape today consists of disturbed sites such as parks, lawns, vacant lots, pasturelands, fields, fence rows, thickets, and along highway and railroad rights-of-way. These disturbed sites are homes to a large array of wildflowers, especially the weedy species that tolerate varied environmental conditions. The distributions of these plants are wide-ranging and the same species in Florida may be found in the Appalachians, the Midwest, or the Northeast. Many of these species are not native to Florida or to the United States, being introduced accidentally or intentionally.

Weedy species found in a variety of disturbed sites include rattle-box *(Crotalaria spectabilis)*, butterweed *(Senecio glabellus)*, creeping oxeye *(Wedelia trilobata)*, common dandelion *(Taraxacum officinale)*, spiny-leaved sow thistle *(Sonchus asper)*, poorman's pepper *(Lepidium virginicum)*, and common chickweed *(Stellaria media)*.

Goldenasters, Chrysopsis
scabrella, *in a vacated lot.
Photo taken in November.*

Flat-topped goldenrods
(Euthamia tenuifolia) *in a
pasture. Photo taken in
November.*

Blazing stars (Liatris
gracilis) *and flat-topped
goldenrods* (Euthamia
tenuifolia) *growing along a
road right-of-way. Photo
taken in November.*

Begger-ticks (Bidens mitis)
*gracing a fence row and road
right-of-way.*

Mass of bladderworts (Utricularia fibrosa) in a wetland. Photo taken in May.

A cypress dome. This body of water is surrounded by pond cypress (Taxodium ascendens), grasses, and other vegetation. Photo taken in December when the cypress trees have shed their leaves.

Begger-ticks (Bidens mitis) growing along a ditch. Photo taken in November.

Wetlands. Marshes (salt and freshwater), wet prairies (inland and coastal), bogs, swamps, floodplains, cypress domes, ditches, and riverine habitats form much of the wet places in Florida. Many acres of wetlands are extinct, polluted, and they continue to be destroyed and polluted at an alarmingly rapid rate to make way for housing, commercial developments and roads. Florida has lost 54 percent of its original 20.3 million acres of wetlands. Each wetland has its own unique ecological features as well as its particular plant species. Cypress, sawgrass *(Cladium jamaicense)*, red maple *(Acer rubrum)*, and swamp blackgum *(Nyssa sylvatica)* may be found in various wetlands. Wildflowers include the milkweed *(Asclepias perennis)*, pale meadow beauty *(Rhexia mariana)*, buttonbush, *(Cephalanthus occidentalis)*, hooded pitcherplant *(Sarracenia minor)*, and sundews *(Drosera brevifolia* and *D. capillaris)*.

Pipeworts (Eriocaulon decangulare) *along a pond's edge. Photo taken in June.*

Hammocks. Scattered throughout the state are wooded "islands" of vegetation that are often surrounded by expanses of grasses or other vegetation from a different community type. Hammocks are either dry *(xeric)* or wet *(mesic)*, and a variety of names have been assigned to the different types of hammocks occurring throughout Florida. The photo shows a live oak-hardwood hammock that is surrounded by pine flatwoods. Note the parklike appearance and the size of the live oaks. Wildflowers growing in this site included paint brush *(Carphephorus corymbosus)*, yellow jessamine *(Gelsemium sempervirens)*, senna symeria *(Seymeria cassioides)*, and the purple violet, *Viola septemloba*.

Live oak/hardwood hammock. Note the parklike appearance. Photo taken in February when most of the leaves had fallen from the trees.

STRUCTURAL CHARACTERISTICS
OF WILDFLOWERS

An extensive, technical vocabulary has been developed to describe and characterize plants. For example, there are more than 50 words to indicate that a plant is not smooth (glabrous); that is, words to describe the types of hairs or condition of hairiness. It can be helpful to know if a plant is hairy or lacks hairs, but for the most part it is not absolutely necessary to know all specific types of hairs.

Following are some very basic terms used to characterize the flower, fruit, leaf, and stem—terms that are essential to basic knowledge of wildflowers.

◆ The Flower

Most wildflowers have colored *petals* (collectively called the *corolla*) that are immediately above (subtended by) *sepals* (usually green), collectively the *calyx*. The number of petals and sepals present should always be noted. Either structure may be free or united to varying degrees. Extreme fusion of the petals results in the corolla being tubular or trumpet-shaped (consider *Phlox* [Polemoniaceae], *Campsis* [Bignoniaceae], *Glandularia* [Verbenaceae], *Lonicera* [Caprifoliaceae], and morning-glories [Convolvulaceae]) or bell-shaped or urn-shaped (*Vaccinium* and *Gaylussacia* [Ericaceae]). The term *perianth*, in descriptive botany, refers collectively to both calyx and corolla. This term is often used in describing plants such as lilies (Liliaceae family) where the petals and sepals are not clearly differentiated and are colored the same. There are those wildflowers, such as tread

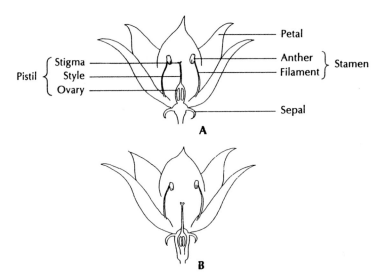

Parts of a flower. A. Flower with a superior ovary. B. Flower with an inferior ovary.

softly *Cnidoscolus stimulosus* (Euphorbiaceae), and members of the buckwheat (Polygonaceae) and poke (Phytolaccaceae) families that lack petals, but have colored sepals that resemble petals (petaloid).

Members of the hisbiscus family (Malvaceae) have *bracts* located below the sepals. A bract is a modified or reduced leaf and is often green. Bracts occur in one or more rows (series or clusters). Those in multiple rows often overlap each other (imbricated). A series or whorl of bracts collectively surrounding a single flower or flower cluster, as in asters, is called an *involucre*. *Phyllary* is another term often used for an involucre bract. The variations occurring in the bracts of plants are often used in identifications.

It is important to identify both female and male parts of the flower. The *pistil*, or female part, consists of the basal *ovary* where seeds are produced, the midregion or *style*, and the terminal apex or *stigma*, which receives the pollen from the male flower. Some plants have two or more styles or the single style has two or more bifurcations. For example, members of the

wood sorrel family (Oxalidaceae) have five styles, those of the phlox family (Polemoniaceae) have three-branched styles, and those of the verbena family (Verbenaceae) have two-branched styles.

The male part is the *stamen*, whose expanded apices, the *anthers*, produce pollen. Each anther typically is attached to a threadlike stalk, the *filament*. Several unrelated species of plants produce sterile stamens called *staminodia*. Noting the number of stamens, their attachment to one another, and their attachment and position in relation to the petals will be useful in your identifications.

Most flowers are *bisexual*, a condition where both male and female reproductive parts occur in the same flower. A *unisexual* flower contains only either female or male parts. A pistillate flower, for example, contains only the female parts, whereas a staminate flower contains only the male parts. Both male and female flowers may occur on the same plant, as happens in cattails and *Sagittaria*. There are some plants, such as the alicia *(Chapmannia floridana)* of the bean family (Fabaceae) that have both bisexual and unisexual flowers on the same plant.

Flowers are often called *regular* (**radial**) or *irregular* (bilateral) based on the arrangement or symmetry of the petals and sepals. Examples of regular flowers are the pine lily (Liliaceae) and Venus' looking-glass (Campanulaceae). Irregular flowers occur in several unrelated families including violets (Violaceae), lobelias (Campanulaceae), milkweeds (Asclepiadaceae), certain mints (Lamiaceae), certain figworts (Scrophulariaceae), and certain beans or peas (Fabaceae). In many irregular flowers, both the corolla and calyx are two-lipped (bilabiate), the upper lip distinctly different from the the lower lip.

◆ **The Inflorescence**

Many flowers are solitary, but many also occur in groups or clusters. An inflorescence has to do with the arrangement of multiple flowers on a plant. Knowing this arrangement for each wildflower can be helpful in its identification. The common basic inflorescence-types are the *spike, raceme, panicle, corymb, umbel,* and *cyme*. It is not always easy to see how a particular plant fits into one of the above arrangements.

Spike. A spike is elongated and unbranched with a central axis (peduncle) along which sessile (stalkless) or nearly sessile flowers are arranged. The lower flowers are the first to open. Examples: ladies'-tresses (Orchidaceae) and cottonweed (Amaranthaceae).

Raceme. A raceme is similar to a spike except that each flower has a simple stalk (pedicel) nearly equal in length. The lower flowers are the first to open. Examples: lupines (Fabaceae) and poke (Phytolaccaceae).

Panicle. A panicle is similar to a raceme except the flower pedicels themselves are branched and each branch bears a flower. Examples: deer-tongue (Asteraceae) and beardtongue (Scrophulariaceae).

Types of inflorescences. A. Spike. B. Raceme. C. Panicle. D. Corymb. E. Umbel. F. Cyme. The largest flowers in the diagrammatic diagram (lowermost) are the oldest.

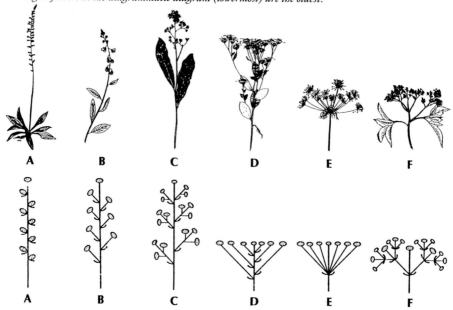

Corymb. The flowers of a corymb form a more or less flat-topped appearance and the pedicels are of unequal lengths. The outermost flowers are the oldest and first to open. Examples: palafoxia and flat-topped goldenrod (Asteraceae).

Umbel. In this arrangement all pedicels arise from a common point. An umbel may be simple or compound. Examples: Mock bishop's-weed, water hemlock, and Queen Anne's lace (Apiaceae).

Cyme. Flowers with this branched inflorescence often have a flat-topped appearance. The first-formed flower terminates the pedicel; therefore, the central flowers are the oldest and first to open. Examples: elderberry (Caprifoliaceae), marsh pinks (Gentianaceae), and milkweeds (Asclepiadaceae).

◆ **The Fruit**
    A fruit is basically a ripened ovary. The type of fruit of a plant is often used as an identifying character, especially at the family and generic levels.
    At maturity, fruits are either dry or fleshy. If the dried or ripened fruit opens (i.e., by sutures, pores, or caps), it is said to be *dehiscent. Indehiscent* fruits do not open. The seeds are released when the fruit wall rots. Nearly all fleshy fruits are indehiscent.
    Some common types of fruit occurring in the wildflowers in this guide are discussed below.

Indehiscent
◆ *Achene (akene)*—a wingless, one-seeded fruit with a thin wall separable from the seed. Begger-ticks, sunflowers, and dandelions (Asteraceae) produce achenes.

◆ *Nutlet*—a small nut as in the verbenas (Verbenaceae), skullcaps (Lamiaceae), and docks (Polygonaceae).

◆ *Utricle*—a small, one-seeded, bladdery fruit with the seed loosely surrounded by the fruit wall. Alligator-weeds and pigweeds (Amaranthaceae) produce utricles.

◆ *Drupe*—has a fleshy wall that encloses the seed lying within an inner pit. Examples are fruits of the olive (Oleaceae), beautyberry (Verbenaceae) and poison ivy (Anacardiaceae).

◆ *Berry*—a fleshy fruit with few to many seeds embedded in a fleshy pulp; no hard inner core. Grapes (Vitaceae) and maypops (Passifloraceae) are examples.

◆ *Aggregate (syncarp)*—a fleshy fruit formed from fusion of several ovaries of a single flower and borne on an inner, enlarged receptacle. Blackberries (Rosaceae) are examples.

Dehiscent
◆ *Follicle*—a pod that splits open along one suture at maturity as in milkweeds (Asclepiadaceae).

◆ *Schizocarp*—a dry fruit that splits into one-seeded parts. Mock bishop's-weed (Apiaceae) and heliotropes (Boraginaceae) produce schizocarps.

◆ *Legume*—a pod that splits open along two sutures as in peas and peanuts (Fabaceae). A specialized type of legume is the *loment* ("sticktight") found in beggarweeds *(Desmodium)*. This legume is constricted between each seed and divides transversely into one-seeded segments.

◆ *Capsule*—a dry fruit that develops from a compound pistil. Most capsules are many-seeded. There are different types of capsules depending how they split open: (a) pores near the top of the capsule as in poppies (Papaveraceae) and the lotus lily (Nymphaeaceae); (b) irregular as in lobelias (Campanulaceae); (c) several segments as in yucca (Agavaceae), morning-glories (Convolvulaceae), and irises (Iridaceae). A *pyxis* is a capsule with the top coming off like a lid as in portulacas (Portulacaceae). A *silique* is an elongated capsule that splits down two sides as in the tansy mustard *Descurainia pinnata*) and wild radish, *Raphanus raphanistrum* (Brassicaceae). A *silicle*, also found in members of the mustard family such as in poorman's pepper *(Lepidium virginicum)*, is a short and squatty silique.

◆ The Leaf

A leaf arises from a node on the stem. The basic parts of a leaf are the *leaf stem (petiole), blade,* and *midvein* or *midrib.* Leaves occur singly (**simple** or **unifoliate**) or are divided into leaflets (**compound**). Compound leaves are palmately or pinnately arranged. In the former the leaflets arise from a common point. Leaflets of a pinnate compound leaf arise at intervals along the rachis. Each leaflet may be stalkless (sessile) or stalked (petioled). Leaflets may be odd- or even-numbered. In some plants such as the sensitive briar *(Schrankia microphylla)* and other mimosa-types (Fabaceae), the compound leaf may in turn bear an additional set of leaves, a condition known as twice pinnately or bipinnately compound.

Most species of wildflowers have their leaves borne on the stem (*cauline* leaves). Species, such as the yellow colic-root *(Aletris lutea)*, paint brush (*Carphephorus corymbosus)* and rayless sunflower *(Helianthus radula)*, have most of their leaves at the base of the flowering stalk *(scape)*. These are called *basal* leaves and may occur in rosettes. Many plants have both cauline and basal leaves.

The leaf shape, arrangement, venation pattern, nature of the leaf margins or edges, apex, and base, and the presence or absence of the petiole should be noted when identifying a wildflower. Some plants, such as camphorweed, *Heterotheca subaxillaris* and climbing aster, *Aster carolinianus*, have leaves whose bases hug or clasp the stem.

Leaf Shape. A large number of descriptive terms are used to describe the shapes of leaves. The more common shapes are *linear* (narrow or grasslike), *oblong, elliptic, lanceolate, oblanceolate, ovate,* and *obovate.* Authors do not always agree which term best describes the shape of leaves of the same species. Some plants may have leaves that are intermediate between two shapes.

Parts of a leaf.

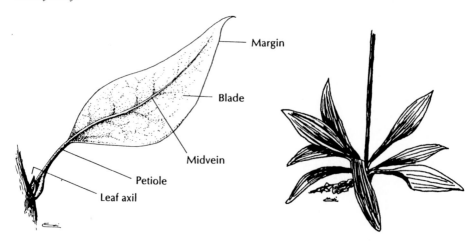

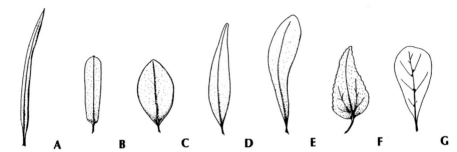

Leaf shapes. A. Linear. B. Oblong. C. Elliptic. D. Lanceolate. E. Oblanceolate. F. Ovate. G. Obovate.

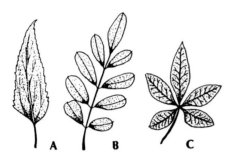

Types of leaves. A. Simple. B. Pinnately compound. C. Palmately compound.

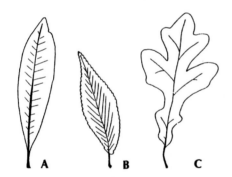

Leaf margins. A. Entire. B. Toothed. C. Lobed.

Leaf Arrangement. Two very useful terms, *alternate* and *opposite*, describe the arrangment of leaves on the stem. If the leaves are arranged singly (unpaired) on the stem, they are said to be alternate. If the leaves are paired, the arrangement is opposite. If three or more leaves arise at the same point (node) on the stem, the leaves are *whorled*. Some leaves have one or more small, leaflike *stipules* at the base of the petiole. Stipules are usually green and paired. Stipules may also occur at the bases of the flower pedicels. Stipules either remain attached to the plant or drop off.

Leaf Margin. A leaf whose outer margin lacks teeth or serrations is said to be *entire*. Several terms used in the more technical manuals describe the *toothed* condition of the leaf margin, but these have been avoided for the most part, emphasizing if the leaf margin is toothed or entire. Some leaves have the blade cut from the margin to or near the midvein which results in a segmented or *lobed* condition.

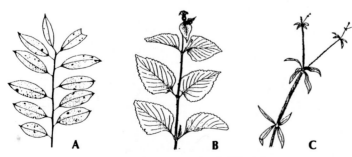

Leaf arrangements. A. Alternate. B. Opposite. C. Whorled.

· G L O S S A R Y ·

achene (akene): A one-seeded, nonsplitting, hard fruit having a thin wall separable from the seed.

aerial root: Roots on the stem of vines used in climbing or holding. Also, the pendant roots of epiphytes (air plants).

aggregate: A fleshy fruit type formed from fusion of several ovaries of a single flower. Blackberry is an example.

alternate: An unpaired arrangement—in contrast to being "opposite." Alternate leaves are located singly on a stem.

anther: The apical, pollen-producing part of the stamen.

apex: The tip.

awl-shaped: Tapering from the base to a slender point.

awn: A stiff bristle.

axil: The upper angle between two structures (e.g., the leaf axil is between the leaf and stem).

axillary: In or arising from an axil.

beard: A cluster, tuft, or group of relatively stiff hairs. Beards occur on the sepals of the prairie iris *(Iris hexagona)* and on some petals of certain violets.

berry: A fleshy, nonsplitting, one to many-seeded fruit lacking a stone.

bifurcate: Forked.

bilabiate: Two-lipped.

bipinnate: Twice pinnate. See pinnate.

bisexual: Having both male and female reproductive organs in the same flower. A bisexual flower is also called a perfect flower. Opposite is unisexual.

blade: The expanded part of a leaf, sepal, or other part.

bract: A reduced or modified leaf just below a flower or flower cluster. In Asteraceae, the bract is also called an involucre bract.

calyx: The outer (usually green) whorl or series of the perianth. Collectively the sepals.

calyx lobe: The free extension of a fused calyx.

calyx tube: The tubular or basal part of a fused calyx.

capsule: A dry, splitting fruit that develops from a compound pistil.

cauline: Pertaining to the stem. A leaf on the stem is a cauline leaf.

ciliate: Having marginal hairs or bristles.

clasping: When the leaf base wraps partially or wholly around the stem.

cleft: A deep cut.

column: The structure in orchids formed by fusion of the stamens and style.

compound leaf: A leaf that is composed of two or more leaflets. The opposite of a compound leaf is a simple leaf.

compressed: Flattened laterally.

corolla: The inner (usually colored) whorl or series of the perianth. Collectively the petals.

corona: A petal-like, crownlike extension of the basal part of the perianth as in *Hymenocallis* lilies.

corymb: A flat-topped inflorescence type where the outermost flowers are the first to open.

culm: The flowering stem of grasses and sedges.

cyathium: A cuplike structure enclosing the reduced flowers of *Euphorbia, Chamaesyce,* and other members of Euphorbiaceae.

cyme: Usually a flat-topped inflorescence type where the innermost or central flowers open first.

deciduous: Shedding, not persistent. Opposite is evergreen.

dehiscent: To open or split open. Opposite is indehiscent.

deltoid: Triangular.

dichasium: An inflorescence type where the first flower to open lies between two lateral flowers.

dioecious: Having male or female flowers (unisexual) and these produced on separate plants.

disk (disc): The central part of a head that consists of tubular or disk florets (in asters and other members of Asteraceae).

dissected: A deep cut or division.

drupe: A fleshy, nonsplitting fruit usually with one seed that is surrounded by a hard covering. An olive is a drupe.

elliptic: A shape where the middle is wider than the two, tapered end.

endemic: Native. Distribution is usually restricted.

entire: Pertaining to the leaf margin that is even, lacking teeth or other indentations.

even-pinnate: When the terminal leaflets of a compound leaf are paired. Opposite is odd-pinnate.

evergreen: Retaining the leaves in the dormant state. Opposite is deciduous.

eye: A marked center on a flower, usually of a different color.

fascicle: A cluster or bundle.

filament: The stalk of a stamen bearing the terminal anther or anthers.

floret: A small flower of a cluster as in members of Asteraceae.

flower stem: The stalk that bears a flower or flower cluster. Scape.

filiform: Slender, threadlike.

fimbriate: Fringed.

floral tube: An enlongated, tubular receptacle that bears the sepals, petals and stamens. Hypanthium.

fruit: A ripened ovary.

follicle: A dry fruit that splits open along one side.

gland-dotted: Glands that appear as dots on the leaf or some other structure.

glandular: Bearing glands. The glands may be stalked or not stalked (e.g., like dots).

glomerule: A small, compact cluster.

grain: A one-seeded, indehiscent fruit with the seed coat fused to the outer wall. Corn is an example.

hairy: Having hairs of various types.

head: A tight cluster of sessile florets.

herbaceous: Not woody.

hood: An arching, strongly concaved part or top such as the hood of the hooded pitcherplant *(Sarracenia minor)*.

hypanthium: A varied-shaped expansion of the floral axis producing sepals, petals, and stamens. See floral tube.

indehiscent: Nonsplitting. Opposite is dehiscent.

inferior ovary: Condition where the ovary lies below the floral parts. Opposite is superior ovary.

inflorescence: The part of a plant where the flowers are located. Having to do with the arrangement of flowers.

insectivorous: Insect-eating.

internode: That part of the stem between two adjacent nodes.

involucre: A series or whorl of bracts surrounding a single flower or flower cluster as in members of Asteraceae.

keel: A conspicuous, longitudinal ridge. The two lower petals of a pea-shaped flower.

labellum: The lip or lower petal of an orchid.

lanceolate: A shape that is broadest near the base and gradually tapered to the apex. Opposite is oblanceolate.

leaflet: One leaf of a compound leaf.

legume: A type of fruit that splits open on both dorsal and ventral sutures. Found in many beans and peas (Fabaceae).

linear: A long, narrow shape where the sides are parallel.

lip: An expanded lobe of a united corolla or calyx. Labellum of an orchid.

loment: A type of fruit (legume) with constrictions between the seeds thereby producing one-seeded segments as in beggarweed *(Desmodium)* of the bean and pea family.

margin: The outer edge or border of a structure such as the leaf margin.

midrib: The main, central vein of a leaf or leaflet. Midvein.

midvein: See midrib.

monoecious: Having separate male and female flowers (unisexual) that are on the same plant.

node: The site on stem where a branch or leaf emerges.

nut: Usually a one-seeded, nonsplitting fruit with a hard shell.

nutlet: A small nut.

oblanceolate: A shape where the apex is broadest and gradually narrowed to the base. Opposite is lanceolate.

oblique: Unequal or slant-sided as in the leaf bases of *Chamaesyce* (Euphorbiaceae).

oblong: A shape where the sides parallel each other. Longer than broad.

obovate: A shape that is longer than broad; the apex is wider than the base. Opposite is ovate.

ocrea: A ciliated or nonciliated sheath located at the stem nodes in members of Polygonaceae. Ocreae is the plural form.

odd-pinnate: When the terminal leaflet of a compound leaf is unpaired. Opposite is even-pinnate.

opposite: A paired arrangement in contrast to alternate. A part directly across another as paired leaves on a stem.

ovate: A shape that is broader below the middle with the ends round. Egg-shaped. Opposite is obovate.

ovoid: Pertaining to being egg-shaped.

palmate: Divided, lobed, or veined in a radiate or digitate fashion like a hand.

panicle: An inflorescence type that is a branching raceme.

pappus: The modified calyx found in many members of Asteraceae.

pedicel: The stalk or stem of a single flower in a cluster.

pedicellate: Bearing a stalk.

peduncle: The stalk of a single flower or a flower cluster.

perianth: Collectively the corolla and calyx.

petal: A segment of the corolla.

petaloid: Like or resembling a petal.

petiolate: Having a petiole or leaf stem.

petiole: The stalk of a leaf.

phyllary: An involucre bract.

pinnate: A leaf type that is featherlike; that is, the leaflets are on either side of the rachis or main axis. Also, a type of featherlike venation in a leaf.

pistil: The female part of a flower consisting basically of the ovary, style, and stigma.

pistillate flower: The female flower; lacking stamens. Opposite is staminate.

pod: A type of capsule such as the legume of many beans and peas (Fabaceae).

prostrate: Lying flat on the ground.

pyxis: A type of capsule where the top comes off like a lid.

raceme: A type of inflorescence with stalked flowers emerging off a main axis.

ray: The outermost, strap-shaped floret in the head of an aster and other members of the Asteraceae.

receptacle: Terminal part of a pedicel or peduncle bearing a flower or a head of flowers.

reflexed: Bent or curved downward or backward.

rhizome: An underground rootlike stem.

rhombic: Diamond-shaped.

revolute: Rolled backward or downward.

rosette: A basal arrangement of leaves where they radiate from a center.

samara: A winged, one or two-seeded indehiscent fruit as in maple trees.

saprophyte: An organism that obtains food from decaying organic matter. Usually lacks chlorophyll.

scape: A leafless flowering stem.

schizocarp: A dry fruit that splits into one-seeded parts.

sepal: A single part of the calyx.

sessile: Lacking a stalk, stem, pedicel, or petiole. Opposite is stalked.

silicle: A short, squatty silique usually as long as wide as in certain mustards (Brassicaceae).

silique: A long, slender, podlike fruit as in certain mustards (Brassicaceae).

simple leaf: A single leaf. Opposite is compound leaf.

smooth: Hairless. The equivalent of being glabrous.

spadix: A fleshy, stalklike part bearing flowers as in members of Araceae.

spathe: A modified leaf or bract enclosing a structure of an inflorescence.

spatulate: Spoonlike. Oblong.

spike: A type of inflorescence where the flowers are sessile on an unbranched, elongated stalk.

spikelet: A small spike with each flower subtended by a bract or scale. The floral unit of grasses.

spur: A tubular projection off a petal or sepal.

stalked: Having a petiole, pedicel, or peduncle. Opposite is sessile.

stamen: The male reproductive organ of a flower.

staminate flower: The male flower; having stamens. Opposite is pistillate.

staminode: A sterile stamen.

standard (banner): The upper petal of a pea-shaped flower.

stigma: Apex of the pistil that receives the pollen.

stipule: A leaflike appendage located at the base of the leaf petiole. Stipules are usually paired and green.

style: The part (usually elongated and narrow) of the pistil between the stigma and ovary.

subtend: To be under or near. To occur immediately below.

succulent: Fleshy or juicy.

superior ovary: Condition where the ovary lies above the floral parts. Opposite is inferior ovary.

tendril: A slender, twining appendage of a branch or leaf used in climbing as in many grapes (Vitaceae) and cucumbers (Cucurbitaceae).

trifoliate: Having three leaflets.

umbel: A type of inflorescence where all the pedicels of a flower emerge from a common point.

undulate: Wavy.

unifoliate: With one leaf. Opposite is compound.

unisexual: One set of reproductive organs occurring in the same flower. Opposite is bisexual.

utricle: A small, one-seeded bladdery fruit with the seed closely surrounded by the fruit wall.

verticil: A whorl. See whorl.

whorl: An arrangement where three or more leaves or flowers are located at the same point. See verticil.

wing: The two, lateral petals of a pea-shaped flower. A membranous appendage or extension as on a seed, stem, or other part.

FLORIDA WILDFLOWERS ◆

Arrowhead or Duck Potato
Sagittaria graminea
Michaux

Family: Alismataceae (water-plantain).

Flowers: Petals 3, white. Sepals 3, green. Flowers in terminal whorls (2–12). Male flowers uppermost: stamens less than 20, filaments hairy and equal to or shorter than the anthers. Sepals deciduous. Female flowers lowermost: sepals persistent, stamens lacking.

Leaves: Basal, stalked, grasslike, ovate, or with dilated tips; leaf blades may be absent.

Habitat: Marshy areas and margins of shallow waters.

Distribution: Throughout the state.

Flowering time: All year.

Comment: Plants under water often have narrow sharp-pointed leaves than plants emersed. Flower stem slender, to 24 in. (60 cm) tall. Synonyms: *Sagittaria cycloptera* and *S. mohrii.*

Sagittaria lancifolia
L.

Family: Alismataceae (water-plantain).

Flowers: Petals 3, white. Sepals 3, green. Flowers in terminal whorls (5–12). Male flowers uppermost: stamens 28–30, filaments hairy, linear and longer than the anthers. Sepals deciduous. Female flowers lowermost: sepals persistent, stamens lacking.

Leaves: Basal, stalked, elliptic, linear or ovate.

Habitat: Marshes, ditches, ponds, and swamps.

Distribution: Throughout the state.

Flowering time: All year.

Comment: Flower stem to 3 ft. (1 m) tall or more, taller than the leaves. Seminole Indians used this plant for shock treatment from an alligator bite. Synonym: *Sagittaria falcata.*

Wapato, Duck Potato, or Common Arrowhead
Sagittaria latifolia
Willdenow

Family: Alismataceae (water-plantain).

Flowers: Petals 3, white. Sepals 3, green. Flowers in terminal whorls (2–10). Male flowers uppermost: stamens 25–40, filaments smooth, linear and longer than the anthers. Sepals deciduous. Female flowers: sepals reflexed, stamens lacking.

Leaves: Mostly arrow-shaped, stalked, smooth or hairy, emersed or emerged.

Habitat: Marshes, ditches, ponds, and swamps.

Distribution: Throughout the state.

Flowering time: Summer, fall.

Comment: Plant smooth, flower stalk to 3 ft. (1 m) tall or more, taller than the leaves. Indians ate the starch-rich tubers. Synonyms: *Sagittaria ornithorhyncha* and *S. pubescens.*

White-tops or Star Rush
Rhynchospora colorata
(L.) Pfeiffer

Family: Cyperaceae (sedge).

Flowers: Head solitary, terminal. Flowers tiny, centrally clustered around the bracts. Bracts reflexed, apex green, base white. Bracts linear, usually fewer than 7; white portion of largest bract usually less than 1 in. (25 mm) in length.

Leaves: Primarily basal, linear, smooth, shorter than the flowering stem.

Habitat: Moist pinelands and prairies.

Distribution: Throughout the state.

Flowering time: Late winter, spring, summer, fall.

Comment: Flowering stem smooth, ribbed, 4–20 in. (10–50 cm) tall. Synonym: *Dichromena colorata.*

Star Rush
Rhynchospora latifolia
(Baldwin) Thomas

Family: Cyperaceae (sedge).

Flowers: Head solitary, terminal. Flowers tiny, centrally clustered around the bracts. Bracts reflexed, apex green, base white. Bracts lanceolate, 7 or more; white portion of largest bract usually longer than 1 in. (25 mm).

Leaves: Primarily basal, linear, smooth, shorter than the flowering stem.

Habitat: Moist pinelands and wet marshes.

Distribution: Throughout the state.

Flowering time: Spring, summer, early fall.

Comment: Flowering stem smooth, ribbed, 12–28 in. (30–70 cm) tall. Synonym: *Dichromena latifolia.*

Saw Palmetto
Serenoa repens
(Bartram) Small

Family: Arecaceae (palm).

Flowers: Petals 3, white. The many small, fragrant flowers occur on elongated, branched inflorescences. Sepals 3. Stamens 6. Mature fruit black.

Leaves: Fan-shaped; leaf stems 3-sided, toothed.

Habitat: Pinelands and hammocks.

Distribution: Throughout the state.

Flowering time: Spring, summer.

Comment: Ripened fruit was a staple food for Florida Indians. Today the flowers are a source of honey.

Spoonflower
Peltandra sagittifolia
(Michaux) Morong

Family: Araceae (arum or calla).

Flowers: Perianth absent. Flowers small, occurring on a fleshy, cylindrical stalk (spadix) surrounded by a sheathing spathe. Spathe green below, white and flared-open above. Mature red berries occur in clusters.

Leaves: Basal, arrow-shaped on stalked stems.

Habitat: Swampy woods and marshes.

Distribution: Central and north Florida.

Flowering time: Spring.

Comment: Plant contains calcium oxalate crystals that irritate the mouth when eaten raw. Synonym: *Peltandra glauca*.

Yellow-eyed Grass
Xyris caroliniana
Walter

Family: Xyridaceae (yellow-eyed grass).

Flowers: Petals 3, white. Flowers on a scaly, compact, conelike spike terminating a leafless stem. Spike ⁹⁄₁₆–1⅜ in. (15–35 mm) long.

Leaves: Linear, to ³⁄₁₆ in. (4 mm) wide, 8–24 in. (20–60 cm) long, blades twisted, bases bulbous and dark brown. Leaves longer than the sheath of the flower stem.

Habitat: Pine flatwoods and sand pine scrub.

Distribution: Throughout the state.

Flowering time: Summer, fall.

Comment: Flower stem stout, smooth, twisted, to 28 in. (70 cm) tall. Synonyms: *Xyris flexuosa* and *X. pallescens*.

Pipewort
Eriocaulon decangulare
L.

Family: Eriocaulaceae (pipewort).

Flowers: Heads hard, white, buttonlike, of minute flowers. Male florets have 2 or 3 petals and 2 sepals. Female florets have 2 petals and 2 sepals. Anthers black in mature heads.

Leaves: In dense basal tufts, linear, smooth. Air spaces occur in the septate leaves where attached.

Habitat: Moist pinelands, ditches, and marshes.

Distribution: Throughout the state.

Flowering time: Spring, summer, fall.

Comment: Flower stem ribbed, smooth, leafless, stout, to 3 ft. (1 m) tall or more. This rushlike plant works well in dried floral arrangements.

Bog-buttons
Lachnocaulon anceps
(Walter) Morong

Family: Eriocaulaceae (pipewort).

Flowers: Heads gray-white, buttonlike, hairy, 4 to 7 mm wide. Each minute floret has 3 sepals, but no petals. Stamens 3, filaments hairy. Anthers yellow in the mature heads.

Leaves: In dense, basal tufts, linear, ¾–2¾ in. (2–7 cm) long. Air spaces lacking in the leaves where attached.

Habitat: Moist pinelands and marshes.

Distribution: Throughout the state.

Flowering time: Spring, summer.

Comment: Flower stem leafless, hairy or smooth, to 18 in. (45 cm) long; roots dark, fibrous. Synonyms: *Lachnocaulon floridanum* and *L. glabrum.*

Bantam-buttons
Syngonanthus flavidulus
(Michaux) Ruhland

Family: Eriocaulaceae (pipewort).

Flowers: Heads yellow-white, hemispherical; yellowish bracts on the underside of the heads. Each minute floret has 3 petals and 3 sepals. Stamens 3. Anthers yellow in mature heads.

Leaves: In dense basal tufts, bases hairy, bluish-green, ¾–1½ in. (2–4 cm) long. Air spaces lacking in the leaves where attached.

Habitat: Moist, low grounds.

Distribution: Throughout the state.

Flowering time: Midwinter, spring, summer, early fall.

Comment: Roots pale-colored, thickened, unbranched. Plant can be used in dried floral arrangements.

Crow-poison
Zigadenus densus
(Desrousseaux) Fernald

Family: Liliaceae (lily).

Flowers: Heads of many, 6-parted, white-pink flowers. Flowers in racemes. Stamens 6. Base of each petal has a gland.

Leaves: Basal, grasslike or linear.

Habitat: Moist pinelands and swamps.

Distribution: Central and north Florida.

Flowering time: Spring.

Comment: Stem leafless, to 3 ft. (1 m) tall or more. Root stock poisonous. Older flowers turn pinkish. Plant also locally known as Osceola's Plume. Synonym: *Tracyanthus angustifolius*.

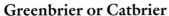

Greenbrier or Catbrier
Smilax auriculata
Walter

Family: Smilacaceae (greenbrier).

Flowers: Corolla whitish-green. Flowers small, fragrant, occurring in stalked, axillary umbels. Berries 2 or 3 seeded, black at maturity.

Leaves: Alternate, often oblong with parallel sides and projecting, basal lobes. Midvein and 2 principal lateral veins on the lower leaf surface about equally pronounced. Stems of the umbels not longer than the stem of the subtending leaf.

Habitat: Pinelands, open woods, and thickets.

Distribution: Throughout the state.

Flowering time: Spring.

Comment: Vine climbing or trailing, woody, usually spineless.

Greenbrier or Catbrier
Smilax laurifolia
L.

Family: Smilacaceae (greenbrier).

Flowers: Corolla whitish-green. Flowers small, occurring in stalked, axillary umbels. Berries 1-seeded, blue-black at maturity.

Leaves: Alternate, entire, narrow, thick, leathery at maturity. Midvein on lower leaf surface more pronounced than the principal lateral veins. Stems of the umbels about as long as the stem of the subtending leaf.

Habitat: Swamps and damp woods.

Distribution: Throughout the state.

Flowering time: Spring, summer, fall.

Comment: Vine woody, high-climbing, spiny or spineless.

Wild Sarsaparilla Vine
Smilax glauca
Walter

Family: Smilacaceae (greenbrier).

Flowers: Corolla yellowish-green. Flowers small, occurring in stalked, axillary umbels. Berries 1- to 3-seeded, bluish-black at maturity.

Leaves: Alternate, whitish or gray beneath, broad, base rounded. Leaves may be mottled with pale areas. Stems of the umbels are slender and longer than the stem of the subtending leaf.

Habitat: Pine flatwoods, thickets, and hammocks.

Distribution: Central and north Florida.

Flowering time: Spring.

Comment: Vine woody, spiny, climbing, often forming thickets.

Adam's Needle
Yucca filamentosa

Family: Agavaceae (yucca).

Flowers: Corolla bell-shaped, whitish-green. Flowers clustered at the end of a central stalk. Petals roundish, sharp-tipped. Stamens 6. Capsule oblong, erect.

Leaves: Basal rosette of sharp, rigid, elongated, thick leaves with margins fraying into curly, filamentous threads.

Habitat: Dry woods and sandy soils.

Distribution: Central and north Florida.

Flowering time: Spring, summer.

Comment: Stem woody, reaching several meters tall. Synonym: *Yucca flaccida*.

Spanish Dagger or Spanish Bayonet
Yucca aloifolia
L.

Family: Agavaceae (yucca).

Flowers: Corolla bell-shaped, white. Flowers clustered at the end of a thick, stocky trunk. Fruit pendulous.

Leaves: Sharp-pointed, to 24 in. (60 cm) long. Margins often brownish, toothed, not fraying into filamentous threads.

Habitat: Dry woods and sandy soils.

Distribution: Throughout the state.

Flowering time: Spring, summer.

Comment: Trunk to 3 ft. (1 m) tall or more. Native to the West Indies and Mexico; escaped from cultivation.

Scrub Beargrass
Nolina brittoniana
Nash

Family: Agavaceae (yucca).

Flowers: Perianth white, 6-parted, apices glandular. Flowers stalked, in erect panicles. Stamens 6, filaments yellowish. Fruit capsule notched at both ends, 3-lobed, lobes sharp-angled.

Leaves: Straplike, recurved, 3–6 ft. (1–2 m) long, in a dense mat at the base of the plant.

Habitat: Sand pine scrub and dry pinelands.

Distribution: Central Florida.

Flowering time: Spring.

Comment: Stem 6 ft. (2 m) tall or more, slightly angulated, stiff.

False Garlic
Nothoscordum bivalve
(L.) Britton

Family: Amaryllidaceae (amaryllis).

Flowers: Perianth 6-parted, star-shaped, creamy-white. Flowers erect, occurring at the end of a long stalk. A sheath occurs where the flowers arise from the stem.

Leaves: Narrow, less than ³⁄₁₆ in. (5 mm) wide, grasslike, flat.

Habitat: Open, grassy sites.

Distribution: Central and north Florida.

Flowering time: Late winter, spring.

Comment: Stem to 20 in. (50 cm) tall. Plant arises from a bulb; lacks an onion or garlic odor. Synonym: *Allium bivalve.*

Wild Onion
Allium canadense
L.

Family: Amaryllidaceae (amaryllis).

Flowers: Perianth 6-parted, white or pinkish, star-shaped. Flowers enclosed by 2 or 3 papery bracts. Floral segments less than ⅜ in. (1 cm) long. Pistil 1. Stamens 6. Floral inflorescence of bulblets entirely or both bulblets and flowers.

Leaves: Linear, smooth, flat, solid, mostly basal and sheathed.

Habitat: Disturbed sites.

Distribution: Central and north Florida.

Flowering time: Spring.

Comment: Herb smooth arising from a bulb. Plant has a distinct onion odor.

Alligator-lily
Hymenocallis palmeri
Watson

Family: Amaryllidaceae (amaryllis).

Flowers: Perianth white, of 6, linear parts surrounding a funnel-shaped membrane (the corona). Flowers solitary, fragrant. Stamens 6, attached to the corona. Pistil narrow, elongated.

Leaves: Linear, to ⅜ in. (1 cm) wide, smooth, surrounded by a basal tubular sheath.

Habitat: Wet woods and prairies.

Distribution: Central and south Florida.

Flowering time: Summer.

Comment: Flower stalk bears a swelling below the flower; stalk smooth, compressed, with 3 papery bracts. Plant arises from a bulb and gets to 20 in. (50 cm) tall. Synonym: *Hymenocallis tridentata*.

Spider Lily
Hymenocallis latifolia
(Miller) Roemer

Family: Amaryllidaceae (amaryllis).

Flowers: Perianth white, of 6 linear parts surrounding a funnel-shaped membrane (the corona). Flowers 8–16, fragrant. Stamens 6, attached to the corona. Anthers red.

Leaves: Broadly linear, flat, smooth, 2¾ in. (7 cm) or less wide.

Habitat: Mangrove swamps and coastal swales.

Distribution: Central and south Florida.

Flowering time: Spring, summer, fall.

Comment: Flower stalk bears a swelling below the flower; stalk smooth, compressed, to 32 in. (80 cm) tall. Synonyms: *Hymenocallis collieri* and *H. keyensis*.

String-lily or Swamp Lily
Crinum americanum
L.

Family: Amaryllidaceae (amaryllis).

Flowers: Perianth white, of 6 linear lobes. Corona lacking. Petals joined basally. Flowers fragrant, subtended by 2 papery bracts. Stamens 6, anthers brownish-red.

Leaves: Linear, margins finely toothed.

Habitat: Marshes, wet woods, and swamps.

Distribution: Throughout the state.

Flowering time: Spring, summer, fall.

Comment: Flower stalk gets to 32 in. (80 cm) tall.

Atamasco-lily or Rain-lily
Zephyranthes atamasco
(L.) Herbert

Family: Amaryllidaceae (amaryllis).

Flowers: Perianth 6-parted, united, white to pinkish. Flower solitary, terminal, on a smooth leafless stalk. Sepals and petals pointed, not tapering. Stigmas 3. Stamens 6, shorter than the pistil.

Leaves: Linear, bases sheathed, smooth, flat, sharp-edged.

Habitat: Wet meadows and pinelands.

Distribution: Central and north Florida.

Flowering time: Winter, spring, summer.

Comment: Flower stalk smooth, leafless to 10 in. (25 cm) tall. Stalk bears a swelling below flower and a membranous sheath that splits in half. Seminole Indians apparently used the bulbs for toothaches. Synonyms: *Atamasco atamasco* and *A. treatiae*.

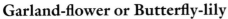

Garland-flower or Butterfly-lily
Hedychium coronarium
Koenig

Family: Zingiberaceae (ginger).

Flowers: Corolla 4-lobed, white. Flowers large, fragrant, clustered near the end of tall, leafy stems.

Leaves: Alternate, large, lanceolate.

Habitat: Swamps and marshes.

Distribution: Central Florida.

Flowering time: Summer, fall, winter.

Comment: Native to tropical Asia.

Spring Ladies'-tresses
Spiranthes vernalis
Engelmann and Gray

Family: Orchidaceae (orchid).

Flowers: Flowers small, white, densely twisted in a single spiral-spike. Lip flared, margins crinkled. Flowers usually fragrant.

Leaves: Slender, often thick, grasslike, basal or on the stem.

Habitat: Wet, grassy areas.

Distribution: Throughout the state.

Flowering time: Spring, summer.

Comment: Stem nearly leafless, to 3 ft. (1 m) or more tall. Terrestrial. Upper part of plant with dense, sharp-pointed hairs. Synonym: *Ibidium vernale.*

Spider Orchid or Long-horned Habenaria

Habenaria quinqueseta
(Michaux) Eaton

Family: Orchidaceae (orchid).

Flowers: White, axillary, in spikelike racemes. Lip (labellum) 3-parted, narrow. Two lateral petals each are unequally two-parted. Upper sepal hooded; sepals green with white border. Spur slender, more than 1½ in. (4 cm) long.

Leaves: Ovate to lanceolate, mainly on the stem, clasping. Lower leaves the larger.

Habitat: Moist pine flatwoods and hammocks.

Distribution: Throughout the state.

Flowering time: Fall, winter.

Comment: Stem leafy, green, to 36 in. (90 cm) tall. Terrestrial. Synonym: *Habenaria habenaria.*

Lawn Orchid

Zeuxine strateumatica
(L.) Schlechter

Family: Orchidaceae (orchid).

Flowers: Corolla white, hoodlike. Lip yellow, fleshy, broadest near the apex. Flowers small, in compact spikes, and sweet-smelling.

Leaves: Alternate, linear, sheathing the stem, overlapping, margins entire, smooth.

Habitat: Disturbed, grassy sites.

Distribution: Throughout the state.

Flowering time: Fall, winter.

Comment: Stem leafy, to 6⅝ in. (17 cm) tall, tinged purple-brown. Terrestrial. Native to Asia.

Lizard's-tail

Saururus cernuus
L.

Family: Saururaceae (lizard's-tail).

Flowers: Corolla and calyx lacking. Flowers white, tiny, and numerous in a slender, drooping spike opposite the leaves.

Leaves: Alternate, stalked, entire, large, heart-shaped.

Habitat: Shallow water, wet woods, and swamps.

Distribution: Throughout the state.

Flowering time: Midwinter, spring, summer.

Comment: Stem hairy, reddish, to 3 ft. (1 m) tall. Plant often forms extensive colonies. Only representative we have of this family.

Wild Buckwheat

Eriogonum tomentosum
Michaux

Family: Polygonaceae (buckwheat or knotweed).

Flowers: Petals lacking. Sepals 6 (3 outer, 3 inner), white or pinkish, hairy on the back. Flowers occur in clusters; inflorescence branched. Styles 3. Stamens 9, filament bases hairy.

Leaves: Nonshedding, both basal and stem leaves present. Stem leaves sessile, in whorls of 3 or 4. Lower leaf surface with dense, white- or tan-colored hairs.

Habitat: Sandhills and dry pinelands.

Distribution: Central and north Florida.

Flowering time: Spring, summer, fall, early winter.

Comment: Stem woody, branched, hairy, tan, to 3 ft. (1 m) tall.

Scrub Buckwheat
Eriogonum longifolium Nutt. var.
gnaphalifolium
Gandoger

Family: Polygonaceae (buckwheat or knotweed).

Flowers: Petals lacking. Sepals 6, whitish-green, linear. Flowers small, about 15–20 in a cluster, somewhat nodding, covered with long silky hairs. Inflorescence branched. Styles 3. Stamens 9.

Leaves: Stem leaves alternate and few. Most leaves are basal and narrow or oblanceolate. Stem leaves reduced upward. Upper leaf surface green and hairy, lower surface whitish.

Habitat: Sandhills and dry pinelands.

Distribution: Central Florida Ridge.

Flowering time: Late winter, spring, summer, fall.

Comment: Single stem may be branched. Stem covered with white hairs, to 3 ft. (1 m) tall. Synonym: *Eriogonum floridanum.*

Wireweed
Polygonella gracilis
(Nuttall) Meissner

Family: Polygonaceae (buckwheat or knotweed).

Flowers: Petals lacking. Flowers in small, spikelike racemes. Sepals white to pink, united, 5 (3 inner, 2 outer). Styles 3. Stamens 8.

Leaves: Alternate, entire, linear-spatulate. Lower leaves soon drop from the stem.

Habitat: Sandhills and dry pinelands.

Distribution: Throughout the state.

Flowering time: Summer, fall.

Comment: Stem slender, branches occurring at the internodes, to 32 in. (80 cm) tall or more. Ocreae with rounded margins. Synonyms: *Delopyrum gracile* and *D. filiforme.*

Hairy Jointweed
Polygonella basiramia
(Small) Nesom and Bates

Family: Polygonaceae (buckwheat or knotweed).

Flowers: Petals absent. Flowers small, in spikelike racemes. Sepals 5, white. Styles 3. Stamens 8.

Leaves: Alternate, narrow. Leaves often shed early.

Habitat: Sand pine scrub.

Distribution: Central Florida. Plant rare, localized in Highlands and Polk counties.

Flowering time: Summer, fall.

Comment: Plant branches into several woody stems close to the ground. Ocreae ciliated. Synonyms: *Delopyrum basiramia* and *Polygonella ciliata* var. *basiramia*.

Sandhill Wireweed
Polygonella fimbriata
(Elliott) Horton

Family: Polygonaceae (buckwheat or knotweed).

Flowers: Petals absent. Flowers in spikelike racemes. Sepals 5-parted, white or tinged pink. Inner sepals fringed. Styles 3. Stamens 8.

Leaves: Alternate, linear, clustered.

Habitat: Scrub, pinelands, and sandhills.

Distribution: Throughout the state.

Flowering time: Summer, fall.

Comment: Stem smooth, woody, brittle, to 3 ft. (1 m) tall, branches emerging at the internodes. Ocreae with long bristles. Synonym: *Thysanella robusta*.

Jointweed or October-flower
Polygonella polygama
(Ventenat) Engelmann and Gray

Family: Polygonaceae (buckwheat or knotweed).

Flowers: Petals lacking. Flowers small, fragrant, in spikelike racemes. Sepals white to pinkish, 5 (3 inner, 2 outer), ovate. Styles 3. Stamens 8.

Leaves: Alternate, entire, linear to narrowly spatulate.

Habitat: Sandhills, pinelands, and sandy soils.

Distribution: Throughout the state.

Flowering time: Summer, fall.

Comment: Stem to 24 in. (60 cm) tall, woody, brittle, diffusely branched; branches emerging at the internodes. Ocreae nonciliated, pointed on one side.

Dotted Smartweed
Polygonum punctatum
Elliott

Family: Polygonaceae (buckwheat or knotweed).

Flowers: Petals lacking. Sepals 5, whitish-green, gland-dotted. Heads densely or loosely flowered in straight or arching racemes.

Leaves: Alternate, entire, lanceolate, smooth or nearly so, stalked, greenish-red.

Habitat: Wet areas.

Distribution: Throughout the state.

Flowering time: Late winter, spring, summer, fall.

Comment: Stem jointed, single or branched, to 3 ft. (1 m) tall. Ocreae bristles ⅜–¾ in. (1 or 2 cm) long, stiff. Synonym: *Persicaria punctata.*

Cottonweed
Froelichia floridana
(Nuttall) Moquin-Tandan

Family: Amaranthaceae (amaranth or pigweed).

Flowers: Petals lacking. Flowers small, cottony, in spikes longer than wide. Calyx 5-lobed. Stamens 5, united.

Leaves: Opposite, mostly basal, entire, lanceolate or linear, clasping. Leaves woolly below. Leaf midvein reddish.

Habitat: Sandhills, pinelands, and other dry sites.

Distribution: Throughout the state.

Flowering time: All year.

Comment: Stem hairy, reddish, to 3 ft. (1 m) tall or more.

Globe Amaranth
Gomphrena serrata
L.

Family: Amaranthaceae (amaranth or pigweed).

Flowers: Petals lacking. Heads white, globular or nearly so, of papery, cottony-haired flowers. Heads subtended by 2, greenish leaf-like bracts.

Leaves: Opposite, lance-elliptic, entire, hairs flattened on the leaf surfaces.

Habitat: Disturbed sites.

Distribution: Throughout the state.

Flowering time: All year.

Comment: Stem hairy, low-growing, branched, spreading. Synonyms: *Gomphrena dispersa* and *G. decumbens*.

Bloodleaf

Iresine diffusa

Humboldt and Bonpland ex Willdenow

Family: Amaranthaceae (amaranth or pig-weed).

Flowers: Petals lacking, sepals 5, whitish-green. Flowers unisexual, small, in dense or widely branched, plumelike panicles. Male flowers with 5 stamens. Female flowers with calyx hairy at the base.

Leaves: Opposite, lanceolate, stalked, smooth or hairy.

Habitat: Hammocks and disturbed sites.

Distribution: Throughout the state.

Flowering time: All year.

Comment: Stem smooth, to 3 ft. (1 m) tall or more. Synonym: *Iresine celosia.*

Alligator-weed

Alternanthera philoxeroides

(Martius) Grisebach

Family: Amaranthaceae (amaranth or pig-weed).

Flowers: Petals lacking. Sepals 5, smooth. Flower spikes silvery-white, papery, long-stalked. Each flower is subtended by 3 bracts. Pistil 1. Stamens 5, united.

Leaves: Opposite, elliptic to oblanceolate, sessile or tapered to a short petiole.

Habitat: Wet, disturbed sites and margins of ponds and ditches.

Distribution: Throughout the state.

Flowering time: All year.

Comment: Flower stem hollow, emerging from a trailing or mat-forming stem, nearly smooth except for leaf axils. Native to South America. Synonym: *Achyranthes philoxeroides.*

Poke or Pokeberry
Phytolacca americana
L.

Family: Phytolaccaceae (pokeweed).

Flowers: Petals lacking. Sepals 5, greenish-white to pinkish, in terminal racemes. Stamen number variable. Ripe berries small, purple-black.

Leaves: Alternate, lanceolate, smooth, stalked, entire.

Habitat: Disturbed sites.

Distribution: Throughout the state.

Flowering time: Spring, summer, fall.

Comment: Stem smooth, to 9 ft. (3 m) tall, branched, often reddish in older plants. Native to tropical America. Young plants can be eaten as greens if properly cooked. Older plants are poisonous. Synonym: *Phytolacca rigida.*

Rouge Plant
Rivina humilis
L.

Family: Phytolaccaceae (pokeweed).

Flowers: Petals lacking. Sepals 4, white or pink. Flowers in racemes. Stamens 4. Berry bright red.

Leaves: Alternate, entire, lanceolate to ovate-elliptic, apex pointed.

Habitat: Thickets and disturbed sites.

Distribution: Central and south Florida.

Flowering time: All year.

Comment: Stems to 3 ft. (1 m) tall, vinelike, sometimes partly woody below. Plant is used as an ornamental.

Common Chickweed
Stellaria media
(L.) Cyrillo

Family: Caryophyllaceae (pink).

Flowers: Petals 5, white, deeply clefted (appears as 10 petals). Flowers numerous, stalked, in axillary cymes. Petals shorter than the sepals. Styles 3. Sepals 5, ovate. Stamen number variable.

Leaves: Opposite, ovate or elliptic, entire, base round. Leaf stalks short, hairy.

Habitat: Disturbed sites.

Distribution: Central and north Florida.

Flowering time: Winter, spring.

Comment: Stem low-growing, weak, succulent, hairs arranged in lines. Synonym: *Alsine media*.

Wire Plant
Stipulicida setacea
Michaux

Family: Caryophyllaceae (pink).

Flowers: Petals 5, white. Flowers minute, in terminal clusters with bracts below. Stigmas 3. Sepals 5, separate, margins transparent. Stamens 3.

Leaves: Stem leaves opposite, minute, scale-like. Basal leaves spatulate, occurring in small rosettes which may be absent at flowering time.

Habitat: Dry pinelands and scrub.

Distribution: Throughout the state.

Flowering time: Spring, summer, fall.

Comment: Stem smooth, wiry, branched, 2 to 8 in. (5–20 cm) tall. Bristly stipules occur at the stem joints. Synonym: *Stipulicida filiformis*.

White Waterlily
Nymphaea ordorata
Aiton

Family: Nymphaeaceae (waterlily).

Flowers: Petals many, lanceolate, white or pinkish. Flowers solitary, noncupped, fragrant. Sepals 4. Stamens many.

Leaves: Large, round, floating, base narrowly clefted. Green above, purplish below.

Habitat: Sluggish bodies of water.

Distribution: Throughout the state.

Flowering time: Spring, summer, fall.

Comment: Seeds and flower buds are edible. Synonyms: *Castalia odorata* and *C. lekophylla.*

Dog Banana or Pawpaw
Asimina reticulata
Chapman

Family: Annonaceae (custard apple).

Flowers: Petals 6, white. Outer 3 petals oblong, spreading; bases of inner 3 petals often purplish. Sepals 3. Flowers axillary, nodding, appearing before the leaves.

Leaves: Alternate, elliptic to oblong, leathery, entire.

Habitat: Pine flatwoods.

Distribution: Central and south Florida.

Flowering time: Winter, spring, summer.

Comment: Stem woody, branched, to 3 ft. (1 m) tall or more. Fruit eaten by animals. Endemic to Florida. Synonym: *Pityothamnus reticulatus.*

Flag Pawpaw
Asimina obovata
(Willdenow) Nash

Family: Annonaceae (custard apple).

Flowers: Petals 6, white. Outer petals the shorter, bases may be purplish. Flower pedicels with reddish hairs. Sepals 3. Berry yellow-green.

Leaves: Alternate, leathery, oblanceolate to oblong, smooth or with sparse reddish hairs.

Habitat: Sand pine scrub and pine flatwoods.

Distribution: Central and south Florida.

Flowering time: Winter, spring.

Comment: Shrub or small tree, to 6 ft. (2 m) tall or more. Endemic to Florida. Synonym: *Pityothamnus obovatus.*

Carolina Poppy
Argemone albiflora
Hornemann

Family: Papaveraceae (poppy).

Flowers: Petals 4 or 5, crinkled, white. Flowers large, cup-shaped. Sepals 2 or 3. Stamens many. Fruit a spiny capsule.

Leaves: Alternate, toothed, lanceolate to obovate, sessile, clasping, spiny.

Habitat: Dry soils and disturbed sites.

Distribution: Central and north Florida.

Flowering time: Spring, summer, fall.

Comment: Stem branched, spiny, to 3 ft. (1 m) tall or more. Synonym: *Argemone alba.*

Peppergrass or Poorman's Pepper
Lepidium virginicum
L.

Family: Brassicaceae (mustard).

Flowers: Petals 4, whitish-yellow. Flowers small, in terminal, elongated racemes. Petals longer than the sepals. Sepals 4. Stamens usually 2. Seedpod (silicle) round, stalked, apex shallow-notched.

Leaves: Alternate, deeply dissected, toothed. Basal rosettes usually absent at time of flowering.

Habitat: Dry fields, roadsides, and disturbed sites.

Distribution: Throughout the state.

Flowering time: All year.

Comment: Stem branched, sparsely haired, to 24 in. (60 cm) tall. Plant has a pungent taste.

Dwarf Sundew
Drosera brevifolia
Pursh

Family: Droseraceae (sundew).

Flowers: Petals 5, white. Flowers small, in 1-sided racemes. Flower stem hairy, glandular. Sepals 5. Stamens 5.

Leaves: In rosettes. Leaf stalk short, hairy, glandular. Blades longer than they are wide.

Habitat: Damp pinelands and bogs.

Distribution: Central and north Florida.

Flowering time: Late winter, spring.

Comment: Carnivorous. Stalked glands on leaves produce sticky secretions that trap insects which are then digested.

Virginia Willow
Itea virginica
L.

Family: Saxifragaceae (saxifrage).

Flowers: Petals 5, white. Flowers small, densely occurring in terminal, finger-shaped racemes. Flower clusters droop at the tip. Calyx 5-lobed, tube cup-shaped. Stamens 5.

Leaves: Alternate, elliptic-obovate, pointed, minutely toothed.

Habitat: Stream banks, wet woods, and swamps.

Distribution: Throughout the state.

Flowering time: Midwinter, spring, early summer.

Comment: Woody shrub, gets to 6 ft. (2 m) tall or more.

Summer Hawthorn
Crataegus flava
Aiton

Family: Rosaceae (rose).

Flowers: Petals 5, separate, white. Flowers terminal, singly or in clusters (cymes) on slender, hairy pedicels. Styles 5. Sepals 5, narrow, hairy-glandular. Stamens many. Fruit 1-seeded.

Leaves: Alternate, thin, veiny, spatulate. Leaf base narrow, margins toothed, glandular, petiole hairy. Often 3-lobed at the leaf apex.

Habitat: Woods and dry fields.

Distribution: Central and north Florida.

Flowering time: Late winter, spring.

Comment: Small tree or shrub with scattered thorns on the branches. Synonyms: *Crataegus michauxii* and *C. floridana*.

Blackberry
Rubus betulifolius
Small

Family: Rosaceae (rose).

Flowers: Petals 5, white. Flowers solitary or in terminal clusters. Calyx 5-lobed, green. Stamens many. Ripen fruit black, edible.

Leaves: Alternate, compound, toothed; green on both leaf surfaces.

Habitat: Thickets, roadsides, fence rows, and fields.

Distribution: Central and north Florida.

Flowering time: Late winter, spring.

Comment: Plant with spines; first season's canes erect.

Sand Blackberry
Rubus cuneifolius
Pursh

Family: Rosaceae (rose).

Flowers: Petals 5, white. Flowers solitary or in terminal clusters. Calyx 5-lobed, green. Stamens many. Ripe fruit black, edible.

Leaves: Alternate, compound, leaflets 3–5, toothed; white and downy on the lower leaf surface.

Habitat: Thickets, roadsides, fields, and sandy soils.

Distribution: Throughout the state.

Flowering time: Late winter, spring, summer, fall.

Comment: Stems erect, prickly.

Southern Dewberry
Rubus trivialis
Michaux

Family: Rosaceae (rose).

Flowers: Petals 5, white, may be tinged pinkish. Flowers often solitary. Calyx 5-lobed, green. Stamens many. Ripe fruit black, edible.

Leaves: Alternate, compound, leaflets 3–5, toothed, somewhat leathery. Green on both leaf surfaces. Leaves turn reddish.

Habitat: Sandy soils of roadsides, fields, and thickets.

Distribution: Throughout the state.

Flowering time: Winter, spring.

Comment: Stems prickly, trailing, prostrate. Synonyms: *Rubus lucidus, R. continentalis,* and *R. rubrisetus.*

Red Chokeberry
Pyrus arbutifolia
(L.) L.f.

Family: Rosaceae (rose).

Flowers: Petals 5, white, tinged with pink. Flowers less than ⅝ in. (1.5 cm) wide in compound corymbs. Styles 5. Sepals 5. Stamens many. Fruit berrylike, smooth, red.

Leaves: Alternate, simple, elliptic, toothed, densely haired or nearly smooth below, deciduous.

Habitat: Moist pinelands.

Distribution: Central and north Florida.

Flowering time: Late winter, spring.

Comment: Small shrub or tree, to 15 ft. (5 m) tall or more, thornless, new branches hairy. Synonyms: *Aronia arbutifolia* and *Sorbus arbutifolia.*

Scrub Plum
Prunus geniculata
Harper

Family: Rosaceae (rose).

Flowers: Petals 5, white (may be tinged pink). Flowers sessile and usually solitary. Style 1. Calyx pinkish, 5-lobed, lobes finely toothed. Stamens many.

Leaves: Alternate, toothed, smooth, ⅜ to ⅝ in. (1–1.5 cm) long, petiole red, broadly elliptic to ovate, deciduous.

Habitat: Sand pine scrub.

Distribution: Central Florida Ridge.

Flowering time: Late winter, early spring.

Comment: Shrub densely branched, branches zigzag to 4½ ft. (1.5 m) tall.

Gopher Apple
Licania michauxii
Prance

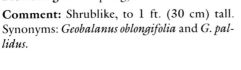

Family: Chrysobalanaceae (chrysobalana).

Flowers: Petals 5, whitish. Flowers small, in terminal, spikelike panicles. Calyx 5-lobed, tube globose. Fruit ovoid, white, tinged reddish or purplish.

Leaves: Leathery, shiny above, and entire; oblanceolate or obovate.

Habitat: Dry pinelands, scrub, and other areas with sandy soils.

Distribution: Throughout the state.

Flowering time: Spring, summer.

Comment: Shrublike, to 1 ft. (30 cm) tall. Synonyms: *Geobalanus oblongifolia* and *G. pallidus.*

◇   ◇   ◇

Summer-farewell
Dalea pinnata
(Walter ex J. F. Gmelin) Barneby

Family: Fabaceae (bean or pea).

Flowers: Corolla reduced to 1 petal. Flowers white, in terminal, stalked, globose, headlike spikes. Bracts prominent, overlapping, broad, reddish-brown. Calyx hairy, 5-lobed, lobes feathery. Stamens 5, alternating with 4 petaloid, infertile stamens.

Leaves: Alternate, odd-pinnately compound. Leaflet segments linear to filiform, gland-dotted, smooth.

Habitat: Dry pinelands and sand pine scrub.

Distribution: Throughout the state.

Flowering time: Summer, fall.

Comment: Stem smooth, branched, somewhat woody, leafy, to 3 ft. (1 m) tall. Synonyms: *Petalostemon pinnatum* and *Kuhnistera pinnata*.

Galactia elliottii
Nuttall

Family: Fabaceae (bean or pea).

Flowers: Corolla pea-shaped, white, sometimes tinged pink. Flowers few, in axillary racemes. Calyx 4-lobed, hairy upper 2 lobes fused. Pod to 2 in. (5 cm) long, compressed, hairy.

Leaves: Alternate, odd-pinnately compound. Leaflets 5–9, stalked, oblong, elliptic or ovate, entire, smooth or nearly so above, hairy below.

Habitat: Pinelands, thickets, and open, sandy soils.

Distribution: Central and south Florida.

Flowering time: Spring, summer, fall.

Comment: Vine twining, prostrate, hairy, base somewhat woody.

Tephrosia chrysophylla
Pursh

Family: Fabaceae (bean or pea).

Flowers: Corolla pea-shaped, white, pink, or red. Flowers in terminal racemes opposite to and longer than the adjacent leaves. Pistil hairy. Calyx 5-lobed. Stamens 10 (9 united, 1 free).

Leaves: Odd-pinnately compound. Leaflets 5–7. Leaf petiole hairy flattened, equal to or shorter than the length of the lowest leaflet. Leaflets entire, ovoid or wedge-shaped, shallowly notched, apex spine-tipped. Parallel veins prominent on the ventral leaflet surface. Upper surface of leaflets nearly hairless, shiny; lower surface hairy.

Habitat: Pinelands.

Distribution: Central and north Florida.

Flowering time: Spring, summer, fall.

Comment: Stem prostrate, reddish, hairy. Flowers white, becoming pink and red. Synonym: *Cracca chrysophylla*.

White Sweet Clover
Melilotus alba
Desrousseaux

Family: Fabaceae (bean or pea).

Flowers: Corolla pea-shaped, white. Flowers small, fragrant, in slender, long-stalked, axillary, spikelike racemes. Upper petal longer than the laterals. Calyx lobes as long as the tube. Legume ovoid, dark brown, 1 or 2 seeded, 2.5–4 mm long.

Leaves: Leaflets 3, oblong or oblanceolate, toothed, ⅜–1 in. (1–2.5 cm) long.

Habitat: Disturbed sites.

Distribution: Throughout the state.

Flowering time: All year.

Comment: Upper stem hairy; lower part nearly hairless. Plant branched, to 3 ft. (1 m) tall or more. Native to Europe.

Amorpha herbacea
Walter

Family: Fabaceae (bean or pea).

Flowers: Corolla white or blue-violet, with 1 petal. Flowers many, in elongated terminal, spikelike racemes. Calyx purplish, 5-lobed, gland-dotted. Stamens 10. Pod few-seeded, glandular, hairy.

Leaves: Alternate, odd-pinnately compound. Leaflets many, entire, gland-dotted, stalked, mostly oblong. Midvein of leaflets terminating as a glandular knob.

Habitat: Dry pinelands.

Distribution: Throughout the state.

Flowering time: Spring, summer.

Comment: Shrub woody below, herbaceous above, to 4½ ft. (1.5 m) tall. Plant covered with a grayish down. Flowers sweet smelling.

Polygala setacea
Michaux

Family: Polygalaceae (milkwort).

Flowers: Heads cylindrical, pointed. Flowers small, whitish-green.

Leaves: Alternate, scalelike, less than 2 mm wide.

Habitat: Pinelands.

Distribution: Throughout the state.

Flowering time: All year.

Comment: Stem slender, smooth, to 20 in. (50 cm) tall.

Tread Softly
Cnidoscolus stimulosus
(Michaux) Engelmann and Gray

Family: Euphorbiaceae (spurge).

Flowers: Petals lacking. Inflorescence terminal, few-flowered. Calyx white, united, lobes 5, petal-like. Stamens 10, united at the base.

Leaves: Alternate, broad, stalked, palmately 3- to 5-lobed or dissected.

Habitat: Dry woods, old fields, and other dry areas.

Distribution: Throughout the state.

Flowering time: All year.

Comment: Stem to 3 ft. (1 m) tall, but usually less. Stems and leaves covered with stinging hairs. Synonym: *Bivonea stimulosa*.

Chamaesyce hypericifolia
(L.) Millspaugh

Family: Euphorbiaceae (spurge).

Flowers: Petals and sepals lacking. Flowers small, in a cuplike structure the cyathium. Petal-like appendages whitish. Cyathia 1 mm long, in stalked, axillary clusters (cymes). Clusters subtended by a pair of leafy bracts, otherwise leafless. Capsules 3-lobed, smooth, broadest near middle, less than 1.4 mm long. Seeds about 1 mm long, wrinkled, brown.

Leaves: Opposite, elliptic, bases oblique, margins finely toothed, petioles short.

Habitat: Pinelands and disturbed sites.

Distribution: Central and south Florida.

Flowering time: All year.

Comment: Stem ascending, smooth, to 24 in (60 cm) tall, often reddish-green. Sap milky.

Eyebane
Chamaesyce hyssopifolia
(L.) Small

Family: Euphorbiaceae (spurge).

Flowers: Petals and sepals lacking. Flowers small, in a cuplike structure the cyathium. Petal-like appendages whitish. Cyathia 1–1.5 mm long, in numerous, axillary leafy-bracted clusters. Capsules 3-lobed, smooth, broadest at the base, 1.6 mm long or more. Seeds about 1 mm long, with transverse ridges, gray.

Leaves: Opposite, elliptic to lanceolate, bases oblique, margins finely toothed, petioles short.

Habitat: Disturbed sites.

Distribution: Throughout the state.

Flowering time: All year.

Comment: Stem ascending, smooth, to 24 in. (60 cm) tall, green or greenish-red. Sap milky.

Milk Purslane
Chamaesyce maculata
(L.) Small

Family: Euphorbiaceae (spurge).

Flowers: Petals and sepals lacking. Flowers small, in a cuplike structure the cyathium. Petal-like appendages narrow, whitish or pink. Capsules 3-lobed, hairy, about 1.5 mm long and wide. Seeds 1 mm long, unequally 4-sided, grayish or brownish.

Leaves: Opposite, linear-oblong, to ⅝ in. (15 mm) long, bases oblique, margins finely toothed. A reddish, central blotch often occurs in the leaves.

Habitat: Disturbed sites.

Distribution: Throughout the state.

Flowering time: Spring, summer, fall.

Comment: Plant prostrate, often mat-forming. Stem reddish, radiating from a center. Upper part of the stem with long hairs, lower part hairless. Sap milky. Synonyms: *Chamaesyce supina* and *Euphorbia maculata*.

Hairy Spurge
Chamaesyce hirta
(L.) Millspaugh

Family: Euphorbiaceae (spurge).

Flowers: Petals and sepals lacking. Flowers small, in a cuplike structure the cyathium. Cyathia about 1 mm long, in axillary, stalked, terminal, roundish clusters. Peduncles leafless. Appendages of glands small. Capsules hairy, about 1 mm wide. Seeds 4-sided, brownish.

Leaves: Opposite, ⅜–1⅛ in. (1–3 cm) long, elliptic to lanceolate, often with some purplish-red, bases oblique, margins finely toothed, hairy.

Habitat: Disturbed sites.

Distribution: Throughout the state.

Flowering time: All year.

Comment: Stem hairy, erect, often branching near the base, reddish-green, to 16 in. (40 cm) tall. Sap milky. Synonym: *Euphorbia hirta.*

Spurge
Euphorbia polyphylla
Engelmann

Family: Euphorbiaceae (spurge).

Flowers: Corolla and calyx lacking. Flowers in a cuplike structure the cyathium. Glands maroon, petaloid appendages white or pinkish, oblong. Styles 3. Male flowers near the base of cyathium. Stamen 1, anther maroon. Capsule smooth, 4 or 5 mm wide.

Leaves: Alternate, linear, numerous, overlapping.

Habitat: Pinelands and disturbed sites.

Distribution: Central and south Florida.

Flowering time: All year.

Comment: Stem leafy, to 1 ft. (30 cm) tall. Sap milky. Synonym: *Tithymalopsis polyphylla.*

Beach Tea
Croton punctatus
Jacquin

Family: Euphorbiaceae (spurge).

Flowers: Petals white. Flowers small, in racemes. Male and female flowers separate, but on the same plant. Male flowers lack petals. Stamens 10–12. Capsule broader than long.

Leaves: Alternate, ovate to lanceolate or broadest near the base, entire, long-stalked, silvery with tiny, star-shaped hairs.

Habitat: Coastal dunes and beaches.

Distribution: Throughout the state.

Flowering time: All year.

Comment: Stem often woody at the base, much branched, hairy, to 3 ft. (1 m) tall.

Silver Croton
Croton argyranthemus
Michaux

Family: Euphorbiaceae (spurge).

Flowers: Petals 5, white, hairy. Flowers small, in terminal racemes. Male and female flowers separate, but on the same plant. Sepals 5, united, whitish-green, hairy. Stamens 8. Pistil 3. Capsule 3-seeded.

Leaves: Alternate, stalked, entire, lanceolate. Green above, silvery or brownish below.

Habitat: Dry pinelands and sandhills.

Distribution: Central and north Florida.

Flowering time: Spring, summer, fall.

Comment: Plant woody, densely covered with brownish, star-shaped hairs. Plant sap was once used for scratches and cuts. The pineland croton *(Croton linearis),* a similar species of central and south Florida, has narrowly linear leaves with white-yellowish hairs on the ventral leaf surfaces.

Croton glandulosus
L.

Family: Euphorbiaceae (spurge).

Flowers: Petals 5, white. Flowers small, in terminal racemes. Male and female flowers separate, but on the same plant. Stigmas 3. Sepals 5, hairy. Stamens 10. Capsule 3-seeded.

Leaves: Alternate, stalked, toothed, lanceolate to oblong. A pair of disc-shaped glands occurs on the leaf petiole at base of the blade.

Habitat: Pinelands, scrub, and disturbed sites.

Distribution: Throughout the state.

Flowering time: All year.

Comment: Plant weedy, rough to the touch, stem branched, to 3½ in. (9 cm) tall. Plant covered with tiny, star-shaped hairs. Synonym: *Croton arenicola*.

Inkberry or Gallberry
Ilex glabra
(L.) Gray

Family: Aquifoliaceae (holly).

Flowers: Corolla 6-lobed, whitish-green. Flowers small, in axillary clusters. Male flowers clustered, female flowers solitary. Stamens 6. Fruit fleshy, black when ripe, bitter.

Leaves: Alternate, evergreen, obovate to elliptic, usually broadened upward, apex toothed.

Habitat: Damp pinelands.

Distribution: Throughout the state.

Flowering time: Winter, spring, summer.

Comment: Shrub or small tree to 6 ft. (2 m) tall or more. Branches hairy.

Dahoon Holly
Ilex cassine
L.

Family: Aquifoliaceae (holly).

Flowers: Corolla white. Flowers small, in axillary clusters. Male and female flowers separate. Fruit red or orangish.

Leaves: Alternate, evergreen, often elliptic, 2–4 in. (5–10 cm) long, entire or slightly toothed above the middle. Dark green, smooth above; pale, hairy below.

Habitat: Low woods and swamps.

Distribution: Throughout the state.

Flowering time: Spring.

Comment: Shrub or tree to 36 ft. (12 m) tall. Bark grayish, branches with fine hairs.

Yaupon Holly
Ilex vomitoria
Aiton

Family: Aquifoliaceae (holly).

Flowers: Petals 5, white, united at the base. Male and female flowers separate. Flowers small, in axillary clusters or solitary. Fruit red.

Leaves: Alternate, evergreen, ¾–1½ in. (2–4 cm) long, oval or elliptic, shallowly toothed. Leaves smooth, dark green, shiny above and paler below.

Habitat: Sandy woods and thickets.

Distribution: Throughout the state.

Flowering time: Spring.

Comment: Shrub or small tree, to 24 ft. (8 m) tall. The early southern, white settlers and Indians made a tea from dried and roasted leaves of yaupon holly.

Redroot
Ceanothus microphyllus
Michaux

Family: Rhamnaceae (buckthorn).

Flowers: Petals 5, white. Flowers tiny, in globular clusters. Sepals 5. Stamens 5.

Leaves: Alternate, evergreen, entire, oblong or ovoid, to ⅜ in. (10 mm) long. Petiole short, hairy. Leaves with 3 main veins.

Habitat: Dry pinelands.

Distribution: Central and north Florida.

Flowering time: Late winter, spring.

Comment: Plant low-growing, bushy. Synonym: *Ceanothus serpyllifolius*.

Loblolly Bay
Gordonia lasianthus
(L.) Ellis

Family: Theaceae (tea or camellia).

Flowers: Petals 5, margins fringed. Flowers showy, solitary, white with a yellow center. Sepals 5. Stamens many, adhering to the bases of the petals.

Leaves: Alternate, evergreen, smooth, elliptic to oblanceolate.

Habitat: Bayheads and swamps.

Distribution: Central and north Florida.

Flowering time: Spring, summer, fall.

Comment: Shrub or small tree.

Lechea deckertii
Small

Family: Cistaceae (rock-rose).

Flowers: Petals 3, white. Flowers small. Sepals 5, outer 2 shorter than the inner 3. Calyx with a few hairs or none at all.

Leaves: Alternate, linear, smooth above, sparsely hairy below.

Habitat: Scrub and sandhills.

Distribution: Throughout the state.

Flowering time: Summer, fall.

Comment: Plant woody below, less so above, wiry-branched, to 1 ft. (30 cm) tall. Synonym: *Lechea myriophylla.*

Long-leaf Violet
Viola lanceolata
L.

Family: Violaceae (violet).

Flowers: Petals 5, white. Purplish lines on the lower petals. Flowers solitary, stalked, spurred. Sepals 5. Stamens 5.

Leaves: Basal, linear or lanceolate, smooth, margins shallow-toothed. Leaf bases tapered.

Habitat: Damp areas.

Distribution: Throughout the state.

Flowering time: Winter, spring.

Primrose-leaved Violet
Viola primulifolia
L.

Family: Violaceae (violet).

Flowers: Petals 5, white. Purplish veins on lower petals. Flowers solitary, stalked, spurred. Sepals 5. Stamens 5.

Leaves: Basal, ovate to widely lanceolate, margins scalloped. Leaf bases rounded, extending onto the leaf petiole as wings.

Habitat: Damp areas.

Distribution: Central and north Florida.

Flowering time: Winter, spring.

Mock Bishop's-weed
Ptilimnium capillaceum
(Michaux) Rafinesque

Family: Apiaceae (celery).

Flowers: Petals 5, tiny, white. Sepals 5, minute. Stamens 5. Flowers in umbels that are taller than the leaves. Forked, threadlike bracts occur below the flowers.

Leaves: Alternate, forked, threadlike, entire.

Habitat: Wet woods and margins of ponds and ditches.

Distribution: Throughout the state.

Flowering time: Spring, summer, fall.

Comment: Stem slender, branched, to 32 in. (80 cm) tall.

Water Dropwort
Oxypolis filiformis
(Walter) Britton

Family: Apiaceae (celery).

Flowers: Petals few, white, in compound umbels. Bracts threadlike.

Leaves: Linear, reduced, septate, bladeless.

Habitat: Low grounds and margins of ditches and swamps.

Distribution: Throughout the state.

Flowering time: Summer, fall.

Comment: Stem smooth, branched at the top, hollow, rushlike, to 6 ft. (2 m) tall.

Water Hemlock
Cicuta mexicana
Coulter and Rose

Family: Apiaceae (celery).

Flowers: Petals 5, whitish-green. Flowers stalked, in compound terminal and lateral umbels. Sepals 5. Stamens 5. Bracts lacking.

Leaves: Alternate on main stem. Leaflets opposite, lanceolate, toothed, stalked.

Habitat: Wet grounds.

Distribution: Throughout the state.

Flowering time: Spring, summer, fall.

Comment: Stem to 3 ft. (1 m) tall or more, smooth, hollow, purplish. Poisonous. Synonym: *Cicuta curtissii.*

Wild Carrot or Queen Anne's Lace
Daucus carota
L.

Family: Apiaceae (celery).

Flowers: Flat clusters of many, lacy-white flowers in terminal umbels. The central flower of each umbel is maroon. Stiff, narrow, 3-forked bracts lie below each main flower cluster. Older clusters curl, forming a cupped "bird's nest."

Leaves: Alternate, stalked, ferny, segments lanceolate.

Habitat: Fields, roadsides, and other disturbed sites.

Distribution: North Florida

Flowering time: Summer, fall.

Comment: Stem hairy, to 3 ft. (1 m) tall or more. Plant has a distinct carrot odor. Native to Europe.

Fragrant Eryngium
Eryngium aromaticum
Baldwin

Family: Apiaceae (celery).

Flowers: Heads round, compact, whitish-blue, supported by 3-branched, spinose bracts.

Leaves: Alternate, usually deeply divided into 5, narrow, entire segments. Lobes sharp-tipped. Stem leaves dense, uniformly distributed.

Habitat: Scrub and dry pinelands.

Distribution: Throughout the state.

Flowering time: Fall.

Comment: Stem smooth, ribbed, erect, lower branches on or near the ground.

Button Snakeroot
Eryngium yuccifolium
Michaux

Family: Apiaceae (celery).

Flowers: Heads compact, nonspiny, of small, whitish-green flowers. Bracts toothed and shorter than the heads.

Leaves: Alternate, linear, veins parallel. Margins spiny. Lower leaves stiff, elongated, linear to lanceolate.

Habitat: Dry pinelands and open woods.

Distribution: Throughout the state.

Flowering time: Spring, summer, fall.

Comment: Stem solitary, branched above, to 3 ft. (1 m) tall or more. Synonym: *Eryngium synchaetum*.

Marsh Pennywort
Hydrocotyle umbellata
L.

Family: Apiaceae (celery).

Flowers: Petals 5, tiny, white. Sepals 5. Stamens 5. Flowers axillary, in simple umbels.

Leaves: Shiny, ovoid, margins scalloped; the long petiole attaches to the leaf's center. Leaf blades ¾–2 in. (2–5 cm) wide.

Habitat: Wet grounds and shallow water of canals and ponds.

Distribution: Throughout the state.

Flowering time: All year.

Comment: Stem creeping or floating, often mat-forming, succulent, rooting at the nodes.

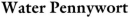

Water Pennywort
Hydrocotyle bonariensis
Lamarck

Family: Apiaceae (celery).

Flowers: Petals 5, whitish. Flowers small, usually in compound umbels, peduncles longer than the leaves. Stamens 5.

Leaves: Shiny, ovoid, margins shallowly lobed; the long petiole attaches to the leaf's center.

Habitat: Wet margins of swamps, ponds, ditches, and moist beach dunes.

Distribution: Throughout the state.

Flowering time: Spring, summer, fall.

Comment: Stem creeping or floating, often mat-forming, branched, rooting at the nodes, succulent.

Wild Chervil
Chaerophyllum tainturieri
Hooker

Family: Apiaceae (celery).

Flowers: Petals 5, white. Flowers small, clustered in compound umbels. Umbels sessile or nearly so. Involucre bracts ovate, ciliate. Sepals minute or lacking. Stamens 5. Fruit ¼–⁵⁄₁₆ in. (6–8 mm) long, ribbed, beaked.

Leaves: Alternate, hairy, stalked, pinnately compound, dissected. Leaf segments over 0.5 mm wide.

Habitat: Disturbed sites.

Distribution: Central and north Florida.

Flowering time: Spring.

Comment: Annual weedy herb, stem unbranched or branched above, hairy, to 28 in. (70 cm) tall. Lower stem hairs pointed downward.

Spermolepis divaricata
(Walter) Rafinesque

Family: Apiaceae (celery).

Flowers: Petals 5, white, free. Flowers minute, in compound umbels. Involucre bracts absent. Sepals obsolete. Stamens 5, interpetal. Fruit with many small bumps.

Leaves: Alternate, smooth, leaves dissected nearly to the base. Leaf segments about 0.5 mm wide, linear to filiform. Lower leaves stalked.

Habitat: Disturbed sites.

Distribution: Throughout the state.

Flowering time: Spring.

Comment: Stem slender, branched above, smooth, to 28 in. (70 cm) tall.

Tarflower
Befaria racemosa
Ventenat

Family: Ericaceae (heath).

Flowers: Petals usually 7, white-pinkish, separate. Flowers fragrant, sticky, in terminal racemes or panicles. Calyx 7-lobed. Stamen number variable.

Leaves: Alternate, evergreen, leathery, entire, ovate to elliptic, sticky.

Habitat: Scrub and pine flatwoods.

Distribution: Throughout the state.

Flowering time: Spring, summer, fall.

Comment: Shrub woody, branched; stem hairy, to 3 ft. (1 m) tall or more.

Dwarf Huckleberry

Gaylussacia dumosa
(Andrzejowski) Torrey and Gray

Family: Ericaceae (heath).

Flowers: Corolla 5-lobed, white. Flowers small, bell-shaped, in axillary elongated racemes. Calyx 5-lobed, lobes with stalked glands. Floral tube hairy, glandular. Mature berry black.

Leaves: Alternate, elliptic or spatulate, short-stalked or sessile.

Habitat: Pinelands and scrub.

Distribution: Throughout the state.

Flowering time: Late winter, spring.

Comment: Stem glandular, hairy. Plant gets to 16 in. (40 cm) tall. Synonyms: *Lasiococcos dumosa* and *L. orocola*.

Rusty Lyonia

Lyonia ferruginea
(Walter) Nuttall

Family: Ericaceae (heath).

Flowers: Corolla 5-lobed, white, urn-shaped. Flowers small, fragrant, in axillary umbel-like clusters. Calyx 5-lobed, lobes triangular. Stamens 10, filaments hairy.

Leaves: Alternate, ovate, obovate or elliptic, stiff, scurfy and rusty-colored on the lower surface. Leaf margins turn downward.

Habitat: Scrub and dry pinelands.

Distribution: Throughout the state.

Flowering time: Winter, spring.

Comment: Shrub or small tree, to 12 ft. (4 m) tall, twigs rusty-colored. Synonym: *Xolisma ferruginea*.

Staggerbush

Lyonia mariana
(L.) D. Don

Family: Ericaceae (heath).

Flowers: Corolla 5-lobed, white-pinkish, urn-shaped. Flowers 7–14 mm long, in clusters on leafless branches. Calyx 5-lobed, lobes narrow, to 9 mm long. Stamens 10, filaments hairy.

Leaves: Alternate, entire, stalked, smooth or nearly so, elliptic to lanceolate, 1½–3½ in. (4–9 cm) long.

Habitat: Moist pinelands.

Distribution: Central and north Florida.

Flowering time: Spring.

Comment: Shrub gets to 4½ ft. (1.5 m) tall. Synonym: *Neopieris mariana.*

Staggerbush

Lyonia fruticosa
(Michaux) Torrey

Family: Ericaceae (heath).

Flowers: Corolla 5-lobed, white, urn-shaped. Flowers small, fragrant, in axillary umbel-like clusters. Calyx 5-lobed, lobes shorter than corolla lobes. Stamens 10, filaments hairy.

Leaves: Alternate, stiff, ovate, obovate to elliptic, margins not turned downward. Leaves reduced near flowering shoot. Rust-colored scales on the lower leaf surfaces.

Habitat: Dry pinelands and scrub.

Distribution: Throughout the state.

Flowering time: Late winter, spring, early summer.

Comment: Scrub to 6 ft. (2 m) tall or more. Young stems hairy. Synonym: *Xolisma fruticosa.*

Indian Pipe
Monotropa uniflora
L.

Family: Ericaceae (heath).

Flowers: Flowers waxy, pipe-shaped, solitary, translucent. The nodding, 5-petaled, white-pink flowers turn black with age. Sepals lacking. Stamens 10.

Leaves: Alternate, small, scale-like.

Habitat: Scrub and deciduous woods.

Distribution: Central and north Florida.

Flowering time: Summer, fall.

Comment: Herb parasitic or saprophytic. Stem thick, fleshy, to 8 in. (20 cm) tall. Synonym: *Monotropa brittonii*. Some workers place this plant in the family Pyrolaceae (pyrola).

Highbush Blueberry
Vaccinium corymbosum
L.

Family: Ericaceae (heath).

Flowers: Corolla white or pinkish, urn-shaped. Flowers usually in clusters, ³⁄₁₆ in. (5 mm) or more long; longer than broad. Calyx 5-lobed, lobes triangular. Stamens 10. Mature berry black, edible.

Leaves: Alternate, elliptic to elliptic-ovate or lanceolate, over ⅝ in. (1.5 cm) long, margins finely toothed. Deciduous.

Habitat: Pinelands, swamps, and bayheads.

Distribution: Central and north Florida.

Flowering time: Late winter, spring.

Comment: Shrub loosely branched, to 9 ft. (3 m) tall. Synonyms: *Vaccinium elliottii* and *Cyanococcus elliottii*.

Darrow's Blueberry
Vaccinium darrowii
Camp

Family: Ericaceae (heath).

Flowers: Corolla urn-shaped, white. Calyx 5-lobed. Stamens 10. Mature berry blue, edible.

Leaves: Alternate, less than ⅝ in. (1.5 cm) long, light blue-green. Leaves evergreen. Stalked glands lacking on the lower surfaces of the leaves.

Habitat: Pine flatwoods and sandhills.

Distribution: Central and north Florida.

Flowering time: Late winter, spring.

Comment: Shrub, to 3 ft. (1 m) tall or more. Synonym: *Vaccinium myrsinites* var. *glaucum.*

Shiny Blueberry
Vaccinium myrsinites
Lamarck

Family: Ericaceae (heath).

Flowers: Corolla urn-shaped, tinged whitish-red. Flowers small, in umbel-like clusters or in short racemes. Calyx 5-lobed, lobes triangular. Stamens 10. Mature berry blue-black, edible.

Leaves: Alternate, less than ¾ in. (2 cm) long, ovate, spatulate to elliptic, glossy-green, sessile, minutely toothed. Evergreen. Small, stalked glands occur on the somewhat pale, lower leaf surface.

Habitat: Sandhills and pine flatwoods.

Distribution: Throughout the state.

Flowering time: Winter, spring.

Comment: Shrub branched, to 24 in. (60 cm) tall (usually less). Synonym: *Cyanococcus myrsinites.*

Deerberry
Vaccinium stamineum
L.

Family: Ericaceae (heath).

Flowers: Corolla urn-shaped, small, white. Flowers small, pendulous, in racemes. Calyx 5-lobed, smooth. Stamens extend beyond the short corolla. Mature berry dark blue, edible.

Leaves: Alternate, elliptic to oblong, pale beneath. Deciduous. Gland-tipped teeth occur near the leaf bases.

Habitat: Pine flatwoods, hammocks, and sandhills.

Distribution: Central and north Florida.

Flowering time: Late winter, spring.

Comment: Shrub, to 3 ft. (1 m) tall or more. Synonyms: *Polycodium stamineum, P. floridanum,* and *P. ashei.*

Swamp Honeysuckle
Rhododendron viscosum
(L.) Torrey

Family: Ericaceae (heath).

Flowers: Corolla funnelform, white-pink. Flowers sticky, fragrant, in terminal clusters. Calyx 5-lobed. Corolla tube, calyx, and flower pedicels with long-stalked glands. Style long. Stamens 5, filaments extend beyond the corolla tube.

Leaves: Alternate, stalked, slightly toothed, elliptic or broadened upward.

Habitat: Wet woods and swamps.

Distribution: Central and north Florida.

Flowering time: Spring, summer, early fall.

Comment: Scrub to 15 ft. (5 m) tall, flowers appearing after the leaves. Synonym: *Azalea serrulata.*

Agarista populifolia
(Lamarck) Judd

Family: Ericaceae (heath).

Flowers: Corolla 5-lobed, urn-shaped, white. Flowers in axillary, sessile or nearly so, racemes. Calyx hairy, 5-lobed, lobes triangular. Stamens 10, anthers awnless, filaments hairy and S-shaped.

Leaves: Alternate, ovate, entire or wavy, blades with fine-netted veins. Petioles hairy.

Habitat: Wet woods and swamps.

Distribution: Central Florida.

Flowering time: Spring.

Comment: Evergreen shrub, branches weakly ascending, to 12 ft. (4 m) tall. Synonyms: *Leucothoe populifolia* and *L. acuminata.*

Dog-hobble
Leucothoe axillaris
(Lamarck) D. Don

Family: Ericaceae (heath).

Flowers: Corolla 5-lobed, urn-shaped, white. Flowers in axillary, sessile racemes. Style hairy. Calyx 5-lobed, lobes longer than the tube. Stamens 10, anthers awnless, filaments hairy and straight. Capsule depressed.

Leaves: Alternate, elliptic to lanceolate, entire or shallowly toothed. Petioles hairy.

Habitat: Moist woods, thickets, and along streams.

Distribution: Central and north Florida.

Flowering time: Spring.

Comment: Evergreen shrub, loosely branched, to 6 ft. (2 m) tall. Synonym: *Leucothoe catesbaei.*

Fetterbush
Leucothoe racemosa
(L.) Gray

Family: Ericaceae (heath).

Flowers: Corolla 5-lobed, urn-shaped, white. Flowers in terminal racemes. Calyx 5-lobed, lobes short and triangular. Stamens 10, anthers awned, filaments straight. Capsule depressed.

Leaves: Alternate, elliptic, finely toothed. Petioles hairy.

Habitat: Moist woods, swamps, and bogs.

Distribution: Central and north Florida.

Flowering time: Spring.

Comment: Deciduous-leaved shrub; older twigs hairless. Synonyms: *Eubotrys racemosa* and *E. elongata.*

Pineland Pimpernel
Samolus valerandi
L.

Family: Primulaceae (primrose).

Flowers: Corolla 5-lobed, white. Calyx 5-lobed, lobes triangular. Terminal racemes usually branched and leafy. Fertile stamens 5, attached to upper part of corolla tube and opposite the petals. Infertile stamens present between the corolla lobes.

Leaves: Oblanceolate, stalked, smooth. Stem and basal leaves present at flowering time. Stem leaves alternate. Lower leaves with winged petioles.

Habitat: Wet brackish and fresh water areas, especially of coastal sites.

Distribution: Throughout the state.

Flowering time: Spring, summer, fall.

Comment: Stem smooth, branched, to 14 in. (35 cm) tall, smooth. Synonyms: *Samolus floribundus* and *S. parviflorus.*

Tough Bumelia or Tough Buckthorn
Bumelia tenax
(L.) Willdenow

Family: Sapotaceae (sapodilla).

Flowers: Corolla 5-lobed, white, each lobe with a lateral pair of appendages. Flowers in clusters (cymes). Calyx 5-lobed. Infertile stamens present. Fruit an ovoid, black berry.

Leaves: Alternate, evergreen, oblanceolate. Upper surface smooth, lower leaf surface with rufous-silky hairs.

Habitat: Dry pinelands and scrub.

Distribution: Central and south Florida.

Flowering time: Spring.

Comment: Shrub thorny with long spines, to 27 ft. (9 m) tall, stem silky-haired. Synonyms: *Bumelia megacocca* and *B. lacuum*.

Storax
Styrax americana
Lamarck

Family: Styracaceae (storax or snowbell).

Flowers: Corolla 5-lobed, lobes hairy, white. Flowers fragrant, axillary, solitary or in short clusters. Sepals 5. Stamens 10.

Leaves: Alternate, stalked, oblanceolate, entire or weakly toothed, smooth or nearly so.

Habitat: Open, wet woods.

Distribution: Central and north Florida.

Flowering time: Spring.

Comment: Woody shrub to 3 ft. (1 m) tall or more. Synonym: *Styrax pulverulenta*.

Olive
Osmanthus megacarpa
(Small) Small ex Little

Family: Oleaceae (olive).

Flowers: Corolla white, 4-lobed, petals nearly united. Flowers small, fragrant, in axillary, few-flowered clusters. Calyx 4-lobed. Stamens 2, anthers large. Fruit globose, dark purple, ¾–1 in. (2–2.5 cm) in diameter.

Leaves: Opposite, simple, shiny, oblanceolate, stalked, entire.

Habitat: Sand pine scrub.

Distribution: Central Florida.

Flowering time: Late winter, spring.

Comment: Shrub or small tree. The olive *Osmanthus americana* of moist woods and hammocks of central and north Florida has ovoid fruit ⅜ in. (1 cm) in diameter or less.

Pigmy Fringe Tree
Chionanthus pygmaea
Small

Family: Oleaceae (olive).

Flowers: Corolla white, lobes 4, linear and about ⅜ in. (1 cm) long. Flowers axillary, in drooping panicles. Sepals 4. Stamens 2, anthers blunt-tipped. Fruit purplish, ¾ to 1 in. (2–2.5 cm) long.

Leaves: Opposite, entire, elliptic, leathery.

Habitat: Sand pine scrub and sandhills.

Distribution: Central Florida. Limited to the central Florida scrub from Marion County south to Highlands County.

Flowering time: Spring, summer, fall.

Comment: Small shrub 3–6 ft. (1–2 m) tall. Plant endangered.

Fringe Tree
Chionanthus virginica
L.

Family: Oleaceae (olive).

Flowers: Corolla white, deeply 4-lobed; lobes linear, ¾ or 1⅛ in. (2 or 3 cm) long. Flowers terminal, in drooping panicles. Sepals 4. Stamens 2, anthers pointed. Fruit blackish, about ½ in. (14 mm) long.

Leaves: Opposite, simple, entire, elliptic or oval, smooth above, smooth or hairy below.

Habitat: Wet woods and stream banks.

Distribution: Central and north Florida.

Flowering time: Spring, summer.

Comment: Small tree to 30 ft. (10 m) tall.

Rustweed
Polypremum procumbens
L.

Family: Loganiaceae (logania).

Flowers: Petals 4, fused, white, hairy within the throat. Flowers tiny, sessile, in a terminal leafy cyme. Sepals 4. Stamens 4.

Leaves: Opposite, linear, toothed. Leaf bases connected by stipular membranes.

Habitat: Disturbed sites and dry pinelands.

Distribution: Throughout the state.

Flowering time: Spring, summer, fall.

Comment: This annual is mat-forming with diffuse, smooth branches radiating from a central crown. Older plants become reddish-brown.

Miterwort
Mitreola sessilifolia
(Gmelin) G. Don

Family: Loganiaceae (logania).

Flowers: Corolla 5-lobed, white, hairy within the throat. Flowers tiny, in short, 2-branched, 1-sided spikes. Sepals 5. Stamens many.

Leaves: Opposite, entire, smooth, elliptic to ovate, base round, sessile. Leaf bases connected by stipular membranes.

Habitat: Wet areas.

Distribution: Throughout the state.

Flowering time: Summer, fall.

Comment: Stem smooth, 4-angled, to 20 in. (50 cm) tall (usually less). Synonym: *Cynoctonum sessilifolium.*

Miterwort
Mitreola petiolata
(Gmelin) Torrey and Gray

Family: Loganiaceae (logania).

Flowers: Corolla 5-lobed, white, hairy within the throat. Flowers tiny, in short, 2-branched, 1-sided spikes. Sepals 5. Stamens many.

Leaves: Opposite, elliptic, ovate to lanceolate, entire, base tapered, short-stalked. Leaf bases connected by stipular membranes.

Habitat: Wet areas.

Distribution: Throughout the state.

Flowering time: Summer, fall.

Comment: Stem smooth, 4-angled, to 28 in. (70 cm) tall (usually less). Synonym: *Cynoctonum mitreola.*

Narrow-Leaved Sabatia
Sabatia brevifolia
Rafinesque

Family: Gentianaceae (gentian).

Flowers: Corolla 5-lobed, white, yellow eye. Floral branches alternate. Style bilobed. Calyx lobes 5, linear, shorter than the corolla lobes. Stamens 5.

Leaves: Opposite, narrowly elliptic to linear, entire, sessile.

Habitat: Wet pinelands.

Distribution: Throughout the state.

Flowering time: Spring, summer, fall.

Comment: Stem branched, smooth, to 28 in. (70 cm) tall. Synonym: *Sabatia elliottii.*

Sabatia difformis
(L.) Druce

Family: Gentianaceae (gentian).

Flowers: Corolla 5-lobed, white, yellow eye lacking. Floral branches opposite. Style bilobed. Calyx lobes 5, linear. Stamens 5.

Leaves: Opposite, entire, sessile, fleshy, lanceolate to ovate, bases broad. Basal leaves absent.

Habitat: Wet pinelands.

Distribution: Central and north Florida.

Flowering time: Spring, summer, fall.

Comment: Stem smooth, square, to 3 ft. (1 m) tall or more.

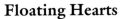
Floating Hearts
Nymphoides aquatica
(J. F. Gmelin) Kuntze

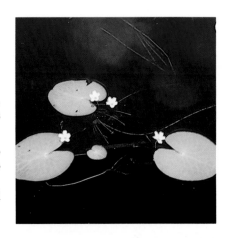

Family: Gentianaceae (gentian).

Flowers: Petals 5, white, united at the base. Style bilobed. Sepals 5, barely united. Stamens 5.

Leaves: Ovoid, to 8 in. (20 cm) across, entire, green above. Lower surface purple, pebbly, veiny.

Habitat: Slow-moving lakes, ponds, and swamps.

Distribution: Throughout the state.

Flowering time: Spring, summer.

Comment: Plant smooth, aquatic, and resembles a water lily. Stem bears 1 floating leaf and a cluster of flowers. Some workers place this plant in the family Menyanthaceae.

Asclepias perennis
Walter

Family: Asclepiadaceae (milkweed).

Flowers: Corolla deeply lobed, petals 5, white. Corolla lobes reflexed. Flowers clustered in umbels. Stamens 5, attached to the stigma.

Leaves: Opposite, stalked, smooth, elliptic to lanceolate.

Habitat: Wet woods, swamps, and along rivers.

Distribution: Central and north Florida.

Flowering time: Spring, summer, fall.

Comment: Stem single or several, smooth, to 20 in. (50 cm) tall. Sap milky.

Curtiss' Milkweed
Asclepias curtissii
Gray

Family: Asclepiadaceae (milkweed).

Flowers: Corolla deeply lobed, petals 5, whitish-green. Corolla lobes reflexed. Flowers sparsely haired, in umbels. Stamens 5, attached to the stigma.

Leaves: Opposite, elliptic to ovate, short-stalked, smooth or nearly so.

Habitat: Scrub and sandhills.

Distribution: Central Peninsular Florida. Endemic.

Flowering time: Spring, summer, fall.

Comment: Stem hairy, often does not stand erect. Synonym: *Oxypteryx curtissii.*

Hedge Bindweed
Calystegia sepium
(L.) R. Brown

Family: Convolvulaceae (morning-glory).

Flowers: Corolla funnel-shaped, solitary, axillary, white (may be tinged purplish). Style 1. Two ovate bracts cover the 5, separate sepals. Stamens 5.

Leaves: Alternate, entire, stalked, smooth or nearly so, narrowly or broadly triangular or arrow-shaped.

Habitat: Moist, disturbed sites.

Distribution: Central and north Florida.

Flowering time: All year.

Comment: Vine smooth or hairy, erect, trailing, twining, or branching. Synonym: *Convolvulus nashii.*

Alamo Vine
Merremia dissecta
(Jacquin) Hallier

Family: Convolvulaceae (morning-glory).

Flowers: Corolla white, funnel-shaped, throat purple or rose. Style 1. Sepals 5, separate, large, smooth, pointed. Stamens 5.

Leaves: Alternate, deeply dissected or lobed, lobes 7–9, margins toothed.

Habitat: Thickets and disturbed sites.

Distribution: Throughout the state.

Flowering time: All year.

Comment: Vine twining, smooth or hairy. Flower remains open all day long.

Stylisma patens
(Desrousseaux) Myint

Family: Convolvulaceae (morning-glory).

Flowers: Corolla 5-lobed, white. Corolla length more than twice that of the sepals. Flowers tubular, solitary, stalked. Styles 2. Sepals 5, separate, smooth or nearly so. Stamens 5, filaments hairy.

Leaves: Opposite, linear, entire, smooth or hairy, over ¾ in. (2 cm) long. Leaves reduced upward.

Habitat: Scrub and dry pinelands.

Distribution: Throughout the state.

Flowering time: Spring, summer, fall.

Comment: Vine prostrate, twining. Synonyms: *Bonamia patens* and *Stylisma angustifolia*.

Stylisma villosa
(Nash) House

Family: Convolvulaceae (morning-glory).

Flowers: Corolla 5-lobed, white. Corolla length more than twice that of the sepals. Flowers tubular, solitary, stalked. Styles 2. Sepals 5, separate, densely long-haired. Stamens 5.

Leaves: Alternate, oblong-lanceolate, entire, hairy, over ¾ in. (2 cm) long.

Habitat: Scrub and dry pinelands.

Distribution: Central and south Florida.

Flowering time: Spring, summer, fall.

Comment: Vine prostrate, twining, hairy. Synonym: *Bonamia villosa.*

Moonflowers
Ipomoea alba
L.

Family: Convolvulaceae (morning-glory).

Flowers: Corolla white with yellow radial stripes. Corolla tube long, slender. Flowers large, showy, fragrant. Calyx 5-lobed, lobes narrowly pointed. Style 1. Stamens 5.

Leaves: Alternate, smooth, heart-shaped or 3–5 lobed.

Habitat: Hammocks, mangroves, and disturbed sites.

Distribution: Central and south Florida.

Flowering time: All year.

Comment: Vine twining, smooth. Blooms at night or early morning. Synonym: *Calonyction aculeatum.*

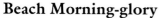
Beach Morning-glory
Ipomoea imperati
(Vahl) Grisebach

Family: Convolvulaceae (morning-glory).

Flowers: Corolla funnel-shaped, white, throat yellow. Style 1. Sepals 5, separate, elliptic to ovate, equal or nearly so. Stamens 5.

Leaves: Alternate, succulent, shape variable, base lobed, apex rounded or notched, smooth.

Habitat: Coastal dunes and beaches.

Distribution: Throughout the state.

Flowering time: Spring, summer, fall.

Comment: Stem smooth, trailing, rooting at the nodes. Synonym: *I. stolonifera*

Wild Potato Vine
Ipomoea pandurata
(L.) G. F. W. Meyer

Family: Convolvulaceae (morning-glory).

Flowers: Corolla funnel-shaped, white, throat lavender or pinkish. Pedicels smooth. Style 1. Calyx 5-lobed, lobes oblong, overlapping, smooth or nearly so. Stamens 5.

Leaves: Alternate, ovate, entire, base straight or nearly so, often hairy below.

Habitat: Thickets and margins of wet woods.

Distribution: Central and north Florida.

Flowering time: Spring, summer, fall.

Comment: Stem twining, trailing, smooth or sparsely haired.

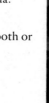

Creeping Morning-glories
Evolvulus sericeus
Swartz

Family: Convolvulaceae (morning-glory).

Flowers: Corolla 5-lobed, white to bluish, funnel-shaped. Flowers solitary, axillary, about ⅜ in. (1 cm wide) and shorter than the leaves. Styles 2, each with 2 slender branches. Calyx 5-lobed, hairy. Stamens 5.

Leaves: Alternate, entire, linear to oblong, ⅜–1⅛ in. (1–3 cm) long with flattened hairs.

Habitat: Sandy soils and wet woods.

Distribution: Throughout the state.

Flowering time: Spring, summer.

Comment: Stem silky-haired, ascending or prostrate, not climbing.

Scorpion-tail
Heliotropium angiospermum
Murray

Family: Boraginaceae (borage or forget-me-not).

Flowers: Corolla 5-lobed, small, white. Flowers in 1-sided, terminal, curved helicoid spikes. Spikes may be paired. Calyx 5-lobed. Stamens 5.

Leaves: Alternate, elliptic or lanceolate, entire, hairy, stalked.

Habitat: Disturbed sites and shell mounds.

Distribution: Central and south Florida.

Flowering time: All year.

Comment: Plant gets to 3 ft. (1 m) tall. Plant blackens when dried. Synonym: *Schobera angiosperma*.

Seaside Heliotrope
Heliotropium curassavicum
L.

Family: Boraginaceae (borage or forget-me-not).

Flowers: Corolla 5-lobed, small, white with a yellow eye. Flowers in 1-sided, terminal, curved helicoid spikes. Spikes usually paired. Calyx 5-lobed. Stamens 5.

Leaves: Alternate, narrowly oblanceolate, pale green, entire, smooth, sessile or nearly so.

Habitat: Saline soils and coastal sites.

Distribution: Throughout the state.

Flowering time: All year.

Comment: Stem low-growing, succulent, mat-forming or ascending, smooth, to 24 in. (60 cm) long. Plant blackens when dried.

Frog-fruit or Carpetweed
Phyla nodiflora
(L.) Greene

Family: Verbenaceae (vervain).

Flowers: Corolla 2-lipped, upper lip 2-lobed, lower lip 3-lobed. Flowers small, purplish-white, in tight, long-stalked heads that are longer than broad. Calyx 2-lipped, lobes united. Stamens 4.

Leaves: Opposite, stalked, obovate or spatulate, smooth, toothed near the apex, base tapered.

Habitat: Damp, sandy soils.

Distribution: Throughout the state.

Flowering time: All year.

Comment: Stems prostrate, creeping, rarely more than 4 in. (10 cm) tall. Synonym: *Lippia nodiflora*.

Turk's-turban or Sky-rocket
Clerodendrum indicum
(L.) Kuntze

Family: Verbenaceae (vervain).

Flowers: Corolla 5-lobed, white, tube elongated, glandular. Style 2-branched, extends beyond the corolla. Calyx 5-lobed, lobes triangular, green changing to red. Stamens 4.

Leaves: Whorled, short-stalked, smooth, entire, lanceolate, oblong or oblanceolate.

Habitat: Disturbed sites.

Distribution: Throughout the state.

Flowering time: All year.

Comment: Stem to 9 ft. (3 m) tall, smooth, stout, hollow, branches whorled. Escaped ornamental. Native to the East Indies. Synonym: *Siphonanthus indicus.*

Hyptis verticillata
Jacquin

Family: Lamiaceae (mint).

Flowers: Corolla 5-lobed, white. Flowers small, in separated, sessile, clusters (verticils) on axillary terminal spikes. Style 2-lobed. Calyx 5-lobed, 2 or 3 mm long. Stamens 4.

Leaves: Opposite, stalked, toothed, tapered at the base, lanceolate.

Habitat: Hammocks and disturbed sites.

Distribution: Central and south Florida.

Flowering time: Summer, fall, early winter.

Comment: Stem smooth or sparsely haired. Plant gets to 6 ft. (2 m) tall or more. Native to tropical America.

Musky Mint
Hyptis alata
(Rafinesque) Shinners

Family: Lamiaceae (mint).

Flowers: Corolla 5-lobed, white, purple-spotted. Flowers small, in stalked, axillary, hemispheric heads. Bracts pale green, hairy. Calyx 5-lobed. Stamens 4, resting on the lower lip of the flower.

Leaves: Opposite, lanceolate to ovate, toothed, base narrow. Lower leaves stalked; upper leaves reduced, sessile. Leaves extend into the inflorescence.

Habitat: Moist, open areas.

Distribution: Throughout the state.

Flowering time: All year.

Comment: Stem square, usually unbranched, sparsely haired, green-purple, stout, to 9 ft. (3 m) tall.

Narrow-leaved Mountain-mint
Pycnanthemum tenuifolium
Schrader

Family: Lamiaceae (mint).

Flowers: Corolla 2-lipped, hairy, white to pinkish. Upper lip 2-lobed, lower lip 3-lobed. Flowers in dense, flat-topped, clusters. Style 2-lobed. Calyx 5-lobed, hairy. Stamens 4.

Leaves: Opposite, linear, 1–1.5 mm wide, entire, sessile or nearly so.

Habitat: Open fields and thickets.

Distribution: North Florida.

Flowering time: Summer.

Comment: Stem square, branched above, smooth, to 3 ft. (1 m) tall or more. Synonym: *Koellia flexuosa*.

Horsemint or Spotted Beebalm
Monarda punctata
L.

Family: Lamiaceae (mint).

Flowers: Corolla 2-lipped, white or yellowish, spotted purplish. Upper lip bearded at apex, middle lobe of lower lip notched at apex. Flowers in clusters (verticils) around the stem and subtended by leaflike bracts that are green on the lower surface and pink on the upper surface. Style 2-branched. Calyx 5-lobed. Stamens 2.

Leaves: Opposite, stalked, elliptic or lanceolate, toothed, base narrow.

Habitat: Disturbed sites.

Distribution: Central and north Florida.

Flowering time: Late spring, summer, fall.

Comment: Stem square, leafy, hairy, to 3 ft. (1 m) tall.

Common Nightshade
Solanum americanum
Miller

Family: Solanaceae (nightshade).

Flowers: Corolla star-shaped, white with yellow, protruding stamens. Flowers axillary, usually in stalked, nodding clusters. Calyx 5-lobed. Stamens 5, surrounding the style. Mature berry shiny black.

Leaves: Alternate, entire or toothed, stalked, sparsely haired, triangular-ovate.

Habitat: Disturbed sites, woods, and thickets.

Distribution: Throughout the state.

Flowering time: All year.

Comment: Stem branched, smooth or nearly so, nonprickly, based may be woody, to 3 ft. (1 m) tall (usually less). Plant poisonous.

Horse-nettle
Solanum carolinense
L.

Family: Solanaceae (nightshade).

Flowers: Corolla star-shaped, white or purplish with yellow, protruding stamens. Flowers few, in terminal racemes. Calyx 5-lobed. Stamens 5, surrounding the style. Mature berry yellow.

Leaves: Alternate, elliptic-lanceolate to ovate, lobed, stalked, prickly, hairy.

Habitat: Disturbed sites.

Distribution: Central and north Florida.

Flowering time: Spring, summer, fall.

Comment: Stem branched, prickly, hairy, to 3 ft. (1 m) tall. Plant poisonous. Synonym: *Solanum floridanum*.

Soda-apple
Solanum capsicoides
Allioni

Family: Solanaceae (nightshade).

Flowers: Corolla star-shaped, white. Calyx 5-lobed. Stamens 5, surrounding the style. Mature berry orange-red, over ⅜ in. (1 cm) long.

Leaves: Alternate, ovate, lobed or toothed, velvety. Midrib of leaf with erect, yellow spines.

Habitat: Disturbed sites.

Distribution: Central and north Florida.

Flowering time: All year.

Comment: Stem to 3 ft. (1 m) tall, branched, armed with yellowish spines.

Jimson-weed
Datura stramonium
L.

Family: Solanaceae (nightshade).

Flowers: Corolla white to purplish, funnel-shaped, elongated, 5-lobed, lobes spine-tipped. Flowers terminal, solitary, strong-scented. Calyx lobes lanceolate, angled, toothed. Fruit a spiny capsule.

Leaves: Alternate, stalked, sparsely haired, lanceolate, toothed.

Habitat: Disturbed sites.

Distribution: Central and north Florida.

Flowering time: Spring, summer, fall.

Comment: Weedy plant is nearly hairless, to 3 ft. (1 m) tall or more, poisonous.

Sweet Broom
Scoparia dulcis
L.

Family: Scrophulariaceae (snapdragon or fig-wort).

Flowers: Corolla 4-parted, white. Petal bases, stamen filament apices, and styles purplish. Flowers tiny, stalked, axillary, throat hairy. Calyx 4-parted, lobes 3-veined. Stamens 4.

Leaves: Opposite, ovate-lanceolate, whorled, gland-toothed, entire or toothed near apex. Lower leaves the larger.

Habitat: Disturbed sites and open pinelands.

Distribution: Throughout the state.

Flowering time: All year.

Comment: Stem branched, hairy, to 32 in. (80 cm) tall. Plant slightly fragrant.

Blueheart
Buchnera americana
L.

Family: Scrophulariaceae (snapdragon or fig-wort).

Flowers: Corolla 5-lobed, white or purple. Lobes shorter than the tube. Flowers axillary, in loose, terminal spikes. Calyx 5-lobed; lobes unequal. Stamens 4.

Leaves: Opposite, rough, entire or toothed, sessile. Basal leaves obovate, upper leaves reduced, ovate, linear-lanceolate to lanceolate-elliptic.

Habitat: Pinelands, disturbed areas, and meadows.

Distribution: Throughout the state.

Flowering time: All year.

Comment: Stem rough, hairy or nearly so, to 3 ft. (1 m) or more tall. Plant turns black when dried. Some workers separate this plant into two species, *Buchnera americana* and *B. floridana*.

Water Hyssop
Bacopa monnieri
(L.) Pennell

Family: Scrophulariaceae (snapdragon or fig-wort).

Flowers: Corolla bell-shaped, lobes 5, white tinged blue-pink. Flowers small, stalked, axillary. Sepals 5, unequal. Stamens 4.

Leaves: Opposite, hairless, sessile, entire, obovate, usually single-veined.

Habitat: Marshy soils and shallow waters of ditches, ponds, and other low areas.

Distribution: Throughout the state.

Flowering time: All year.

Comment: Stems creeping, often mat-forming, smooth, succulent, odorless. Plant resembles a portulaca. Synonym: *Bramia monnieri*.

Gratiola hispida
(Bentham) Pollard

Family: Scrophulariaceae (snapdragon or figwort).

Flowers: Corolla 2-lipped, 4-lobed, white. Flowers solitary, sessile, axillary. Style 1. Sepals 5, ciliated. Upper 2 stamens fertile.

Leaves: Opposite, sessile, firm, hairy, linear, margins reflexed. Lower leaf surface grooved.

Habitat: Dry pinelands and scrub.

Distribution: Throughout the state.

Flowering time: Spring, summer, fall.

Comment: Stem hairy, low growing, rough, to 10 in. (25 cm) tall. Synonyms: *Gratiola subulata* and *Sophronanthe hispida*.

Mecardonia acuminata
(Walter) Small

Family: Scrophulariaceae (snapdragon or figwort).

Flowers: Corolla 5-lobed, white tinged with lavender, pink veins on posterior side. Flowers solitary, axillary, long-stalked, throat hairy within. Calyx 5-lobed, lobes unequal in size. Fertile stamens 4.

Leaves: Opposite, thickish, elliptic to oblanceolate, apex toothed, short-stalked or sessile.

Habitat: Moist pinelands and moist disturbed sites.

Distribution: Throughout the state.

Flowering time: Spring, summer, fall.

Comment: Stem smooth, square, to 20 in. (50 cm) tall. Plant blackens when dried.

Beardtongue
Penstemon multiflorus
Chapman

Family: Scrophulariaceae (snapdragon or fig-wort).

Flowers: Corolla 5-lobed, white or white-pur-plish. Flowers nodding, in terminal panicles. Style 1. Calyx 5-lobed, hairy. Fertile stamens 4; 1 long, hairy-tipped infertile stamen (stam-inode).

Leaves: Stem leaves opposite, entire or some-what toothed, gland-dotted, sessile, oblan-ceolate. Basal leaves stalked, in rosettes. Up-permost leaves reduced.

Habitat: Dry pinelands, scrub, and disturbed sites.

Distribution: Throughout the state.

Flowering time: Spring, summer, fall.

Comment: Stem smooth, to 3 ft. (1 m) tall or more.

Southern Plantain
Plantago virginica
L.

Family: Plantaginaceae (plantain).

Flowers: Corolla 4-lobed, tiny. Flowers in dense, spikelike heads. Flower stalk hairy, leaf-less, hollow. Sepals 4, united at the base. Sta-mens 4.

Leaves: Mostly basal, oblanceolate to elliptic, hairy, entire or toothed, to 4 mm wide.

Habitat: Disturbed soils of lawns, roadsides, and old fields.

Distribution: Throughout the state.

Flowering time: Winter, spring, summer.

Common Plantain
Plantago major
L.

Family: Plantaginaceae (plantain).

Flowers: Corolla 4-lobed, tiny. Flowers in dense, spikelike heads. Flower stalk leafless, solid. Sepals 4, united at the base. Stamens 4.

Leaves: Mostly basal, ovate, hairy, entire or toothed, to 4 in. (10 cm) wide.

Habitat: Disturbed sites.

Distribution: Throughout the state.

Flowering time: All year.

Comment: Native to Eurasia. This species and the English plantain were used for cuts, sores, and snake and insect bites. A tea brewed from the seeds was taken for diarrhea, dysentery, and bleeding mucous membranes.

English Plantain
Plantago lanceolata
L.

Family: Plantaginaceae (plantain).

Flowers: Corolla 4-lobed, tiny. Flowers in dense, spikelike heads. Flower stalk leafless, 5-angled, solid. Sepals 4, united at the base. Stamens 4. Stamens and stigmas protrude from the heads.

Leaves: Mostly basal, elliptic to lanceolate, ribbed, hairy or smooth.

Habitat: Disturbed sites.

Distribution: Throughout the state.

Flowering time: Spring, summer, fall.

Comment: Native to Eurasia.

Elytraria caroliniensis
(J. F. Gmelin) Persoon

Family: Acanthaceae (acanthus).

Flowers: Corolla 5-lobed, white or blue. Flowers in terminal, bracteated spikes. Bracts ciliate. Calyx 4 or 5-lobed, lobe tips hairy. Stamens 2, inside the floral tube.

Leaves: Stem leaves reduced to overlapping, stiff scales. Main leaves in a basal rosette, linear to spatulate, to 8 in. (20 cm) long.

Habitat: Wet pinelands, floodplains, and grassy ditches.

Distribution: Throughout the state.

Flowering time: Spring, summer, fall.

Comment: Stem smooth, to 20 in. (50 cm) tall. Synonym: *Tubiflora carolinensis*.

Buttonbush
Cephalanthus occidentalis
L.

Family: Rubiaceae (madder).

Flowers: Corolla 4-lobed, creamy-white. Flowers small, fragrant, massed tightly in long-stalked, ball-shaped heads. The projecting pistils make the globose head to resemble a pin cushion. Calyx 4-lobed. Stamens 4.

Leaves: Opposite or in whorls of 3, short-stalked, ovate to elliptic, margins entire.

Habitat: Marshes and similar areas.

Distribution: Throughout the state.

Flowering time: Spring, summer, fall.

Comment: Small shrub, to 9 ft. (3 m) tall.

Innocence
Hedyotis procumbens
(J. F. Gmelin) Fosberg

Family: Rubiaceae (madder).

Flowers: Corolla 4-lobed, white. Flowers erect, in clusters or solitary. Calyx 4-lobed. Stamens 4.

Leaves: Opposite, ovate or elliptic, entire. Leaf bases connected by stipular membranes.

Habitat: Dry pinelands, sandhills, and disturbed sites.

Distribution: Throughout the state.

Flowering time: Winter, spring.

Comment: Stem sparsely haired, low-growing, creeping. Synonym: *Houstonia procumbens.*

Hedyotis corymbosa
(L.) Lamarck

Family: Rubiaceae (madder).

Flowers: Corolla 4-lobed, white-pinkish. Flowers small, axillary, on slender stalks. Calyx 4-lobed, lobes ciliated. Corolla shorter than the calyx. Stamens 4.

Leaves: Opposite, linear to lanceolate, glandular, sessile or nearly so. Leaf bases connected by stipular membranes.

Habitat: Disturbed sites.

Distribution: Throughout the state.

Flowering time: Spring, summer, fall.

Comment: Stem smooth or nearly so, square, to 20 in. (50 cm) (usually less), branched. Synonym: *Oldenlandia corymbosa.*

Hedyotis uniflora
(L.) Lamarck

Family: Rubiaceae (madder).

Flowers: Corolla 4-lobed, white-pinkish. Flowers small, in axillary, sessile or short-stalked clusters. Calyx 4-lobed, hairy. Corolla shorter than the calyx. Stamens 4.

Leaves: Opposite, sessile, hairy, elliptic to ovate-lanceolate. Leaf bases connected by stipular membranes.

Habitat: Disturbed, sandy sites.

Distribution: Throughout the state.

Flowering time: Spring, summer, fall.

Comment: Stem hairy, lower branches often lying on the ground, to 20 in. (50 cm) long. Synonyms: *Oldenlandia fasciculata* and *O. uniflora*.

Spermacoce assurgens
Ruiz and Pavon

Family: Rubiaceae (madder).

Flowers: Corolla 4-lobed, white, hairy inside. Flowers small, in terminal and axillary, hemispheric clusters. Stigmas 2. Calyx 4-lobed, lobes ovate and shorter than the tube. Stamens 4. Capsule hairy, obovoid, 2 mm long.

Leaves: Opposite, bases narrow, sessile, elliptic, veins prominent, margins with short hairs. Larger leaves mostly over 3/16 in. (5 mm) wide.

Habitat: Moist woods, pinelands, and disturbed sites.

Distribution: Throughout the state.

Flowering time: All year.

Comment: Plant erect or spreading, stem sparsely hairy, to 16 in. (40 cm) tall. Synonym: *Borreria laevis*.

Spermacoce prostrata
Aublet

Family: Rubiaceae (madder).

Flowers: Corolla white, 4-lobed, lobes ovate. Flowers small, in dense headlike clusters (cymes) in the leaf axils. Flowers pointing in all directions. Calyx 4-lobed, lobes sharply pointed, green with white margins. Stamens 4. Capsule sparsely hairy, elliptic, about 1 mm long.

Leaves: Opposite, bases narrow, short-petioled, linear to narrowly lanceolate, veins prominent, margins with short hairs. Larger leaves mostly less than 3/16 (5 mm) wide.

Habitat: Pinelands.

Distribution: Throughout the state.

Flowering time: All year.

Comment: Plant erect or spreading, stem slender, erect, branching, sparsely hairy, to 16 in. (40 cm) tall. Synonym: *Borreria ocimoides*.

Mexican Clover
Richardia brasiliensis
(Moq.) Gomez

Family: Rubiaceae (madder).

Flowers: Corolla star-shaped, 6-lobed, white. Flowers small, in sessile, flat, terminal heads or clusters. Fruit hairy.

Leaves: Opposite, lanceolate to elliptic, hairy. Leaf bases connected by stipular membranes.

Habitat: Lawns and other disturbed sites.

Distribution: Thoughout the state.

Flowering time: All year.

Comment: Stem hairy, rough, spreading. Plant usually low-growing. Native to South America. Similar to *R. scabra*.

Buttonweed

Diodia virginiana
L.

Family: Rubiaceae (madder).

Flowers: Corolla 4-lobed, white. Corolla lobes hairy within. Flowers sessile, axillary. Calyx 2-lobed, hairy. Stamens 2.

Leaves: Opposite, linear to lanceolate, sessile, margins ciliated. Leaf bases connected by stipular membranes.

Habitat: Moist woods, pinelands, and swamps.

Distribution: Throughout the state.

Flowering time: All year.

Comment: Stem smooth or sparsely haired, reddish-green, weak-branched. Plant usually low-growing. Synonyms: *Diodia tetragona* and *D. hirsuta*.

Poor Joe

Diodia teres
Walter

Family: Rubiaceae (madder).

Flowers: Corolla 4-lobed, white-pinkish. Corolla lobes smooth within. Flowers sessile, axillary. Calyx 4-lobed, hairy. Stamens 4.

Leaves: Opposite, linear to lanceolate, sessile, somewhat rigid. Leaf bases connected by stipular membranes.

Habitat: Open, dry areas.

Distribution: Throughout the state.

Flowering time: Spring, summer, fall.

Comment: Stem erect or spreading, hairy to sparsely haired. Synonyms: *Diodia rigida* and *Diodella rigida*.

Bedstraw
Galium tinctorium
L.

Family: Rubiaceae (madder).

Flowers: Corolla 3-lobed, white. Flowers small, axillary. Stamens 4.

Leaves: Whorled, usually 5 or 6 per node, entire, linear to narrowly oblanceolate.

Habitat: Moist thickets and disturbed sites.

Distribution: Throughout the state.

Flowering time: Spring, summer.

Comment: Stem erect, weakly branched, rough to the touch.

Southern Elderberry
Sambucus canadensis
L.

Family: Caprifoliaceae (honeysuckle).

Flowers: Corolla 5-lobed, white. Flowers small, occurring in flat-topped clusters (umbels). Sepals 5, small. Stamens 5.

Leaves: Opposite, pinnately compound. Leaflets 5–9, toothed; lower leaflets usually trifoliate.

Habitat: Roadsides and thickets.

Distribution: Throughout the state.

Flowering time: All year.

Comment: Small tree or bush. Black fruit eaten by birds; also used for pies, jellies, and jams. Synonym: *Sambucus simpsonii.*

White Lobelia
Lobelia paludosa
Nuttall

Family: Campanulaceae (bluebell or harebell).

Flowers: Corolla 2-lipped, 5-lobed; 2 upper lobes and 3 lower lobes. Flowers white or pale blue in terminal, spikelike racemes. Calyx 5-lobed; lobes narrow, entire or barely toothed. Stamens 5, united around the style.

Leaves: Alternate, spatulate or elliptic, sessile, entire or toothed. Upper stem leaves reduced or absent. Basal leaves may be present at flowering time.

Habitat: Wet pinelands and swamps.

Distribution: Throughout the state.

Flowering time: All year.

Comment: Stem to 32 in. (80 cm) tall.

White-topped Aster
Aster reticulatus
Pursh

Family: Asteraceae (aster or daisy).

Flowers: Heads of drooping white ray florets and yellow disk florets. Heads stalked, in terminal branches. Bracts hairy, whitish with green midrib.

Leaves: Alternate, strongly veined, toothed, pale beneath, elliptic to ovate, sessile or nearly so.

Habitat: Moist pinelands.

Distribution: Throughout the state.

Flowering time: All year.

Comment: Stem to 3 ft. (1 m) or more tall, smooth, usually branched. Synonym: *Doellingeria reticulata*.

White-topped Aster
Aster tortifolius
Michaux

Family: Asteraceae (aster or daisy).

Flowers: Heads numerous, small, of a few short, white ray florets and creamy-yellow disk florets. Heads terminal. Outer bracts hairy, white with green tips.

Leaves: Alternate, short, sessile, hairy, entire, broadened near the tips.

Habitat: Oak scrub and dry pinelands.

Distribution: Throughout the state.

Flowering time: Summer, fall.

Comment: Stem hairy, slender, to 3 ft. (1 m) tall. Synonyms: *Sericocarpus bifoliatus* and *S. acutisquamosus*.

Frost Aster
Aster pilosus
Willdenow

Family: Asteraceae (aster or daisy).

Flowers: Heads of many white, ray florets and yellow to red disk florets. Heads many, stalked, axillary. Bracts lanceolate, smooth, tips pointed and ciliate, midrib green, margins whitish. Involucre about ³⁄₁₆ (5 mm) long.

Leaves: Alternate, elliptic to linear, sharp-pointed, sessile, ciliate. Leaves reduced in the inflorescence.

Habitat: Sandhills, cleared floodplains, and coastal hammocks.

Distribution: Central and north Florida.

Flowering time: Spring, summer, fall.

Comment: Stem branched, hairy, to 3 ft. (1 m) tall.

Aster eryngiifolius
Torrey and Gray

Family: Asteraceae (aster or daisy).

Flowers: Heads of about 20, white to pinkish ray florets and many disk florets. Heads terminal, single or sometimes clustered, subtended by a leaflike, spine-tipped bract. Involucre bracts overlapping, spine-tipped.

Leaves: Alternate, sessile, grasslike, reduced upward and bractlike, margins spine-tipped. Basal leaves spreading.

Habitat: Wet flatwoods and bogs.

Distribution: Florida Panhandle.

Flowering time: Spring, summer.

Comment: Stem unbranched, hairy, to 28 in. (70 cm) tall.

Spanish Needles
Bidens alba
(L.) DC.

Family: Asteraceae (aster or daisy).

Flowers: Heads erect with few, white ray florets (sometimes absent) and yellow-orange disk florets. Apices of rays slightly toothed. Tips of outer bracts dilated, hairy. Inner bracts membranous.

Leaves: Opposite, stalked, toothed, lanceolate to ovate, pinnately divided, smooth or nearly so, trifoliate or unifoliate.

Habitat: Disturbed sites.

Distribution: Throughout the state.

Flowering time: All year.

Comment: Stem smooth or nearly so, upper branches angled, to 3 ft. (1 m) tall or more. Synonyms: *Bidens pilosa* and *B. leucantha*.

Pineland Daisy
Chaptalia tomentosa
Ventenat

Family: Asteraceae (aster or daisy).

Flowers: Heads white, of 3-toothed ray florets and white disk florets. Flowers solitary, nodding or erect. Bracts overlapping.

Leaves: Chiefly in basal rosettes, elliptic to oblanceolate, entire or slightly toothed, white-woolly beneath, dark green above.

Habitat: Wet pinelands.

Distribution: Throughout the state.

Flowering time: Winter, spring, early summer.

Comment: Stem hairy, to 1 ft. (30 cm) tall.

Southern Fleabane
Erigeron quercifolius
Lamarck

Family: Asteraceae (aster or daisy).

Flowers: Heads several, of white, pinkish or purplish ray florets and yellow disk florets. More than 100 ray florets in each head.

Leaves: Chiefly basal, oblanceolate or obovate, lobed or toothed, hairy. Stem leaves alternate, reduced, clasping, hairy.

Habitat: Disturbed sites and open woods.

Distribution: Throughout the state.

Flowering time: Late winter, spring, summer.

Comment: Stem hairy, at least near the base, to 28 in. (70 cm) tall.

Fleabane
Erigeron vernus
(L.) Torrey and Gray

Family: Asteraceae (aster or daisy).

Flowers: Heads few, stalked, of white, purplish, or pinkish ray florets and yellow disk florets. Less than 50 ray florets in each head.

Leaves: Chiefly basal, thick, nearly smooth, oval, elliptic to oblanceolate, entire or slightly toothed. Stem leaves alternate, reduced.

Habitat: Wet, shady disturbed sites and pinelands.

Distribution: Throughout the state.

Flowering time: Late winter, spring, summer, fall.

Comment: Stem smooth or sparsely haired, to 24 in. (60 cm) tall.

Daisy Fleabane
Erigeron strigosus
Muhlenberg

Family: Asteraceae (aster or daisy).

Flowers: Heads several, hairy, of 50 to 100 white, pinkish or purplish ray florets and yellow disk florets.

Leaves: Chiefly basal, elliptic to oblanceolate, entire or toothed. Upper stem leaves alternate, stalked, linear, entire or nearly so.

Habitat: Disturbed sites and hammocks.

Distribution: Throughout the state.

Flowering time: Spring, summer, fall.

Comment: Stem branched, smooth to hairy below, to 28 in. (70 cm) tall.

Dog Fennel
Eupatorium capillifolium
(Lamarck) Small

Family: Asteraceae (aster or daisy).

Flowers: Heads of many white, disk florets. Ray florets lacking. Heads fragrant, in diffuse, branched panicles. Bracts overlapping.

Leaves: Upper leaves alternate, lower ones opposite; finely divided, less than 2 mm wide.

Habitat: Pinelands and disturbed sites.

Distribution: Throughout the state.

Flowering time: Summer, fall.

Comment: Stem hairy, to 6 ft. (2 m) tall or more, branches drooping.

Dog Fennel
Eupatorium compositifolium
Walter

Family: Asteraceae (aster or daisy).

Flowers: Heads of many white, disk florets. Ray florets lacking. Heads fragrant, in diffuse, branched panicles. Bracts overlapping.

Leaves: Upper leaves alternate, lower ones opposite; linear, ⅛ in. (3 mm) or more wide.

Habitat: Pinelands and disturbed sites.

Distribution: Throughout the state.

Flowering time: Summer, fall.

Comment: Stem to 3 ft. (1 m) tall or more, branched.

Eupatorium mohrii
Greene

Family: Asteraceae (aster or daisy).

Flowers: Heads white, each of about 5 disk florets. Ray florets lacking. Heads in terminal, roundish corymbs. Bracts overlapping, margins white.

Leaves: Opposite below, alternate above, narrowly elliptic to lanceolate, reflexed, entire or toothed. Principal stem leaves sessile or short-stalked, bases narrow.

Habitat: Pinelands and sandy soils.

Distribution: Throughout the state.

Flowering time: Late spring, summer, fall.

Comment: Stem and branches hairy, to 3 ft. (1 m) tall. Synonym: *Eupatorium recurvans.*

False Hoarhound
Eupatorium rotundifolium
L.

Family: Asteraceae (aster or daisy).

Flowers: Heads of many white, disk florets. Ray florets lacking. Inflorescence (corymb) flattened, broad, branches opposite. Bracts overlapping, golden-dotted, tips pointed.

Leaves: Lower leaves opposite, upper ones alternate; rhombic-ovate to broadly ovate, sessile or nearly so, hairy, margins blunt-toothed. Leaves with 2 lateral veins paralleling the midrib.

Habitat: Pinelands and ditches.

Distribution: Throughout the state.

Flowering time: Summer, fall.

Comment: Stem to 3 ft. (1 m) tall or more, hairy, glandular, leafy.

Eupatorium serotinum
Michaux

Family: Asteraceae (aster or daisy).

Flowers: Heads of many white disk florets. Ray florets lacking. Inflorescence (corymb) broad, terminal. Bracts overlapping, margins blunt and white.

Leaves: Opposite, lanceolate to elliptic, stalked, long-pointed, toothed, base broad. Upper leaf surface smooth or nearly so, lower surface hairy. Leaves with 2 lateral veins paralleling the midrib.

Habitat: Moist, disturbed sites and open hardwoods.

Distribution: Throughout the state.

Flowering time: Summer, fall.

Comment: Stem to 6 ft. (2 m) tall or more, hairy above, smooth below.

Semaphore Eupatorium
Eupatorium mikanioides
Chapman

Family: Asteraceae (aster or daisy).

Flowers: Heads white, of about 5 disk florets. Inflorescence terminal. Ray florets lacking. Bracts overlapping, linear, sharp-tipped, margins green.

Leaves: Opposite, stalked, thickish, blunt-toothed, ovate-deltoid. Uppermost leaves reduced in size, toothless or nearly so.

Habitat: Low pinelands and salt marshes.

Distribution: Throughout the state.

Flowering time: Summer, fall.

Comment: Stem to 3 ft. (1 m) tall or more, round, hairy above, smooth below. Endemic to Florida.

Wild Hoarhound
Ageratina aromaticum
(L.) Spach

Family: Asteraceae (aster or daisy).

Flowers: Heads of less than 20 white, disk florets. Ray florets lacking. Corolla lobes with dense, long hairs. Bracts oblong, overlapping.

Leaves: Opposite, stalked, ovate, margins with round teeth, leaf bases round.

Habitat: Dry, moist woods and disturbed sites.

Distribution: Throughout the state.

Flowering time: Late summer, fall, early winter.

Comment: Stem woody at the base, branches opposite, to 3 ft. (1 m) tall. Floral branches hairy. Flowers fragrant. Synonym: *Eupatorium aromaticum.*

Ageratina jucunda
(Greene) Clewell and Wooten

Family: Asteraceae (aster or daisy).

Flowers: Heads of less than 20 white, disk florets. Ray florets lacking. Corolla lobes smooth or nearly so. Bracts oblong, overlapping. Involucre less than 3/16 in. (5 mm) long.

Leaves: Opposite, stalked, triangular, margins sharp-toothed.

Habitat: Sandhills, open woods, and dry, disturbed sites.

Distribution: Throughout the state.

Flowering time: Late summer, fall, early winter.

Comment: Stem woody at the base, branches opposite, to 3 ft. (1 m) tall. Floral branches hairy. Flowers slightly fragrant. Synonym: *Eupatorium jucundum.*

Eclipta prostrata
(L.) L.

Family: Asteraceae (aster or daisy).

Flowers: Heads white, of several disk florets and fewer ray florets. Flowers terminal, solitary, axillary, stalked. Bracts hairy, in 1 row.

Leaves: Opposite, toothed, sessile or nearly so, linear to lanceolate, hairy.

Habitat: Disturbed sites.

Distribution: Throughout the state.

Flowering time: All year.

Comment: Stem hairy, low-growing, erect, to 3 ft. (1 m) tall. Synonym: *Eclipta alba*.

Hempweed
Mikania cordifolia
(L. f.) Willdenow

Family: Asteraceae (aster or daisy).

Flowers: Heads hairy, of 3 or 4 tubular, white to pinkish florets. Ray florets lacking. Heads in axillary, stalked clusters. Bracts roundish to pointed, ¼–⅜ in. (6–9 mm) long. Flowers fragrant.

Leaves: Opposite, stalked, densely hairy, toothed or entire, base heart-shaped. Leaf petioles hairy.

Habitat: Open thickets and wet areas.

Distribution: Throughout the state.

Flowering time: All year.

Comment: Vine herbaceous, climbing, hairy.

Hempweed
Mikania scandens
(L.) Willdenow

Family: Asteraceae (aster or daisy).

Flowers: Heads of 4, tubular, white to pinkish florets. Ray florets lacking. Heads in axillary, stalked clusters. Bracts pointed, ⅛–³⁄₁₆ in. (3–5 mm) long.

Leaves: Opposite, stalked, entire or sparsely toothed, smooth or nearly so, somewhat triangular. Leaf petiole hairy.

Habitat: Moist thickets, swamps, and disturbed sites.

Distribution: Throughout the state.

Flowering time: All year.

Comment: Vine herbaceous, climbing, smooth or nearly so.

Palafoxia feayi
Gray

Family: Asteraceae (aster or daisy).

Flowers: Heads of tubular, white or pale purple florets. Anthers dark. Ray florets lacking. Heads stalked, in terminal, branching corymbs. Bracts hairy, narrow, green.

Leaves: Alternate, entire, ovate-lanceolate or broadest near base.

Habitat: Dry pinelands, scrub, and sandy thickets.

Distribution: Central and south Florida.

Flowering time: Summer, fall.

Comment: May be shrubby; upper stem hairy and herbaceous, lower stem woody. Plant slender, branching, to 6 ft. (2 m) tall or more. Endemic to Florida.

Pluchea foetida
(L.) DC.

Family: Asteraceae (aster or daisy).

Flowers: Heads sessile, of tubular, creamy-white florets. Ray florets lacking. Heads many, in terminal clusters. Lateral floral branches taller than the center (oldest) ones. Involucre ³⁄₁₆–⁵⁄₁₆ in. (5–7 mm) long.

Leaves: Alternate, sessile-clasping, oblong or lanceolate, toothed, thickish. Upper stem leaves much shorter than the lower ones.

Habitat: Wet areas.

Distribution: Throughout the state.

Flowering time: Summer, fall.

Comment: Stem hairy, to 3 ft. (1 m) tall or more. Plant odiferous.

Blackroot
Pterocaulon virgatum
(L.) DC.

Family: Asteraceae (aster or daisy).

Flowers: Heads of many tiny, whitish to pinkish disk florets. Ray florets lacking. Florets in terminal, often drooping spikes. Bracts overlapping, apices pointed.

Leaves: Alternate, smooth above, hairy below, elliptic or lanceolate, sessile, margins undulating. Upper leaf surface green with a central white stripe. Leaf bases extend onto the stem as wings.

Habitat: Pinelands and disturbed sites.

Distribution: Throughout the state.

Flowering time: Spring, summer, fall.

Comment: Stem hairy, to 28 in. (70 cm) tall, emerging from black roots. Synonym: *Pterocaulon pycnostachyum.*

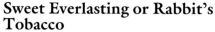

Sweet Everlasting or Rabbit's Tobacco
Gnaphalium obtusifolium
L.

Family: Asteraceae (aster or daisy).

Flowers: Heads discoid, tiny, white. Ray florets lacking. Heads in terminal corymbs or panicles. Bracts white, papery, overlapping.

Leaves: Alternate, narrowly lanceolate or elliptic, sessile, green and nearly smooth above, hairy and white below.

Habitat: Dry, open disturbed sites.

Distribution: Throughout the state.

Flowering time: Summer, fall.

Comment: Stem leafy, hairy, whitish, to 3 ft. (1 m) tall.

Cudweed
Gnaphalium pensylvanicum
Willdenow

Family: Asteraceae (aster or daisy).

Flowers: Heads disklike in spiked, axillary clusters. Bases of heads woolly. Florets whitish. Bracts straw-colored.

Leaves: Stem leaves alternate, entire to wavy, broadly spatulate to oblanceolate. Basal leaves in a rosette, short-lived. Lower and upper surfaces of leaves greenish, but lower surfaces more densely hairy than upper.

Habitat: Open, disturbed sites.

Distribution: Throughout the state.

Flowering time: Winter, spring, summer.

Comment: Stem hairy, often branched, to 16 in. (40 cm) tall. Synonyms: *Gnaphalium spathulatum, G. peregrinum,* and *G. purpureum* var. *spathulatum.*

Cudweed
Gnaphalium falcatum
Lamarck

Family: Asteraceae (aster or daisy).

Flowers: Heads discoid, tiny, whitish to brownish. Ray florets lacking. Heads spikelike, terminal and axillary. Bracts brownish to greenish.

Leaves: Alternate, both basal and stem leaves present. Upper leaves linear to narrowly oblanceolate. Leaf surfaces similar, grayish-green, equally and densely hairy above and below.

Habitat: Disturbed sites and pinelands.

Distribution: Throughout the state.

Flowering time: Winter, spring, summer.

Comment: Stem branched, to 20 in. (50 cm) tall, densely white-woolly. Synonym: *Gnaphalium purpureum* var. *falcatum.*

Dwarf Horseweed
Conyza canadensis
(L.) Cronquist

Family: Asteraceae (aster or daisy).

Flowers: Heads numerous, small. Ray florets white, disk florets yellow. Heads in spreading panicles. Bracts overlapping, smooth.

Leaves: Alternate, numerous, toothed or entire, smooth or sparsely haired, margins ciliated.

Habitat: Disturbed sites.

Distribution: Throughout the state.

Flowering time: All year.

Comment: Stem leafy, smooth, to 4½ ft. (1.5 m) tall. Synonym: *Erigeron canadensis.*

Frostweed
Verbesina virginica
L.

Family: Asteraceae (aster or daisy).

Flowers: Heads long-stalked, in terminal corymbs. Ray florets white, entire or notched. Disk florets white. Bracts lanceolate, hairy, in 2 rows.

Leaves: Alternate, stalked, hairy, toothed, ovate to lanceolate, lower surface pale green. Rough to the touch. Larger leaves lobed. Leaf bases extend down onto the stem.

Habitat: Open woods, thickets, and disturbed sites.

Distribution: Throughout the state.

Flowering time: Spring, summer, fall.

Comment: Stem winged, hairy, to 6 ft. (2 m) tall or more.

Melanthera nivea
(L.) Small

Family: Asteraceae (aster or daisy).

Flowers: Heads stalked, of white, tubular florets. Ray florets lacking. Stamens blackish. Bracts hairy, rough, overlapping.

Leaves: Opposite, long-stalked, toothed, hairy. Leaves broadest near base, often 3-lobed.

Habitat: Dry or moist pinelands, open woods, thickets, and beaches.

Distribution: Throughout the state.

Flowering time: All year.

Comment: Stem branched, 4-angled, mottled with purple, rough. Plant gets to 6 ft. (2 m) tall or more.

Fireweed
Erechtites hieracifolia
(L.) Rafinesque

Family: Asteraceae (aster or daisy).

Flowers: Heads elongated, in panicles. Bases of heads enlarged. Disk florets creamy white. Ray florets lacking. Bracts linear, margins often white, apices pointed.

Leaves: Alternate, sessile, toothed or lobed, sparsley haired, elliptic to lanceolate.

Habitat: Moist, disturbed sites.

Distribution: Throughout the state.

Flowering time: All year.

Comment: Stem branched, grooved, sparsely haired, to 3 ft. (1 m) tall or more.

Hymenopappus scabiosaeus
L'Heritier de Brutelle

Family: Asteraceae (aster or daisy).

Flowers: Heads of white or pinkish, tubular florets. Ray florets lacking. Heads long-stalked, in terminal corymbs. Involucre bracts petal-like, ovate, in 1 or 2 rows. Centers of bracts green, bordered by cream-colored margins.

Leaves: Stem leaves alternate, nearly sessile, bipinnately compound. Basal rosette of pinnately dissected or lobed leaves with long petioles.

Habitat: Dry, open areas and woods.

Distribution: Central and north Florida.

Flowering time: Spring, summer.

Comment: Stem erect, angulate, upper branches hairy, to 32 in. (80 cm) tall. Flowers sweet smelling.

Golden Club or Neverwet
Orontium aquaticum
L.

Family: Araceae (arum or calla).

Flowers: Perianth absent. Flowers of 4 or 6 segments on a cylindrical, golden-yellow, terminal stalk (spadix). The basal, sheathing spathe is reduced. Stamens 4 or 6.

Leaves: Basal, stalked, entire, ovate, oblong or elliptic, sheathed.

Habitat: Shallow swamps, ponds, and streams.

Distribution: Central and north Florida.

Flowering time: Winter, spring.

Wild Taro or Dasheen
Colocasia esculenta
(L.) Schott

Family: Araceae (arum or calla).

Flowers: Perianth lacking. Flowers tiny, located on a fleshy stalk (spadix) surrounded by a yellow-green sheath (spathe). Female flowers near the base of spadix and male flower above.

Leaves: Large, arrowhead-shaped, stalked in the center, smooth, entire. Petiole fleshy, large.

Habitat: Ditches and edges of rivers and swamps.

Distribution: Throughout the state.

Flowering time: Spring, summer, fall.

Comment: Native to the Pacific Islands. Escaped from cultivation. This prolific plant is taking over many waterways and choking out the native plants.

Yellow-eyed Grass
Xyris elliottii
Chapman

Family: Xyridaceae (yellow-eyed grass).

Flowers: Petals 3, yellow. Flowers on a scaly, compact, conelike spike terminating a leafless stem. Spike 7–9 mm long.

Leaves: In basal clumps, narrowly linear (1.5–2.5 mm wide), flat, smooth, to 10 in. (25 cm) long. Leaves often twisted, less than 3 mm wide.

Habitat: Moist flatwoods, lake shores, ditches, and other low areas.

Distribution: Throughout the state.

Flowering time: Spring, summer, fall.

Comment: Flower stem flatten above, to 20 in. (50 cm) tall. The several species of *Xyris* in Florida are difficult to identify and technical manuals should be consulted. Genus only occurs in North America.

Yellow-eyed Grass
Xyris difformis
Chapman

Family: Xyridaceae (yellow-eyed grass).

Flowers: Petals 3, yellow. Flowers on a scaly, compact, conelike spike terminating a leafless stem. Spike ⅜–⅝ in. (10–15 mm) long.

Leaves: Broadly linear (to 14 mm wide), 8–20 in. (20–50 cm) long, bases somewhat fan-shaped, pinkish and mucoid.

Habitat: Pine flatwoods.

Distribution: Throughout the state.

Flowering time: Spring, summer, fall.

Comment: Flower stem flattened above, to 24 in. (60 cm) tall.

Yellow Colic-root
Aletris lutea
Small

Family: Liliaceae (lily).

Flowers: Corolla yellow, tubular, nearly united to the tips. Flowers many, in spikelike racemes. Outer surfaces of flowers covered with small bumps.

Leaves: Mainly in basal rosettes, lanceolate, yellow-green. Stem leaves reduced.

Habitat: Moist pinelands.

Distribution: Throughout the state.

Flowering time: Spring, summer.

Comment: Stem slender, to 3 ft. (1 m) tall or more. *Aletris* is from a Greek word to grind; Aletris apparently was a female slave who ground grain.

Bloodroot or Redroot
Lachnanthes caroliniana
(Lamarck) Dandy

Family: Haemodoraceae (bloodwort).

Flowers: Petals 3, yellow-brown. Flowers dingy, woolly, in terminal clusters. Sepals 3. Stamens 3.

Leaves: Smooth, mostly basal, sword-shape, irislike. Rhizomes and roots when broken show a red sap.

Habitat: Bogs, swamps, and wet pinelands.

Distribution: Throughout the state.

Flowering time: Spring, summer, fall.

Comment: Floral stem to 32 in. (80 cm) tall or more. Upper stem hairy, lower part smooth. Sandhill cranes especially eat this plant. Synonym: *Gyrotheca tinctoria.*

Yellow-star Grass
Hypoxis juncea
J. E. Smith

Family: Hypoxidaceae (yellow-star grass).

Flowers: Perianth star-shaped, 6-pointed, yellow. Petals and sepals are similar. Stamens 6, attached at the base of the perianth.

Leaves: Basal, less than 1 mm wide, 3-veined. Leaves exceed the flower stem; margins rolled inward.

Habitat: Pinelands.

Distribution: Throughout the state.

Flowering time: All year.

Comment: Flower stem leafless, slender, to 10 in. (25 cm) tall. Upper stem area hairy, lower part smooth. Some authors place this plant in the amaryllis family (Amaryllidaceae). A similar species, *Hypoxis leptocarpa,* has flat, linear leaves more than 1 mm wide.

Yellow Blue-eyed Grass
Sisyrinchium exile
Bicknell

Family: Iridaceae (iris).

Flowers: Perianth 6-parted, creamy-yellow with a red-purple eye-ring. Flowers small. Flower stalk has a swelling below the perianth. Stamens 3, united to the style.

Leaves: Narrow, grasslike.

Habitat: Disturbed sites, wet fields, and roadsides.

Distribution: Central and north Florida.

Flowering time: Spring.

Comment: Plant low-growing, radially-spreading. Native to South America. This is our only yellow blue-eyed grass. Synonym: *Sisyrinchium brownei.*

Golden Canna
Canna flaccida
Salisbury

Family: Cannaceae (canna).

Flowers: Petals 3, united, narrow, yellow. Corolla lobes longer than the perianth tube. Flowers in terminal, spikelike racemes. Sepals 3, erect. Style petaloid. Infertile stamens 3, yellow. 1 fertile stamen with a petal-like filament. Capsule warty.

Leaves: Alternate, entire, broad, elongated leaf-stalks sheathed.

Habitat: Marshes and other wet areas.

Distribution: Throughout the state.

Flowering time: All year.

Comment: Stem smooth, leafy, to 3 ft. (1 m) tall or more.

Yellow Fringed Orchid
Platanthera ciliaris
(L.) Lindley

Family: Orchidaceae (orchid).

Flowers: Perianth yellow-orange, lip deeply fringed. Spur longer than the flower pedicel. Flowers occur in terminal, cylindrical spikes.

Leaves: Lanceolate, sharp-pointed, smooth.

Habitat: Wet pinelands.

Distribution: Central and north Florida.

Flowering time: Summer.

Comment: Stem leafy, to 3 ft. (1 m) tall. Terrestrial. Synonym: *Blephariglottis ciliaris*.

Tallowwood or Hog Plum
Ximenia americana
L.

Family: Olacaceae (ximenia or olax).

Flowers: Petals usually 4, separate. Upper surfaces of the petals are covered with dense, reddish-brown, fuzzy hairs. Flowers small, axillary, in umbellate clusters. Sepals 4, small. Stamens 8. Fruit elliptic, yellow, fragrant, to 1 in. (25 mm) long, edible.

Leaves: Alternate, entire, stalked, elliptic to ovate, smooth.

Habitat: Scrub, pinelands, and hammocks.

Distribution: Central and south Florida.

Flowering time: Early winter, spring, fall.

Comment: Bush or small tree to 21 ft. (7 m) tall. Plant armed with sharp, axillary spines. Parasitic on roots of nearby plants.

Purslane
Portulaca oleracea
L.

Family: Portulacaceae (purslane).

Flowers: Petals 5, yellow. Flowers small, sessile, axillary. Pistil 1. Styles 3. Calyx 2-lobed. Stamens many.

Leaves: Alternate and opposite, spatulate or obovate, thick, fleshy, entire. Hairs lacking or inconspicuous in the leaf axils.

Habitat: Disturbed sites.

Distribution: Throughout the state.

Flowering time: All year.

Comment: Stem fleshy, prostrate, mat-forming, smooth, thick, branches opposite or alternate. Native to Europe.

Spatter-dock or Cowlily

Nuphar luteum

Sibthorp and J. E. Smith

Family: Nymphaeaceae (waterlily).

Flowers: Petals yellow, small, numerous. Flowers solitary, stalked, cup-shaped. Sepals usually 6, larger than the petals. Stamens many, anthers larger than the filaments.

Leaves: Large, floating, stalked, base clefted.

Habitat: Sluggish bodies of water.

Distribution: Throughout the state.

Flowering time: All year.

Comment: Seeds edible. Synonyms: *Nymphaea advena, N. macrophylla, N. fluviatilis,* and *N. chartacea.*

Lotus Lily or American Lotus

Nelumbo lutea

(Willdenow)

Family: Nymphaeaceae (waterlily).

Flowers: Petals and sepals many, not clearly differentiated, pale yellow. Flowers solitary, stalked, large. Stamens many, anther tips hooked. Capsule a flattened cone with terminal holes.

Leaves: Circular, usually raised out of the water. Petiole attached to the leaf center. Leaf veiny below.

Habitat: Sluggish lakes, ponds and streams.

Distribution: Throughout the state.

Flowering time: Spring, summer, fall.

Comment: Flower stem 3 ft. (1 m) or more. Tubers and fruits are edible.

Yellow Waterlily
Nymphaea mexicana
Zuccarini

Family: Nymphaeaceae (waterlily).

Flowers: Petals many, bright yellow. Flowers solitary, stalked. Sepals 4, with inconspicuous closely spaced lines. Stamens many.

Leaves: Large, ovate, floating, base clefted. Green above, purplish-red below. Brownish blotches on the leaves.

Habitat: Sluggish lakes, ponds and streams.

Distribution: Throughout the state.

Flowering time: Spring, summer, fall.

Comment: Seeds and flower buds are edible. Synonym: *Castalia flava*.

Swamp Buttercup
Ranunculus carolinianus
DC.

Family: Ranunculaceae (buttercup or crowfoot).

Flowers: Petals 5, yellow. Sepals 5, reflexed. Pistils several. Stamens many. Achenes flattened, smooth, pointed.

Leaves: Alternate, long-stalked, single or compound, lobes irregularly toothed.

Habitat: Wet woods and swamps.

Distribution: Central and north Florida.

Flowering time: Late winter, spring, summer, fall.

Comment: Plant is smooth or nearly so. Stem weakly erect, spreading and reclining.

Yellow Prickly Poppy or Mexican Poppy

Argemone mexicana
L.

Family: Papaveraceae (poppy).

Flowers: Petals 4 to 6, crinkled, yellow. Flowers large, cup-shaped. Sepals 2 or 3. Stamens many. Fruit a spiny capsule.

Leaves: Alternate, toothed, lanceolate to obovate, sessile, clasping, spiny.

Habitat: Open, disturbed sites.

Distribution: Throughout the state.

Flowering time: Winter, spring, summer.

Comment: Stem branched, spiny, to 3 ft. (1 m) tall or more. Synonym: *Argemone leiocarpa*.

Tansy Mustard

Descurainia pinnata
(Walter) Britton

Family: Brassicaceae (mustard).

Flowers: Petals 4, yellowish. Flowers small, in terminal, elongated racemes. Sepals 4, hairy. Stamens 6. Seedpod (silique) 4-sided, smooth, stalked, ³⁄₁₆–⁵⁄₁₆ in. (5–7 mm) long, narrowly club-shaped.

Leaves: Alternate, deeply dissected, ferny. Leaves with hoary-gray hairs.

Habitat: Disturbed sites.

Distribution: Central and north Florida.

Flowering time: Winter, spring.

Comment: Stem hairy, glandular. Synonym: *Sophia pinnata*.

Wild Radish
Raphanus raphanistrum
L.

Family: Brassicaceae (mustard).

Flowers: Petals 4, separate, yellow, distinctly veined. Sepals 4, separate. Stamens 6. Seedpod (silique) longer than broad, often with longitudinal ridges; prominent constrictions between the seeds.

Leaves: Alternate, upper leaves narrow and reduced. Lower leaves the larger and lobed.

Habitat: Disturbed sites.

Distribution: Throughout the state.

Flowering time: Spring.

Comment: Stem hairy, somewhat rough, to 3 ft. (1 m) tall or more. Native of Eurasia.

Hooded Pitcherplant
Sarracenia minor
Walter

Family: Sarraceniaceae (pitcherplant).

Flowers: Petals 5, drooping, yellow. Flower solitary, odorless. Sepals 5, yellow-green. Stamens many.

Leaves: Erect, hollow, hood covers opening; white or translucent spotted.

Habitat: Wet pinelands and marshes.

Distribution: Central and north Florida.

Flowering time: Spring.

Comment: Carnivorous. Insects caught and digested inside the hollow leaves provide nitrogen to the plant. Plant gets to 16 in. (40 cm) tall or more.

Trumpets
Sarracenia flava
L.

Family: Sarraceniaceae (pitcherplant).

Flowers: Petals 5, yellow. Flowers solitary (not shown in photo), with a musty odor. Sepals 5. Stamens many.

Leaves: Erect, hollow, trumpet-shaped, green and yellow. Orifice of leaves not covered by a hood. Neck of hood maroon within.

Habitat: Wet flatwoods, bogs, and acid swamps.

Distribution: Florida Panhandle.

Flowering time: Spring.

Comment: Carnivorous. Insects caught and digested inside the hollow leaves provide nitrogen to the plant. Plant often exceeds 20 in. (50 cm) tall.

Rabbit-bells
Crotalaria rotundifolia
(Walter) Gmelin

Family: Fabaceae (bean or pea).

Flowers: Corolla small, pea-shaped, yellow often with greenish lines. Flowers few in long-stalked racemes. Upper petal the larger. Calyx 5-lobed, hairy, upper 2 sepals the larger. Stamens 10, united, anthers of 2 lengths. Pod inflated, smooth, cylindrical, about 1 in. (25 mm) long.

Leaves: Alternate, unifoliate, short-stalked, hairy, oval to elliptic, spine-tipped.

Habitat: Dry woods and disturbed sandy soils.

Distribution: Throughout the state.

Flowering time: All year.

Comment: Stem hairy, branched, often low-growing. Poisonous. Synonyms: *Crotalaria maritima* and *C. linaria*.

Rattle-box
Crotalaria spectabilis
Roth

Family: Fabaceae (bean or pea).

Flowers: Corolla large, pea-shaped, yellow. Flowers in elongated racemes terminating the main stems. Upper petal with dark lines. Calyx 5-lobed, smooth, purplish. Stamens 10, united, anthers of 2 lengths. Pod inflated, cylindrical, smooth, 1⅛–2 in. (3–5 cm) long.

Leaves: Alternate, unifoliate, round and largest at the free end.

Habitat: Dry pinelands and disturbed sites.

Distribution: Throughout the state.

Flowering time: All year.

Comment: Poisonous. Stem leafy, branched, to 3 ft. (1 m) tall or more. Native to the Old World. Synonym: *Crotalaria retzii.*

Rattle-box
Crotalaria lanceolata
E. Meyer

Family: Fabaceae (bean or pea).

Flowers: Corolla pea-shaped, ⅜ in. (1 cm) or less long, yellow with red-brown lines or spots. Flowers in racemes terminating the main stems. Calyx 5-lobed, hairy. Stamens 10, united, anthers of 2 lengths. Pod inflated, cylindrical, hairy, about 1½ in. (4 cm) long.

Leaves: Alternate, leaflets 3. Leaflets linear to lanceolate, sharp-tipped.

Habitat: Disturbed sites.

Distribution: Central and north Florida.

Flowering time: All year.

Comment: Stem minutely hairy, branched, to 3 ft. (1 m) tall or more. Native to Africa.

Rattle-box
Crotalaria pallida
Aiton

Family: Fabaceae (bean or pea).

Flowers: Corolla pea-shaped, yellow, often streaked reddish-brown. Flowers in racemes terminating the main stems. Calyx 5-lobed, hairy, tube longer than the lobes. Stamens 10, united, anthers of 2 lengths. Pod inflated, cylindrical, 1⅛ or 1½ in. (3 or 4 cm) long.

Leaves: Alternate, leaflets 3. Leaflets elliptic, oval to obovate, nearly smooth above, sparsely pressed-flattened hairs below.

Habitat: Disturbed sites and sandy soils.

Distribution: Throughout the state.

Flowering time: All year.

Comment: Stem leafy, hairs pressed-flattened on the stem, branched, to 3 ft. (1 m) tall or more. Native to Africa. Synonyms: *Crotalaria mucronata* and *C. striata*.

Crotalaria pumila
Ortega

Family: Fabaceae (bean or pea).

Flowers: Corolla small, pea-shaped, yellow, clustered in short racemes. Calyx 5-lobed. Stamens 10, united, of 2 lengths. Pod inflated, small.

Leaves: Alternate, stalked. Leaflets 3, oblanceolate to wedge-shaped, apex rounded, margins entire, smooth, middle leaflet the larger.

Habitat: Pinelands and coastal dunes.

Distribution: Central and south Florida.

Flowering time: All year.

Comment: Stem slender, sparsely haired, often mat-forming.

Partridge-pea
Chamaecrista fasciculata
(Michaux) Greene

Family: Fabaceae (bean or pea).

Flowers: Petals 5, yellow. Purplish-red spots often at the base of petals. Flowers 2 cm or more across, inflorescence stalked, in the leaf axils. Calyx 5-lobed, lobes narrow, smooth. Stamens 10, unequal sizes; some purplish, others yellow. Pod narrow, hairy, 1⅛–2¾ in. (3–7 cm) long.

Leaves: Alternate, even-pinnately compound. Leaflets many, linear, each spine-tipped. Small, saucer-shaped gland on the middle of leaf petiole.

Habitat: Pinelands and open, disturbed sites.

Distribution: Throughout the state.

Flowering time: All year.

Comment: Plant 3 ft. (1 m) tall or more, often bushy; stem reddish-green, smooth or nearly so. Synonyms: *Chamaecrista deeringiana, C. brachiata,* and *Cassia chamaecrista.*

Wild Sensitive Plant
Chamaecrista nictitans
(L.) Moench

Family: Fabaceae (bean or pea).

Flowers: Petals 5, yellow. Flowers solitary or few-flowered, to ⅜ in. (1 cm) wide, in short axillary racemes. Calyx 5-lobed. Stamens 5, unequal sizes. Pod compressed, hairy, 1⅛ (3 cm) long.

Leaves: Alternate, even-pinnately compound. Leaflets small, linear, spine-tipped. Small gland on the petiole below the lowest leaflets.

Habitat: Pinelands and disturbed sites.

Distribution: Throughout the state.

Flowering time: Spring, summer, fall, early winter.

Comment: Bushy, to 28 in. (70 cm) tall, branched. Closes when touched. Synonyms: *Chamaecrista procumbens, C. mohrii, C. multipinnata, C. aspera,* and *Cassia nictitans.*

Sicklepod

Senna obtusifolia
(L.) Irwin and Barneby

Family: Fabaceae (bean or pea).

Flowers: Petals 5, yellow. Flowers few, clustered in terminal or axillary racemes. Calyx 5-lobed, unequal. Stamens 10, some sterile, unequal sizes. Pod sickle-shaped, to 8 in. (20 cm) long.

Leaves: Alternate, even-pinnately compound. Leaflets 2 or 3 pairs, obovate, apex round and spine-tipped, terminal pair the largest. Elongated gland on petiole between or near the lowest pair of leaflets.

Habitat: Disturbed sites.

Distribution: Throughout the state.

Flowering time: Summer, fall.

Comment: Plant poisonous, smooth or nearly so, 3 ft. (1 m) tall or more. Native to tropical America. Synonym: *Cassia obtusifolia*.

Coffee Senna

Senna occidentalis
(L.) Link

Family: Fabaceae (bean or pea).

Flowers: Petals 5, yellow with dark veins. Flowers axillary or solitary in few-flowered racemes. Calyx 5-lobed, unequal sizes. Stamens 10, some sterile, unequal in size. Pod linear, compressed, to 5½ in. (14 cm) long.

Leaves: Alternate, even-pinnately compound. Leaflets 6–12, ovate or lanceolate, tips pointed, margins ciliated. Round, sessile gland on the leaf petiole at the base.

Habitat: Disturbed sites.

Distribution: Throughout the state.

Flowering time: Spring, summer, fall.

Comment: Stem smooth or nearly so, to 6 ft. (2 m) tall. The roasted ground seeds have been used as a coffee substitute. Synonym: *Cassia occidentalis*.

Chamaecrista rotundifolia
(Persoon) Greene

Family: Fabaceae (bean or pea).

Flowers: Petals 5, yellow. Flowers small, long-stalked, axillary. Sepals 5, hairy. Stamens 6, unequal sizes. Anthers large, filaments short. Pod finely hairy, compressed, about 8 in. (20 cm) long.

Leaves: Alternate, leaflets 1 pair. Each leaflet is fused at the oblique base. Leaflets ovoid, spine-tipped, margins finely ciliated. Surfaces smooth, petioles ciliate. Stipules veiny, paired, margins ciliated, narrowly pointed.

Habitat: Disturbed sites.

Distribution: Central Florida.

Flowering time: All year.

Comment: Stem hairy, prostrate, spreading, branches erect. Native to tropical America. Synonym: *Cassia rotundifolia.*

Pencilflower
Stylosanthes hamata
(L.) Taubert

Family: Fabaceae (bean or pean).

Flowers: Flowers sterile or fertile. Fertile flowers lack a perianth. The sterile flowers have yellow corollas and tubular calyces. Style hooked. Stamens 10. Pod a 2-jointed loment.

Leaves: Alternate, leaflets 3, narrowly elliptic, margins ciliate, apex spine-tipped. Veins of lower surface of leaflets prominent. Stipules paired, narrow and tapered to a tip.

Habitat: Pinelands and disturbed sites.

Distribution: Central and south Florida.

Flowering time: All year.

Comment: Stem slender, hairy.

Black Medic
Medicago lupulina
L.

Family: Fabaceae (bean or pea).

Flowers: Corolla pea-shaped, yellow. Flowers small in roundish, compact spikelike, axillary racemes. Calyx bell-shaped, hairy. Stamens 10 (9 united, 1 free). Mature legume coiled, black, to 2.5 mm long.

Leaves: Alternate, leaflets 3, hairy, finely toothed, apices bristle-tipped. Leaflets ovate to elliptic or wedge-shaped, spine-tipped.

Habitat: Disturbed sites.

Distribution: Throughout the state.

Flowering time: Winter, spring, summer.

Comment: Stem 4-angled, hairy to smooth, prostrate, branching from a crown of roots. Native to Europe.

Cowpea
Vigna luteola
(Jacquin) Bentham

Family: Fabaceae (bean or pea).

Flowers: Corolla pea-shaped, bright yellow. Upper petal wider than long. Flowers in long-stalked, terminal racemes. Keel curved, but not spirally-coiled. Style hairy along upper surface. Calyx 2-lipped, upper lobes united. Stamens 10 (9 united, 1 free). Pod hairy, linear.

Leaves: Leaflets 3, ovate or lanceolate, entire, sparsely hairy.

Habitat: Disturbed sites and thickets, especially in the coastal areas.

Distribution: Throughout the state.

Flowering time: All year.

Comment: Vine herbaceous, smooth, trailing or climbing.

Bequilla
Sesbania emerus
(Aublet) Urban

Family: Fabaceae (bean or pea).

Flowers: Corolla pea-shaped. Upper petal yellow mottled with purplish-brown. Keel tip often pink-red. Flowers few, in axillary racemes. Calyx smooth, bell-shaped; lobes shorter than the tube. Stamens 10 (9 united, 1 free). Pod linear, 8 in. (20 cm) long, flattened, many seeded.

Leaves: Opposite, even-pinnately compound. Leaflets entire, about ⅝ in. (15 mm) long, numerous, oblong or linear, spine-tipped. Leaves and stem smooth.

Habitat: Disturbed sites.

Distribution: Throughout the state.

Flowering time: Summer, fall.

Comment: Plant may grow over 3 ft. (1 m) tall. Synonym: *Sesban exaltata*.

Rhynchosia reniformis
DC.

Family: Fabaceae (bean or pea).

Flowers: Corolla small, pea-shaped, yellow. Flowers in nearly sessiled, terminal axillary racemes. Calyx 5-lobed, hairy. Stamens 10 (9 united, 1 free). Pod hairy, glandular, compressed, to ⅝ in. (15 mm) long. Seeds 2.

Leaves: Unifoliate, long-stalked, margins entire. Leaf coarsely veiny, round, with resinous dots.

Habitat: Dry woodlands and clearings.

Distribution: Throughout the state.

Flowering time: All year.

Comment: Stem hairy, branched, erect to 10 in. (25 cm) tall. Synonyms: *Rhynchosia simplicifolia* and *R. intermedia*.

Rhynchosia cinerea
Nash

Family: Fabaceae (bean or pea).

Flowers: Corolla small, pea-shaped, yellow. Flowers congested, in axillary racemes; racemes shorter than the adjacent leaf. Calyx 5-lobed, unequal. Stamens 10 (9 united, 1 free). Pod hairy, to ¾ in. (20 mm) long, brown with black dots. Seeds usually 2.

Leaves: Leaflets 3, leathery, petiole to ¾ in. (20 mm) long. Terminal leaflet the largest, apex rounded.

Habitat: Dry pinelands.

Distribution: Central and south Florida.

Flowering time: All year.

Comment: Stems woody, hairy, trailing or prostrate, radiating from a central crown.

Alicia
Chapmannia floridana
Torrey and Gray

Family: Fabaceae (bean or pea).

Flowers: Petals 5, yellow. Flowers terminal. Calyx hairy, 2-lipped. Flowers bisexual and unisexual. Stamens 10, united. Pod a loment, ⅜–1⅛ in. (1–3 cm) long.

Leaves: Alternate, odd-pinnately compound, 1½–2⅜ in. (4–6 cm) long. Leaflets 3–7, oblanceolate, spine-tipped, margins ciliate.

Habitat: Sandy woods, scrub, and disturbed sites.

Distribution: Central and south Florida.

Flowering time: Spring, summer, fall.

Comment: Stem slender, hairy, viscid, to 32 in. (80 cm) tall. Only species of the genus; endemic.

Indian Clover
Melilotus indica
(L.) Allioni

Family: Fabaceae (bean or pea).

Flowers: Corolla pea-shaped, yellow. Flowers small, fragrant, in slender, stalked, spikelike racemes. Upper and lateral petals about the same length. Calyx lobes as long as the tube. Legume ovoid, yellow or reddish, 2.5 mm or less.

Leaves: Leaflets 3, mostly oblanceolate to obovate.

Habitat: Disturbed sites.

Distribution: Central and north Florida.

Flowering time: Spring, summer.

Comment: Stem to 20 in. (50 cm) tall, branched, sparsely haired. Native to Eurasia.

Indigofera caroliniana
Miller

Family: Fabaceae (bean or pea).

Flowers: Corolla pea-shaped, yellow-brown to pinkish. Flowers in terminal or axillary racemes that are usually longer than the subtending leaves. Calyx 5-lobed. Lower petals (keel) with small, lateral pouches. Stamens 10 (9 united, 1 free), anther tips pointed. Pods hairy, clustered and pointed downward.

Leaves: Alternate, odd-pinnately compound, grayish-green. Leaflets 9–15, small, obovate to oblanceolate, sparsely hairy, spine-tipped.

Habitat: Dry, sandy pinelands and sandhills.

Distribution: Throughout the state.

Flowering time: Spring, summer, fall.

Comment: Shrubby plant to 6 ft. (2 m) tall with slender branches.

False Indigo
Baptisia lanceolata
(Walter) Elliott

Family: Fabaceae (bean or pea).

Flowers: Corolla pea-shaped, yellow. Flowers axillary. Base of pistil hairy. Calyx hairy, 5-lobed, lobes shorter than the tube. Upper 2 lobes shorter than the lateral lobes. Stamens 10, free.

Leaves: Alternate, trifoliate, stalked. Leaflets elliptic to oblanceolate, over 1½ in. (4 cm) long. Midribs of lower leaflet surfaces with flattened hairs.

Habitat: Sandhills, flatwoods, scrub, and pine-oak-hickory woods.

Distribution: Central and north Florida.

Flowering time: Spring.

Comment: Stem reddish-purple, hairy to 3 ft. (1 m) tall. Branches zigzag.

False Indigo
Baptisia lecontei
Torrey and Gray

Family: Fabaceae (bean or pea).

Flowers: Corolla pea-shaped, yellow. Base of pistil hairy. Calyx hairy, 5-lobed, lobes shorter than the tube. Upper 2 lobes shorter than the lateral lobes. Stamens 10, free.

Leaves: Alternate, trifoliate, stalked. Leaflets obovate to oblanceolate, usually less than 1½ in. (4 cm) long. Midribs of lower leaflet surfaces with flattened hairs.

Habitat: Dry pinelands and scrub.

Distribution: Central and north Florida.

Flowering time: Spring, summer.

Comment: Plant bushy-branched, to 3 ft. (1 m) tall, branches zigzag, hairy.

Yellow Wood Sorrel
Oxalis stricta
L.

Family: Oxalidaceae (wood sorrel).

Flowers: Petals 5, yellow, smooth. Styles 5. Sepals 5. Stamens 10, filaments long and short. Capsule ⅜–⅝ in. (8–15 mm) long, hairy.

Leaves: Leaflets 3, clover-shaped, smooth.

Habitat: Fields, open woods, and lawns.

Distribution: Throughout the state.

Flowering time: All year.

Comment: Stem prostrate or erect, hairy. Plant has a sour taste and is often called sourgrass. Synonyms: *Xanthoxalis cymosa, X. rufa,* and *Oxalis dillenii.*

Flax
Linum floridanum
(Planchon) Trelease

Family: Linaceae (flax).

Flowers: Petals 5, lemon-yellow. Flowers located on the upper stem branches. Styles 5, separate. Sepals 5, separate, with marginal glands. Stamens 5. Capsule ovoid.

Leaves: Upper leaves alternate; lower ones opposite. Entire, narrow, sessile, erect, sharp-tipped.

Habitat: Pinelands.

Distribution: Throughout the state.

Flowering time: All year.

Comment: Stem smooth, slender, solitary or branched, to 3 ft. (1 m) tall. Flowers closed by noon. Synonyms: *Cathartolinum floridanum* and *C. macrosepalum.*

Burnut or Puncture Weeds
Tribulus cistoides
L.

Family: Zygophyllaceae (caltrop).

Flowers: Petals 5, yellow. Flowers axillary, solitary, long-stalked. Sepals 5, lanceolate, hairy. Stamens 10, slender. Ovary and fruit spiny.

Leaves: Opposite, evenly compound, hairy. Leaflets elliptic or oblong, terminal pair spine-tipped.

Habitat: Disturbed sites.

Distribution: Throughout the state.

Flowering time: All year.

Comment: Stem hairy, prostrate or low-growing, radiating from the center. Native to tropical America.

Yellow Batchelor's Button
Polygala rugelii
Shuttleworth

Family: Polygalaceae (milkwort).

Flowers: Heads dense, of small, lemon-yellow flowers. Heads about 1⅛ in. (3 cm) long, solitary.

Leaves: Alternate, entire. Lower leaves obovate, upper ones oblanceolate and lanceolate.

Habitat: Low pinelands.

Distribution: Throughout the state.

Flowering time: All year.

Comment: Stem leafy, to 28 in. (70 cm) tall. Synonym: *Pilostaxis rugelii.*

Wild Batchelor's Button
Polygala nana
(Michaux) DC.

Family: Polygalaceae (milkwort).

Flowers: Heads cloverlike, yellow-green.

Leaves: Stem leaves alternate, simple, entire. Leaves mainly in basal rosettes. Basal leaf blades tufted, somewhat spatulate.

Habitat: Wet pinelands.

Distribution: Throughout the state.

Flowering time: All year.

Comment: Plant low-growing. Synonym: *Pilostaxis nana.*

Polygala cymosa
Walter

Family: Polygalaceae (milkwort).

Flowers: Heads yellow-green, in a branched, flat-topped inflorescence (cyme).

Leaves: Alternate, entire. Stem leaves linear, rapidly reduced upward. Basal rosette of lanceolate or linear leaves present at the time of blooming.

Habitat: Wet areas.

Distribution: Throughout the state.

Flowering time: Spring, summer, fall.

Comment: Stem hollow, smooth to 3 ft. (1 m) tall or more. Synonym: *Pilostaxis cymosa.*

Polygala ramosa
Elliott

Family: Polygalaceae (milkwort).

Flowers: Heads yellow, in a branched, flat-topped inflorescence.

Leaves: Alternate, entire. Stem leaves linear. Basal leaves in the rosette are elliptic or spatulate. Basal leaves often absent at the time of blooming.

Habitat: Moist pinelands.

Distribution: Throughout the state.

Flowering time: Spring, summer, fall.

Comment: Stem solid, smooth, to 1 ft. (30 cm) tall. Synonym: *Pilostaxis ramosa.*

Phyllanthus tenellus
Roxburgh

Family: Euphorbiaceae (spurge).

Flowers: Petals lacking. Flowers small, yellowish, in stalked glomerules emerging from the leaf axils. Fruiting pedicels long, slender. Sepals 5. Stamens 5. Capsule smooth. Seeds covered with bumps.

Leaves: Alternate, compound. Leaflets entire, smooth.

Habitat: Disturbed sites and open woods.

Distribution: Throughout the state.

Flowering time: All year.

Comment: Stem smooth, to 3 ft. (1 m) tall. Leaves and flowers restricted to the lateral branches off the main stem. Native to Africa and the Mascarene Islands.

Phyllanthus urinaria
L.

Family: Euphorbiaceae (spurge).

Flowers: Petals lacking. Male flowers with a 6-parted, yellowish-white calyx. Stamens 2 or 3, united. Calyx of female flowers yellowish. Capsule smooth, 2 mm wide. Flowers small attached below each leaflet. Seeds brownish with transverse ribs.

Leaves: Alternate, compound. Leaflets spine-tipped, smooth, except for lower margins, short-stalked, margins ciliate, bases oblique.

Habitat: Disturbed sites.

Distribution: Throughout the state.

Flowering time: Summer, fall.

Comment: Stem smooth or nearly so. Usually less than 3 ft. (1 m) tall. Leaves and flowers restricted to lateral branches off the main stem. Native to the Old World.

Queen's Delight
Stillingia sylvatica
L.

Family: Euphorbiaceae (spurge).

Flowers: Petals lacking. Flowers yellowish in terminal, erect, spikelike racemes. Upper part and much of the spike consists of male flowers; lower part consists of female flowers. Stamens 2. Stigmas 3, red. Capsule 3-lobed.

Leaves: Alternate, narrowly lanceolate to elliptic, glandular, finely toothed.

Habitat: Dry pinelands, sandhills, and hammocks.

Distribution: Throughout the state.

Flowering time: All year.

Comment: Stem smooth, to 3 ft. (1 m) tall. Sap milky. Synonyms: *Stillingia angustifolia,* *S. spathulata,* and *S. tenuis.* The corkwood *(Stillingia aquatica)* is a similar species, but found in swamps and wet soils.

Winged Sumac
Rhus copallina
L.

Family: Anacardiaceae (cashew or sumac).

Flowers: Petals 5, whitish to yellowish. Flowers tiny, in dense, terminal clusters. Fruit small, in red clusters.

Leaves: Alternate, pinnately compound. Leaflets many, oblong to lanceolate, glossy, sessile, entire or toothed, pointed. Leaf stem winged.

Habitat: Thickets and dry woods.

Distribution: Throughout the state.

Flowering time: Spring, summer, fall.

Comment: Shrub or small tree, to 24 ft. (8 m) tall. Synonyms: *Rhus leucantha* and *R. obtusifolia.*

Indian Hemp or Teaweed
Sida rhombifolia
L.

Family: Malvaceae (mallow).

Flowers: Petals 5, united, pale yellow, apex oblique. Flowers mostly solitary, axillary, on slender stalks about ¾ in. (2 cm) long. Base of petals may be red. Calyx 5-lobed, lobes triangular. Bracts lacking. Stamens many, attached to the pistil.

Leaves: Alternate, oblong or lanceolate, finely toothed, 3-veined. Upper leaf surface smooth, lower surface hairy and grayish.

Habitat: Disturbed sites.

Distribution: Throughout the state.

Flowering time: Spring, summer, fall.

Comment: Stem branching, to 3 ft. (1 m) tall (usually less).

Broomweed
Sida acuta
Burman f.

Family: Malvaceae (mallow).

Flowers: Petals 5, to ⅝ in. (1.5 cm) long, yellow-white, bases united. Flowers solitary, axillary, and on stalks about 4 mm long. Calyx 5-lobed, lobes sharp-tipped. Bracts lacking. Stamens many, attached to the pistil.

Leaves: Alternate, lanceolate to ovate and rhombic, toothed, broadest at the base, 3-veined.

Habitat: Disturbed sites.

Distribution: Throughout the state.

Flowering time: All year.

Comment: Stem branching, to 3 ft. (1 m) tall (usually less). Synonym: *Sida carpinifolia*.

Sida cordifolia
L.

Family: Malvaceae (mallow).

Flowers: Corolla 5-lobed, yellow or yellow-orange. Flowers short-stalked, clustered on the upper branches. Calyx hairy, 5-lobed, lobes lanceolate. Bracts below the flowers lacking. Stamens many.

Leaves: Alternate, stalked, ovate to lance-oblong, velvety, base heart-shaped, margins toothed.

Habitat: Disturbed pinelands and hammocks.

Distribution: Throughout the state.

Flowering time: All year.

Comment: Stem woody, densely hairy, to 3 ft. (1 m) tall. Native to tropical America.

Pineland Hibiscus
Hibiscus aculeatus
Walter

Family: Malvaceae (mallow).

Flowers: Petals 5, cream-yellow with a maroon center. Flowers solitary, in upper leaf axils. Stamens 5. Involucre bracts forked at apices.

Leaves: Alternate, 3–5 lobed, ovate to lanceolate, toothed.

Habitat: Wet, disturbed sites and edges of pine flatwoods.

Distribution: North Florida.

Flowering time: Summer, fall.

Comment: Stem rough, with star-shaped hairs, branched above, to 3 ft. (1 m) tall or more.

Hypericum cistifolium
Lamarck

Family: Hypericaceae (St. John's-wort or garcinia).

Flowers: Petals 5, small, yellow. Inflorescence terminal, branched. Styles 3-parted. First flower to open is located between 2 lateral flowers. Sepals 5, ovate or lanceolate. Stamens numerous.

Leaves: Opposite, entire, narrow, elliptic to lanceolate, sessile. Basal groove on leaf lacking. Fascicles of leaves in the leaf axils.

Habitat: Low pinelands and swamps.

Distribution: Throughout the state.

Flowering time: Spring, summer, fall.

Comment: Stem woody, branched, green above and reddish below, to 3 ft. (1 m) tall. Synonym: *Hypericum opacum.*

Sandweed
Hypericum fasciculatum
Lamarck

Family: Hypericaceae (St. John's-wort or garcinia).

Flowers: Petals 5, bright yellow. Flowers sessile, solitary or clustered, axillary and terminal. Styles 3 or united. Sepals 5, linear. Stamens many.

Leaves: Opposite, linear, entire, sessile. Fascicles of leaves in the leaf axils. Largest of the needlelike, evergreen leaves over ½ in. (13 mm) in length.

Habitat: Wet pinelands and other wet areas.

Distribution: Throughout the state.

Flowering time: Late winter, spring, summer, fall.

Comment: Shrub bushy-branched, woody, somewhat flat-topped, to 9 ft. (3 m) tall. Synonym: *Hypericum aspalathoides*.

Hypericum reductum
P. Adams

Family: Hypericaceae (St. John's-wort or garcinia).

Flowers: Petals 5, yellow. Flowers solitary or clustered, axillary and terminal. Styles 3. Sepals 5, needlelike (3 mm long), and white-dotted.

Leaves: Opposite, entire, needlelike, sessile; largest leaf less than ⅜ in. (11 mm) long.

Habitat: Dry pinelands and scrub.

Distribution: Throughout the state.

Flowering time: Spring, summer, fall.

Comment: Plant low-growing less than 20 in. (50 cm) tall, stem woody, often angled and lying on the ground.

St. Peter's Wort
Hypericum tetrapetalum
Lamarck

Family: Hypericaceae (St. John's-wort or garcinia).

Flowers: Petals 4, yellow. Flowers solitary or clustered, axillary and terminal. Styles 3. Outer 2 sepals leaflike and larger than the 2 inner ones. Bracts occur at the base of the flower pedicels.

Leaves: Opposite, entire, ovate to elliptic, sessile, clasping.

Habitat: Damp, sandy soils.

Distribution: Throughout the state.

Flowering time: All year.

Comment: Stem may become woody, often reddish-green, to 3 ft. (1 m) tall. Synonym: *Ascyrum tetrapetalum.*

Pineweed or Orange-grass
Hypericum gentianoides
(L.) BSP.

Family: Hypericaceae (St. John's-wort or garcinia).

Flowers: Petals 5, yellow-orange. Flowers small, on terminal branches. Styles 3. Sepals 5, separate, linear-lanceolate, nearly equal in size. Stamens 5–10.

Leaves: Opposite, entire, sessile, narrow, 2 or 3 mm long.

Habitat: Pinelands and disturbed sites.

Distribution: Throughout the state.

Flowering time: Spring, summer, fall.

Comment: Herb with a wiry-branched stem, to 20 in. (50 cm) tall. Synonym: *Sarothra gentianoides.*

Hypericum crux-andraea
(L.) Crantz

Family: Hypericaceae (St. John's-wort or garcinia).

Flowers: Petals 4, yellow. Flowers solitary or clustered, terminal and axillary. Styles usually 3. Sepals 4, gland-dotted. Outer 2 sepals ovate, veined and larger than the inner 2, lanceolate sepals.

Leaves: Opposite, entire, elliptic, ovate or oblong, sessile, smooth.

Habitat: Sandy soils of pinelands and hammocks.

Distribution: Throughout the state.

Flowering time: Spring, summer, fall.

Comment: Shrublike, to 3 ft. (1 m) tall, stem reddish, base often woody. Synonyms: *Hypericum stans* and *Ascyrum cuneifolium.*

St. Andrew's Cross
Hypericum hypericoides
(L.) Crantz

Family: Hypericaceae (St. John's-wort or garcinia).

Flowers: Petals 4, yellow, oblong to linear. Flowers solitary or clustered, terminal and axillary. Styles 2. Outer 2 sepals ovate, inner 2 narrow, short (or absent).

Leaves: Opposite, entire, linear, elliptic to oblanceolate, sessile, gland-dotted.

Habitat: Wet pinelands.

Distribution: Throughout the state.

Flowering time: Spring, summer, fall.

Comment: Shrublike, base woody, branched, leafy and reddish, to 3 ft. (1 m) tall. Synonyms: *Ascyrum hypericoides* and *A. linifolium.*

Dwarf St. John's Wort
Hypericum mutilum
L.

Family: Hypericaceae (St. John's-wort or garcinia).

Flowers: Petals 5, light yellow, 2 or 3 mm long. Inflorescence many flowered, branched, leafy. Styles 3. Sepals 5, linear, smooth, about equal in size. Stamens few, arising from base of the ovary.

Leaves: Opposite, entire, sessile. Leaves ovate, elliptic to lanceolate, 3- to 5-veined, gland-dotted.

Habitat: Margins of ponds, ditches, and other wet areas.

Distribution: Throughout the state.

Flowering time: Spring, summer, fall.

Comment: Stem usually branched, to 28 in. (70 cm) tall.

Rock-rose
Helianthemum nashii
Britton

Family: Cistaceae (rock-rose).

Flowers: Petals 5, yellow. Flower-clusters several, in elongated panicles. Sepals 5, hairy, inner ones oval or oval-elliptic. Petaled flowers with 15 stamens; apetalous flowers with 5 stamens.

Leaves: Alternate, linear-elliptic to elliptic, midrib prominent beneath. Basal rosette lacking.

Habitat: Scrub.

Distribution: Central and south Florida.

Flowering time: Spring, summer.

Comment: Stem hairy, to 16 in. (40 cm) tall. Synonyms: *Crocanthemum thyrsoideum* and *C. nashii.*

Rock-rose
Helianthemum corymbosum
Michaux

Family: Cistaceae (rock-rose).

Flowers: Petals 5, yellow, about ⅜ in. (1 cm) long. Flowers in dense, terminal cymes. Sepals 5. Stamens many, orange.

Leaves: Alternate, narrowly elliptic to ovate, hairy, silvery-green below and dark green above. No basal rosette of leaves.

Habitat: Hammocks and dry pinelands.

Distribution: Throughout the state.

Flowering time: Late winter, spring, summer.

Comment: Stem erect, spreading, hairy, to 8 in. (20 cm) tall. This species also produces self-pollinated flowers that are small and lack petals. Synonym: *Crocanthemum corymbosum.*

Piriqueta caroliniana
(Walter) Urban

Family: Turneraceae (turnera).

Flowers: Petals 5, pale to deep yellow. Flowers axillary, stalked. Styles 3. Sepals 5. Stamens 5. Fruit a round, green capsule.

Leaves: Alternate, linear, elliptic, oblong or lanceolate, usually toothed or undulating, hairy or smooth, sessile. Lower leaves the larger.

Habitat: Pinelands.

Distribution: Throughout the state.

Flowering time: Spring, summer, fall.

Comment: Stem slender, smooth to hairy, to 20 in. (50 cm) tall. Synonyms: *Piriqueta tomentosa* and *P. viridis.*

Poorman's Patches
Mentzelia floridana
Nuttall

Family: Loasaceae (loasa).

Flowers: Petals 5, yellow. Flowers mostly solitary, axillary, and terminal. Style 3-branched. Sepals 5, lobes lanceolate. Stamens many.

Leaves: Alternate, toothed, 3-lobed, ovate, broadest at the base.

Habitat: Coastal dunes and hammocks.

Distribution: Central and south Florida.

Flowering time: All year.

Comment: Stem branched, to 3 ft. (1 m) tall. Plant brittle and broken parts tenaciously cling to whatever they touch.

Prickly-pear Cactus
Opuntia humifusa
(Rafinesque) Rafinesque

Family: Cactaceae (cactus).

Flowers: Corolla yellow, often with reddish centers. Flowers large, solitary, showy. Pistil 1. Sepals greenish, narrow. Fruit pulpy, reddish, many-seeded.

Leaves: Alternate, small, deciduous.

Habitat: Pinelands and open, dry woods.

Distribution: Throughout the state.

Flowering time: Spring, summer.

Comment: Stems fleshy, spiny. Fruit edible, used in making jellies. Plant gets to 16 in. (40 cm) tall. Synonym: *Opuntia compressa*.

Ludwigia octovalvis
(Jacquin) Raven

Family: Onagraceae (evening-primrose).

Flowers: Petals 4, yellow. Sepals 4, lobes ovate. Stamens 8. Flowers sessile or stalked in the upper leaf axils. Seed capsule to 2 in. (5 cm) long, cylindrical, ribbed.

Leaves: Alternate, narrowly lanceolate or ob-lanceolate, sessile or nearly so, essentially smooth to hairy.

Habitat: Disturbed sites and margins of ditches.

Distribution: Throughout the state.

Flowering time: All year.

Comment: Stem branched, nearly smooth, often woody below, upper herbaceous stem square, to 6 ft. (2 m) tall. Synonyms: *Jussiaea scabra* and *J. angustifolia.*

Seedbox
Ludwigia alternifolia
L.

Family: Onagraceae (evening-primrose).

Flowers: Petals 4, yellow. Sepals 4, somewhat triangular. Style shorter than the sepals. Stamens 4. Capsule cube-shaped.

Leaves: Alternate, elliptic or lanceolate, stalked or sessile, base narrow.

Habitat: Swamps and other wet areas.

Distribution: Central and north Florida.

Flowering time: Spring, summer, fall.

Comment: Stem branched, slightly winged, smooth or nearly so, to 3 ft. (1 m) tall or more.

Ludwigia virgata
Michaux

Family: Onagraceae (evening-primrose).

Flowers: Petals 4, yellow. Flowers in terminal racemes. Styles more than ¼ in. (6 mm) long, longer than the sepals. Sepals 4, elliptic, reflexed, 2 times the length of the capsule. Stamens 4. Seed capsule about ³⁄₁₆ in. (5 mm) long, stalked. Pedicels equaling or longer than the capsules.

Leaves: Alternate, sessile, smooth. Leaves above midstem linear to linear-oblong. Lowest leaves smooth.

Habitat: Wet, sandy pinelands and bogs.

Distribution: Throughout the state.

Flowering time: Spring, summer, fall.

Comment: Stem smooth or sparsely hairy, branched to 3 ft. (1 m) tall.

Ludwigia decurrens
Walter

Family: Onagraceae (evening-primrose).

Flowers: Petals 4, yellow, to ⁷⁄₁₆ in. (12 mm) long. Flowers solitary, sessile or stalked, in the leaf axils. Sepals 4, ovate, to ⅜ in. (10 mm) long. Stamens usually 8. Capsule 4-angled, elongated.

Leaves: Alternate, lanceolate, sessile or short-stalked, drooping, smooth or sparsely hairy.

Habitat: Swamps, marshes, and other wet areas.

Distribution: Central and north Florida.

Flowering time: Spring, summer, fall.

Comment: Stem widely branched, winged, 4-angled, smooth, to 3 ft. (1 m) tall or more. Synonym: *Jussiaea decurrens*.

Primrose Willow
Ludwigia peruviana
(L.) Hara

Family: Onagraceae (evening-primrose).

Flowers: Petals 4 or 5, large, yellow. Flowers showy, solitary, in the upper leaf axils. Sepals 4 or 5, lanceolate. Stamens 8. Seed capsule short, thick.

Leaves: Alternate, ovate, lanceolate to elliptic, entire, hairy, sessile or nearly so.

Habitat: Borders of ditches, ponds, and other wet areas.

Distribution: Throughout the state.

Flowering time: All year.

Comment: Plant often shrubby, herbaceous primarily, branched, densely hairy, 3 ft. (1 m) tall or more. Synonym: *Jussiaea peruviana.*

False Loosestrife
Ludwigia arcuata
Walter

Family: Onagraceae (evening-primrose).

Flowers: Petals 4, yellow. Flowers solitary in the leaf axils. Petals longer than the sepals. Sepals 4, linear-lanceolate. Stamens 4. Capsule usually curved, ¼–⁵⁄₁₆ in. (6–8 mm) long.

Leaves: Opposite, linear to oblanceolate, smooth, thickish, sessile or nearly so.

Habitat: Margins of swamps and lakes and wet disturbed sites.

Distribution: Throughout the state.

Flowering time: Spring, summer, fall.

Comment: Plant low-growing, leafy, creeping, sparsely haired. Synonym: *Ludwigiantha arcuata.*

Cut-leaved Evening Primrose
Oenothera laciniata
Hill

Family: Onagraceae (evening-primrose).

Flowers: Petals 4, pale yellow. Flowers sessile, in the upper leaf axils. Stigmas 4, tubular. Sepals 4, hairy. Stamens 8. Flowers turn red-pink, following blooming. Capsule cylindric, hairy.

Leaves: Alternate, elliptic to oblanceolate, usually deeply lobed, hairy.

Habitat: Disturbed sites.

Distribution: Central and north Florida.

Flowering time: All year.

Comment: Stem low-growing, branching near the base, spreading, sparsely hairy. Synonym: *Raimannia laciniata.*

Weedy Evening-primrose
Oenothera biennis
L.

Family: Onagraceae (evening-primrose).

Flowers: Petals 4, pale yellow, broader near the apex. Stigmas 4, reflexed. Sepals 4, reflexed. Stamens 8. Capsule cylindric, to 1½ in. (4 cm) long.

Leaves: Alternate, lanceolate or elliptic, usually hairy, toothed or nearly so.

Habitat: Disturbed sites.

Distribution: Central and north Florida.

Flowering time: Summer, fall, early winter.

Comment: Stem leafy, hairy or nearly so, to 3 ft. (1 m) tall or more.

Yellow Jessamine
Gelsemium sempervirens
(L.) J. Saint-Hilaire

Family: Loganiaceae (logania).

Flowers: Corolla yellow, 5-lobed, trumpet-shaped. Flowers axillary, solitary or clustered, pedicels with bracts. Pistil 1. Stigmas 4. Sepals 5, separate. Stamens 5, attached to inner part of the corolla tube. Anthers arrow-shaped.

Leaves: Opposite, entire, lanceolate to elliptic, evergreen, stalked.

Habitat: Woods, thickets, and disturbed sites.

Distribution: Throughout the state.

Flowering time: Winter, spring.

Comment: Vine woody, climbing, twining, fragrant. Plant contains poisonous alkaloids.

Physalis angulata
L.

Family: Solanaceae (nightshade).

Flowers: Corolla bell-shaped, yellow-green. Flowers small, solitary, axillary, stalked. Calyx 5-lobed, lobes smooth except the hairy tips. Stamens 5, anthers bluish. Mature berry enclosed by the inflated, thin calyx, often with purplish lines.

Leaves: Alternate, thin, smooth, lanceolate to widely ovate, mostly toothed, stalked.

Habitat: Open woods, thickets, and disturbed sites.

Distribution: Throughout the state.

Flowering time: All year.

Comment: Stem smooth or nearly so, branches square, to 3 ft. (1 m) tall or more.

Ground Cherry
Physalis arenicola
Kearney

Family: Solanaceae (nightshade).

Flowers: Corolla bell-shaped, yellow, often dark inside. Flowers solitary, axillary, short-stalked. Calyx 5-lobed. Stamens 5, anthers yellow. Mature berry yellow, enclosed by the inflated, thin, orangish calyx.

Leaves: Alternate, stalked, ovate or broadest near base, hairs sparse, may be sticky.

Habitat: Pinelands, sandhills, and disturbed sandy soils.

Distribution: Throughout the state.

Flowering time: Spring, summer.

Comment: Stem branched, to 16 in. (40 cm) tall, sparsely haired; star-shaped hairs lacking.

Ground Cherry
Physalis Walteri
Nuttall

Family: Solanaceae (nightshade).

Flowers: Corolla bell-shaped, yellow, with or without a dark center. Flowers solitary, axillary, short-stalked. Calyx 5-lobed, hairy, lobes triangular. Stamens 5, anthers yellow. Mature berry yellow enclosed by the inflated, thin, orangish calyx.

Leaves: Alternate, stalked, ovate to elliptic, entire or wavy, velvety.

Habitat: Pinelands and coastal dunes.

Distribution: Throughout the state.

Flowering time: All year.

Comment: Stem to 24 in. (60 cm) tall, branched. Plant covered with star-shaped hairs. Synonym: *Physalis viscosa*.

Senna Symeria
Seymeria cassioides
(Walter) Blake

Family: Scrophulariaceae (snapdragon or fig-wort).

Flowers: Corolla small, 5-lobed, yellow, bases often with reddish-brown streaks and dots, hairless externally. Flowers solitary, stalked, axillary. Style longer than the stamens. Calyx 5-lobed, smooth, lobes narrow. Stamens 4, not hairy.

Leaves: Opposite, narrow with filiform segments, thickish.

Habitat: Low pinelands.

Distribution: Central and north Florida.

Flowering time: Summer, fall.

Comment: Stem square, smooth or nearly so, bushy-branched, to 24 in. (60 cm) tall. Synonym: *Afzelia cassioides.*

Seymeria pectinata
Pursh

Family: Scrophulariaceae (snapdragon or fig-wort).

Flowers: Corolla small, 5-lobed, yellow, hairy externally. Flowers solitary, stalked, axillary. Calyx 5-lobed, lobes hairy, glandular. Stamens 4, filaments hairy.

Leaves: Opposite, segments lanceolate or linear.

Habitat: Pinelands.

Distribution: Throughout the state.

Flowering time: Summer, fall.

Comment: Stem hairy, moderately branched, to 24 in. (60 cm) tall. Synonym: *Afzelia pectinata.*

Verbascum virgatum
Stokes

Family: Scrophulariaceae (snapdragon or fig-wort).

Flowers: Corolla 5-lobed, yellow. Corolla tube shorter than the lobes. Flowers stalked in spikelike racemes. Each petal has an inner, reddish-brown, hairy blotch at the base. Sepals 5, glandular. Stamens 5, filaments hairy.

Leaves: Stem leaves alternate, toothed, sessile, hairy, to 10 in. (25 cm) long. Rosette leaves stalked.

Habitat: Roadsides, sandhills, and disturbed sites.

Distribution: Central and north Florida.

Flowering time: Late winter, spring, summer.

Comment: Stem leafy, to 3 ft. (1 m) tall or more.

Woolly Mullein
Verbascum thapsus
L.

Family: Scrophulariaceae (snapdragon or fig-wort).

Flowers: Corolla 5-lobed, yellow. Flowers fragrant, in terminal, dense spikes. Sepals 5. Fertile stamens 5, filaments hairy.

Leaves: Stem leaves alternate, elliptic to oblanceolate, sessile, velvety, yellow-green, extending down onto the stem. Basal leaves stalked, in rosettes.

Habitat: Disturbed sites.

Distribution: North Florida.

Flowering time: Summer, fall.

Comment: Stem stout, leafy, usually single, densely haired with star-shaped hairs, 3 ft. (1 m) tall or more. Native of Europe.

Hairy False Foxglove
Aureolaria pectinata
(Nuttall) Pennell

Family: Scrophulariaceae (snapdragon or fig-wort).

Flowers: Corolla 5-lobed, yellow. Flowers showy and bell-shaped. Calyx with stalked glands, 5-lobed, lobes toothed. Stamens 4 (2 long with hairy bases, 2 short), anthers awned at the base.

Leaves: Stem leaves opposite, finely divided, with stalked glands.

Habitat: Dry pinelands.

Distribution: Central and north Florida.

Flowering time: Spring, summer, fall.

Comment: Stem to 3 ft. (1 m) tall or more, branched, branches opposite, densely hairy with stalked glands. Entire plant sticky and glandular. Synonyms: *Dasystoma pectinata* and *Gerardia pectinata*.

Yellow Butterwort
Pinguicula lutea
Walter

Family: Lentibulariaceae (bladderwort).

Flowers: Corolla 2-lipped, lobes 5, yellow. Flower solitary on a slender stalk. Lower lip spurred. Calyx 5-lobed. Stamens 2. Fruit a capsule.

Leaves: Pale green, ovate or oblong, in basal rosettes. Leaves rolled inward from the edge; greasy.

Habitat: Moist, acid pinelands.

Distribution: Throughout the state.

Flowering time: Winter, spring.

Comment: Carnivorous. Sticky leaves trap and digest small insects. Stem leafless, to 16 in. (40 cm) tall. Terrestrial.

Floating Bladderwort
Utricularia inflata
Walter

Family: Lentibulariaceae (bladderwort).

Flowers: Corolla 5-lobed, yellow. Base of lower lip inside raised into a conspicuous palate. Spur notched at tip. Flowers in racemes. Calyx 2-lobed. Stamens 2.

Leaves: Leaf petioles from a radiating whorl of elongated floats. Finely dissected leaves attached to the floats bear tiny, inflated sacs called bladders.

Habitat: Waters of ditches, ponds, and canals.

Distribution: Throughout the state.

Flowering time: All year.

Comment: Carnivorous. Insects and other small, aquatic animals are trapped and digested in the bladders. Plant floating, to 8 in. (20 cm) tall.

Horned Bladderwort
Utricularia cornuta
Michaux

Family: Lentibulariaceae (bladderwort).

Flowers: Corolla 2-lipped, lobes 5, yellow. Lower lip 3-lobed, the larger. Spur slender, ⁵⁄₁₆–⅝ in. (7–14 mm) long. Lower flower overtops the unexpanded buds above. Calyx 2-lobed, entire. Stamens 2.

Leaves: Small, subterranean leaves with minute bladders for trapping insects.

Habitat: Wet soils and margins of ponds.

Distribution: Throughout the state.

Flowering time: All year.

Comment: Carnivorous. Plant terrestrial, to 8 in. (20 cm) tall. Synonym: *Stomoisia cornuta*.

Bladderwort
Utricularia subulata
L.

Family: Lentibulariaceae (bladderwort).

Flowers: Corolla 2-lipped, lobes 5, yellow. Spur of lower lip ³⁄₁₆ in. (5 mm) long or less. Calyx 2-lobed, entire. Stamens 2.

Leaves: Finely, dissected leaves bear bladders at the surface of wet soils. Leaves not readily evident.

Habitat: Moist pinelands.

Distribution: Central and north Florida.

Flowering time: All year.

Comment: Carnivorous, terrestrial, to 18 in. (45 cm) tall. Stem leafless, hairlike, bronze-colored. Synonyms: *Stomoisia juncea* and *S. virgatula*.

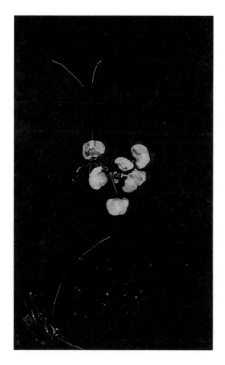

Cone-spur Bladderwort or Humped Bladderwort
Utricularia gibba
L.

Family: Lentibulariaceae (bladderwort).

Flowers: Corolla 2-lipped, lobes 5, yellow. Flowers stalked. Spur ⅛–³⁄₁₆ in. (3–5 mm) long; equal to or shorter than the lower lip of corolla. Calyx 5-lobed; lobes less than ⅛ in. (3 mm) long. Stamens 2.

Leaves: Alternate, usually forked once, finely dissected, bladder-bearing.

Habitat: Shallow water or mud.

Distribution: Central Florida.

Flowering time: Spring, summer, fall.

Comment: Stem creeping, mat-forming in shallow water or on the mud. Synonyms: *Utricularia pumila* and *U. biflora*.

Bladderwort
Utricularia fibrosa
Walter

Family: Lentibulariaceae (bladderwort).

Flowers: Corolla 2-lipped, lobes 5, yellow. Flowers stalked. Spur ¼–⅜ in. (6–10 mm) long; equal to or longer than the lower lip. Calyx 2-lobed, lobes 2 or 3 mm long.

Leaves: Alternate, usually forked 3 or 4 times. Some leaves bear bladders, others do not.

Habitat: Shallow ponds and ditches.

Distribution: Central and north Florida.

Flowering time: All year.

Comment: Stem creeping, usually in mud or peat.

Japanese Honeysuckle
Lonicera japonica
Thunberg

Family: Caprifoliaceae (honeysuckle).

Flowers: Corolla trumpet-shaped, white to yellow, 5-lobed, lobes unequal. Flowers paired, axillary, fragrant. Calyx 5-lobed. Stamens 5.

Leaves: Opposite, entire to toothed, ovate or elliptic. Leaves below inflorescence stalked.

Habitat: Thickets and disturbed woods.

Distribution: Central and north Florida.

Flowering time: Spring, summer, fall.

Comment: Vine woody, climbing or twining. Native to Asia.

Creeping Cucumber
Melothria pendula
L.

Family: Cucurbitaceae (gourd or cucumber).

Flowers: Corolla 5-lobed, yellow or yellow-green. Male flowers smaller and often clustered than the larger, solitary female flowers. Calyx 5-lobed. Stamens 3, fused; lacking in female flowers. Mature berry cucumberlike, blackish.

Leaves: Alternate, simple, stalked, 3–5 lobed, margins spine-tipped, surfaces rough.

Habitat: Disturbed sites, thickets, and pinelands.

Distribution: Throughout the state.

Flowering time: All year.

Comment: Vine slender, climbing using tendrils that are located opposite the leaves.

Wild Balsam Apple
Momordica charantia
L.

Family: Cucurbitaceae (gourd or cucumber).

Flowers: Corolla 5-lobed, yellow. Male flowers smaller than the female flowers. Calyx 5-lobed. Stamens 3; lacking in female flowers. Mature berry warty, golden yellow or orange, splitting revealing the bright red seeds.

Leaves: Alternate, deeply 5–7 lobed, toothed, stalked.

Habitat: Disturbed sites and thickets.

Distribution: Central and south Florida.

Flowering time: All year.

Comment: Vine climbing, using tendrils that are located opposite the leaves. Native to the Old World tropics.

Yellow Buttons
Balduina angustifolia
(Pursh) Robinson

Family: Asteraceae (aster or daisy).

Flowers: Heads terminal, of bright yellow, toothed ray florets and yellow disk florets. Ripen disk becomes hard, pitted, and honey-combed. Bracts ovate, pointed.

Leaves: Alternate, numerous, linear, usually entire.

Habitat: Pinelands, scrub, and sandy areas.

Distribution: Throughout the state.

Flowering time: All year.

Comment: Stem branched, to 3 ft. (1 m) tall. Synonym: *Actinospermum angustifolium.*

Greeneyes
Berlandiera subacaulis
(Nuttall) Nuttall

Family: Asteraceae (aster or daisy).

Flowers: Heads single, ray florets yellow and disk florets green-yellowish. Heads long-stalked, terminal. Bracts broad.

Leaves: Alternate, chiefly basal, lobed, ellip-tic-oblanceolate, downy beneath.

Habitat: Pinelands and dry, disturbed sites.

Distribution: Throughout the state.

Flowering time: All year.

Comment: Stem hairy, to 20 in. (50 cm) tall. Endemic to Florida.

Berlandiera pumila
(Michaux) Nuttall

Family: Asteraceae (aster or daisy).

Flowers: Heads of yellow ray florets and reddish, sterile disk florets. Heads long-stalked, terminal. Bracts broad, overlapping, ciliate.

Leaves: Alternate, ovate to lance-ovate, hairy, lower surfaces paler than the upper, margins toothed, upper leaves sessile.

Habitat: Sandhills and sandy fields.

Distribution: Central and north Florida.

Flowering time: Spring, summer, fall.

Comment: Stem 3 ft. (1 m) tall or more, with grayish hairs, leafy. One or more stems emerge from a basal crown.

Begger-ticks
Bidens mitis
(Michaux) Sherff

Family: Asteraceae (aster or daisy).

Flowers: Heads of bright yellow ray florets and yellow-brown disk florets. Outer bracts (often 8), green, sparsely haired. Inner bracts membranous, yellowish-reddish.

Leaves: Opposite, stalked, margins toothed or entire, linear or narrowly lanceolate. Leaves single or divided into narrow segments. Midvein hairy.

Habitat: Wet, disturbed sites.

Distribution: Throughout the state.

Flowering time: All year.

Comment: Stem smooth or sparsely haired, to 3 ft. (1 m) tall or more. Plant often occurs in larger numbers.

Burmarigold
Bidens laevis
(L.) BSP.

Family: Asteraceae (aster or daisy).

Flowers: Heads erect, of yellow ray florets and yellow disk florets. Outer bracts green, spatulate, succulent; inner ones membranous and yellowish. Heads axillary, stalked.

Leaves: Opposite, toothed or entire, elliptic to lance-elliptic, unlobed, smooth, sessile or stalked.

Habitat: Open, wet areas.

Distribution: Throughout the state.

Flowering time: All year.

Comment: Stems ascending, somewhat succulent, smooth, main branches opposite, to 3 ft. (1 m) tall or more. Plant with long rhizomes, often rooting at the nodes. Synonym: *Bidens nashii.*

Spanish Needles
Bidens bipinnata
L.

Family: Asteraceae (aster or daisy).

Flowers: Heads small, erect. Ray florets pale yellow, few or absent; disk florets yellowish. Outer bracts green, narrow. Seeds clustered, needlelike with 3 or 4, barbed awns.

Leaves: Opposite (uppermost may be alternate), pinnately dissected, stalked.

Habitat: Floodplains and disturbed sites.

Distribution: Central and north Florida.

Flowering time: Summer, fall.

Comment: Stem to 3 ft. (1 m) tall or more, smooth or nearly so.

Sea Dasies or Sea Oxeye
Borrichia frutescens
(L.) DC.

Family: Asteraceae (aster or daisy).

Flowers: Heads of yellow ray florets and yellow disk florets. Bracts overlapping, ovate, spine-tipped. Heads terminate the upper branches.

Leaves: Opposite, thick, grayish, hairy, usually entire, oblanceolate or obovate.

Habitat: Coastal beaches and marshes.

Distribution: Througout the state.

Flowering time: All year.

Comment: Stem leafy, to 3 ft. (1 m) tall or more. Plant aromatic, forming extensive colonies.

Goldenaster
Chrysopsis mariana
(L.) Elliot

Family: Asteraceae (aster or daisy).

Flowers: Heads of yellow ray florets and yellow disk florets. Ray tips lobed. Heads hairy, in corymbs. Bracts narrowly lanceolate, overlapping, hairless. Involucre ⁷⁄₁₆ in. (11 mm) long. Pedicels and bracts with stalked glands.

Leaves: Alternate, gland-dotted. Upper leaves elliptic to narrowly lanceolate, smooth, sessile, mostly entire. Lower leaves with long hairs, elliptic to oblanceolate, toothed, stalked. Basal rosette lacking.

Habitat: Dry pinelands.

Distribution: Central and north Florida.

Flowering time: Spring, fall.

Comment: Stem to 32 in. (80 cm) tall, glands stalked, hairs long. Plant sticky. Synonym: *Heterotheca mariana.*

Goldenaster
Chrysopsis scabrella
Torrey and Gray

Family: Asteraceae (aster or daisy).

Flowers: Heads stalked, of yellow ray florets and yellow disk florets. Bracts overlapping, with stalked glands. Involucre ⁵⁄₁₆ in. (7 mm) long.

Leaves: Stem leaves alternate, linear to narrowly spatulate, entire, sessile, glandular. Basal leaves spatulate or obovate.

Habitat: Pinelands and oak scrub.

Distribution: Throughout the state.

Flowering time: Summer, fall.

Comment: Stem to 3 ft. (1 m) tall, leafy, glands stalked, rough to the touch. Plant sticky and odiferous. Synonym: *Heterotheca scabrella.*

Goldenaster
Chrysopsis subulata
Small

Family: Asteraceae (aster or daisy).

Flowers: Heads of yellow ray florets and yellow disk florets. Heads numerous, cobwebby, drooping. Bracts linear, bristle-tipped, reflexed.

Leaves: Stem leaves numerous, alternate, linear to spatulate, upper margins toothed, often covered with white hairs. Basal leaves spatulate or obovate, smooth or with long, white hairs.

Habitat: Pinelands and disturbed sites.

Distribution: Central and south Florida.

Flowering time: All year.

Comment: Stem smooth or with cobwebby hairs, to 3 ft. (1 m) tall. Synonyms: *Heterotheca subulata* and *H. hyssopifolia* var. *subulata.*

Tickseed
Coreopsis floridana
E. B. Smith

Family: Asteraceae (aster or daisy).

Flowers: Heads of yellow-orange rays with lobed apices and dark brownish disk florets. Heads large, stalked. Outer bracts smooth, short, triangular, greenish with reddish stripes. Inner bracts membranous.

Leaves: Alternate, thickish, entire, hairy or smooth. Lower leaves stalked, spatulate, clasping. Leaves reduced upward.

Habitat: Wet pinelands.

Distribution: Central and north Florida.

Flowering time: Fall, winter.

Comment: Stem smooth, to 3 ft. (1 m) tall or more. Plant succulent.

Tickseed
Coreopsis gladiata
Walter

Family: Asteraceae (aster or daisy).

Flowers: Heads of yellow ray florets with lobed apices and dark purplish disk florets. Heads large, stalked. Outer bracts short, lanceolate.

Leaves: Alternate, entire, spatulate, thickish, hairy or smooth. Upper leaves reduced, lower leaves stalked.

Habitat: Low pinelands, edges of woods and ditches.

Distribution: Throughout the state.

Flowering time: Summer, fall, winter.

Comment: Stem gets to 3 ft. (1 m) tall or more. Synonyms: *Coreopsis angustifolia, C. longifolia,* and *C. heliantholides.*

Tickseed
Coreopsis leavenworthii
Torrey and Gray

Family: Asteraceae (aster or daisy).

Flowers: Heads of yellow ray florets with lobed apices and brownish disk florets. Heads stalked, many. Outer bracts lanceolate to awl-shaped.

Leaves: Opposite, usually entire, linear to ob-lanceolate.

Habitat: Wet pinelands and disturbed sites.

Distribution: Throughout the state.

Flowering time: All year.

Comment: Stem branched, to 3 ft. (1 m) tall or more. Endemic to Florida. Synonym: *Coreopsis lewtonii.*

Dye Flowers
Coreopsis basalis
(Otto and Dietrich) Blake

Family: Asteraceae (aster or daisy).

Flowers: Heads of yellow ray florets with basal red spots and lobed tips. Disk florets reddish-brown. Heads large, stalked. Outer bracts linear.

Leaves: Stem leaves opposite, hairy, divided or dissected. Basal leaves (usually present) stalked with elliptic to ovate lobes.

Habitat: Disturbed sites.

Distribution: Central and north Florida.

Flowering time: Spring, summer.

Comment: Stem branched, hairy or smooth, to 28 in. (70 cm) tall. Native to the western United States. Synonym: *Coreopsis drummondii.*

Lance-leaved Coreopsis or Tickseed
Coreopsis lanceolata
L.

Family: Asteraceae (aster or daisy).

Flowers: Heads of yellow disk florets and bright yellow ray florets. Ray florets wedge-shaped with conspicuous toothed tips. Flowers large at the ends of long stalks. Outer bracts green, lanceolate. Inner bracts membranous, lanceolate.

Leaves: Stem leaves opposite, lance-shaped or elliptic, single with 1 or 2 basal lobes, margins entire, hairy or smooth. Upper leaves reduced and sessile, lower ones petiolate.

Habitat: Disturbed sites, swamp edges, and sandhills.

Distribution: North-central and north Florida.

Flowering time: Spring, summer.

Comment: Stem leafy, with 1–5 nodes below the inflorescence, smooth or hairy, to 40 in. (100 cm) tall. Synonym: *Coreopsis crassifolia*.

Sneezeweed
Helenium flexuosum
Rafinesque

Family: Asteraceae (aster or daisy).

Flowers: Heads of yellow ray florets and globular, brown disk florets. Rays reflexed, tips lobed. Heads usually many and short-stalked.

Leaves: Alternate, slightly toothed, elliptic or lanceolate. Leaf bases extending onto the stem as wings.

Habitat: Flatwoods, fields, and pastures.

Distribution: North-central and north Florida.

Flowering time: Spring, summer, fall.

Comment: Stem often branched, with fine hairs, to 3 ft. (1 m) tall or more. Plant bitter and poisonous.

Helenium pinnatifidum
(Nuttall) Rydberg

Family: Asteraceae (aster or daisy).

Flowers: Heads of yellow ray florets and yellow disk florets. Ray florets fan-shaped, tips lobed. Usually 1 flower/stem. Bracts linear, in 1 row.

Leaves: Alternate, thick, sessile. Basal leaves in rosettes, stem leaves reduced upward. Lower leaves entire or scalloped, widest near the upper end. Some leaves may be purplish-green.

Habitat: Wet pinelands.

Distribution: Throughout the state.

Flowering time: Spring, summer.

Comment: Stem usually unbranched, green-purplish, hairy or smooth, to 32 in. (80 cm) tall.

Spanish Daisy, Sneezeweed, or Bitterweed
Helenium amarum
(Rafinesque) H. Rock

Family: Asteraceae (aster or daisy).

Flowers: Heads numerous, of yellow ray florets and yellow disk florets. Rays hairy on the back, tips lobed. Bracts hairy.

Leaves: Alternate; basal leaves usually absent when plant blooms. Stem leaves narrowly linear, entire, in groups of 3–5.

Habitat: Disturbed sites.

Distribution: Throughout the state.

Flowering time: Spring, summer, fall.

Comment: Stem branched above, smooth, to 20 in. (50 cm) tall. Synonym: *Helenium tenuifolium*.

Flat-topped Goldenrod
Euthamia tenuifolia
(Pursh) Greene

Family: Asteraceae (aster or daisy).

Flowers: Heads tiny and yellow. Heads in widely-branched, level-topped clusters. Ray florets more numerous than the disk florets.

Leaves: Alternate, numerous, 1-veined, linear to filiform, smooth.

Habitat: Pinelands and disturbed sites.

Distribution: Throughout the state.

Flowering time: Summer, fall, winter.

Comment: Stem branched, smooth or slightly haired, to 3 ft. (1 m) tall or more. Synonym: *Euthamia minor.*

Scratch Daisy
Haplopappus divaricatus
(Nuttall) Gray

Family: Asteraceae (aster or daisy).

Flowers: Heads of yellow ray florets and yellow disk florets. Heads small, arising from the leaf axils. Bracts narrow, overlapping, tips pointed, glandular. Involucre 4–6 mm long. Lowermost bracts short, hairy.

Leaves: Alternate, narrowly elliptic to oblanceolate, sessile, entire or toothed, spine-tipped.

Habitat: Pinelands.

Distribution: Central and north Florida.

Flowering time: Summer, fall.

Comment: Stem hairy, glandular, rough, to 3 ft. (1 m) tall or more. Synonym: *Isopappus divaricatus.*

Helianthus agrestis
Pollard

Family: Asteraceae (aster or daisy).

Flowers: Heads large, axillary, long-stalked. Ray florets yellow, disk florets flattened, brownish-purple. Bracts overlapping, lanceolate.

Leaves: Primarily alternate (sometimes opposite below), lanceolate, irregularly toothed, upper surface rough. Leaf margins ciliate at the base. Lower leaf surface paler than the upper.

Habitat: Wet, open disturbed sites and pinelands.

Distribution: Central and south Florida.

Flowering time: Summer, fall.

Comment: Stem branched, hairy, rough, 6 ft. (2 m) tall or more.

Helianthus debilis
Nuttall

Family: Asteraceae (aster or daisy).

Flowers: Heads axillary, long-stalked. Ray florets yellow, disk florets purplish-brown. Bracts overlapping, lanceolate, hairy, extending beyond the head.

Leaves: Alternate, long-stalked, hairy, somewhat triangular, entire or toothed, rough.

Habitat: Coastal beaches.

Distribution: Throughout the state.

Flowering time: All year.

Comment: Stem smooth to rough, branches spreading, to 3 ft. (1 m) tall.

Narrow-leaved Sunflower
Helianthus angustifolius
L.

Family: Asteraceae (aster or daisy).

Flowers: Heads of yellow ray florets and reddish-brown disk florets. Heads large, terminal. Bracts lanceolate or linear, overlapping, hairy. Outer bracts with tips pointed.

Leaves: Alternate above, opposite below, lanceolate to linear, rough, sessile or nearly so, margins entire and revolute. Leaves usually less than 1 cm wide.

Habitat: Moist pinelands and disturbed sites.

Distribution: Central and north Florida.

Flowering time: Summer, fall.

Comment: Stem rough, usually branched above, to 6 ft. (2 m) tall or more.

Helianthus floridanus
Gray

Family: Asteraceae (aster or daisy).

Flowers: Heads of yellow ray florets and yellow disk florets. Heads large, terminal. Bracts lanceolate or linear, overlapping, hairy. Outer bracts often round or bluntly acute.

Leaves: Alternate above, opposite below, lanceolate, rough, sessile or nearly so, margins wavy and turned down. Larger leaves ⅜ in. (1 cm) wide.

Habitat: Moist pinelands and disturbed sites.

Distribution: Central and north Florida.

Flowering time: Summer, fall.

Comment: Stem rough, usually branched above, to 3 ft. (1 m) tall or more.

Helianthus strumosus
L.

Family: Asteraceae (aster or daisy).

Flowers: Heads terminal and axillary, of yellow ray and disk florets. Involucre bracts overlapping, lanceolate, margins ciliate.

Leaves: Mostly opposite, lanceolate, tips pointed, stalked, rough above, paler below and smooth to hairy on the veins.

Habitat: Pinelands.

Distribution: Central and north Florida.

Flowering time: Summer, fall.

Comment: Stem smooth, branched above, to 3 ft. (1 m) tall or more.

Camphorweed
Heterotheca subaxillaris
(Lamarck) Britton and Rusby

Family: Asteraceae (aster or daisy).

Flowers: Heads of yellow ray florets and hairy, yellow disk florets. Heads many, in diffuse corymbs. Bracts linear, overlapping, glandular, hairy.

Leaves: Alternate, broad-based, wavy-edged, clasping, ovate, lanceolate or elliptic, toothed, rough. Upper leaves sessile. Lower leaves the larger. Base of petiole with winged lobes.

Habitat: Pinelands and disturbed sites.

Distribution: Throughout the state.

Flowering time: All year.

Comment: Stem hairy, glandular, to 3 ft. (1 m) tall. Plant odiferous.

Hawkweed
Hieracium gronovii
L.

Family: Asteraceae (aster or daisy).

Flowers: Heads of yellow, ray florets with toothed tips. Disk florets lacking. Heads in terminal, branched panicles. Floral branches with stalked glands. Bracts overlapping, glandular, pointed. Inner bracts ¼–⁵⁄₁₆ in. (6–7 mm) long.

Leaves: Mostly basal, hairy, oblanceolate to lanceolate. Upper stem leaves alternate, reduced.

Habitat: Pinelands and disturbed sites.

Distribution: Throughout the state.

Flowering time: Summer, fall, early winter.

Comment: Stem to 3 ft. (1 m) tall or more, upper part less hairy than lower. Sap milky. An old belief was that hawks obtained their keen eyesight from swooping upon these plants.

Dwarf Dandelion
Krigia virginica
(L.) Willdenow

Family: Asteraceae (aster or daisy).

Flowers: Heads small, of yellow-orange ray florets. Disk florets lacking. Bracts in a single row.

Leaves: Mainly in basal rosettes, oblanceolate to elliptic, lobed or toothed, petiole hairy, bases ciliate.

Habitat: Dry woods, pinelands, and disturbed sites.

Distribution: Central and north Florida.

Flowering time: Winter, spring.

Comment: Stem leafless, sap milky. Plant low-growing.

Indian Plantain

Arnoglossum floridanum
(Gray) Robins

Family: Asteraceae (aster or daisy).

Flowers: Heads of yellowish, cylindrical, disk florets. Ray florets lacking. Heads in broad, terminal inflorescences. Bracts 5, winged.

Leaves: Alternate, smooth, strongly veined, toothed, oval or broadest near the base.

Habitat: Dry pinelands and scrub.

Distribution: Central and north Florida.

Flowering time: Spring, summer, fall.

Comment: Stem smooth, grooved, to 3 ft. (1 m) tall or more. Synonym: *Mesadenia floridana.*

Phoebanthus

Phoebanthus grandiflora
(Torrey and Gray) Blake

Family: Asteraceae (aster or daisy).

Flowers: Heads sunflowerlike, of yellow ray florets and yellow disk florets. Usually 1 large head at the end of the stem. Bracts narrow, bristly.

Leaves: Alternate, rough, entire, linear to lanceolate.

Habitat: Sandhills, oak scrub, and pinelands.

Distribution: Central and south Florida.

Flowering time: Spring, summer, fall.

Comment: Stem tall, rough, leafy, branches few or none.

Goldenaster
Pityopsis graminifolia
(Michaux) Nuttall

Family: Asteraceae (aster or daisy).

Flowers: Heads of yellow ray and disk florets. Bracts linear, pointed, hairs silvery-gray.

Leaves: Alternate, silky-silvery, linear to lanceolate, with silvery-grayish hairs, margins entire. Lower leaves longer and wider than the upper ones.

Habitat: Dry pinelands and sandhills.

Distribution: Throughout the state.

Flowering time: Spring, summer, fall.

Comment: Stem with grayish hairs, branched, leafy, to 3 ft. (1 m) tall. Two varieties occur that differ in size of the heads. Synonyms: *Heterotheca graminifolia, H. g. tracyi, Pityopsis tracyi,* and *P. microcephala.*

False Dandelion
Pyrrhopappus carolinianus
(Walter) DC.

Family: Asteraceae (aster or daisy).

Flowers: Heads lemon-yellow, long-stalked. Disk florets absent. Outer bracts shorter than the inner ones.

Leaves: Alternate, both stem and basal present. Stem leaves few, sessile, reduced. Basal leaves elliptic to oblanceolate, lobed or toothed, stalked.

Habitat: Roadsides, fields, lawns, and other disturbed sites.

Distribution: Throughout the state.

Flowering time: All year.

Comment: Stem to 24 in. (60 cm) tall, smooth below, sparsely hairy above. Sap milky. Synonym: *Sitilias caroliniana.*

Blackeyed Susan
Rudbeckia hirta
L.

Family: Asteraceae (aster or daisy).

Flowers: Heads long-stalked, ray florets yellow to orange, disk florets fertile and dark brown. Bracts hairy, rough.

Leaves: Alternate, toothed to nearly entire, hairy. Upper leaves sessile, reduced. Lower leaves stalked, elliptic or oblanceolate. Leaf surfaces rough.

Habitat: Open fields, along roadsides, and other disturbed sites.

Distribution: Throughout the state.

Flowering time: All year.

Comment: Stem hairy, rough, to 3 ft. (1 m) tall.

Rudbeckia mohrii
Gray

Family: Asteraceae (aster or daisy).

Flowers: Heads of yellow, sterile ray florets and dark, fertile disk florets. Heads long-stalked. Involucre bracts linear to linear-lanceolate.

Leaves: Alternate, narrowly linear.

Habitat: Wet flatwoods and cypress swamps.

Distribution: Florida Panhandle.

Flowering time: Summer, fall.

Comment: Stem smooth, to 3 ft. (1 m) tall or more.

Rudbeckia mollis
Elliott

Family: Asteraceae (aster or daisy).

Flowers: Heads terminal, conical. Ray florets sterile, yellow. Disk florets fertile, purple-black. Involucre bracts lanceolate, hairy.

Leaves: Alternate, elliptic-spatulate to elliptic, entire or with round teeth, sessile or nearly so.

Habitat: Open woods and sandhills.

Distribution: Central and north Florida.

Flowering time: Summer, fall.

Comment: Stem to 3 ft. (1 m) tall or more, branched above, ribbed, lower stem with many gray hairs.

Butterweed
Senecio glabellus
Poir

Family: Asteraceae (aster or daisy).

Flowers: Heads numerous, in corymbs. Disk and ray florets, yellow-orange. Rays toothed. Bracts linear.

Leaves: Alternate, smooth, elliptic to oblanceolate. Larger leaves mainly basal, stalked, lobed. Upper leaves reduced, sessile.

Habitat: Wet, disturbed areas.

Distribution: Throughout the state.

Flowering time: Winter, spring, summer.

Comment: Stem hollow, to 32 in. (80 cm) tall, smooth, ribbed, succulent.

Seaside Goldenrod
Solidago sempervirens
L.

Family: Asteraceae (aster or daisy).

Flowers: Heads many, stalked, of yellow disk and ray florets. Heads usually borne on 1 side of the floral branches. Inflorescence a club-shaped panicle, often leafy at the base.

Leaves: Alternate, smooth, elliptic, entire, somewhat fleshy. Stem leaves numerous, sessile. Uppermost stem leaves reduced, linear, lying close to the stem. Basal leaves long and wide.

Habitat: Open pinelands and coastal sites.

Distribution: Throughout the state.

Flowering time: All year.

Comment: Stem stout, smooth or nearly so, to 6 ft. (2 m) tall or more. Plant somewhat succulent.

Goldenrod
Solidago tortifolia
Elliott

Family: Asteraceae (aster or daisy).

Flowers: Heads numerous, of yellow ray and disk florets. Ray florets less than 10. Heads borne along 1 side of the floral branches. Bracts smooth, pointed, yellowish.

Leaves: Alternate, sparsely haired, apices toothed, linear to narrowly elliptic. Upper stem leaves numerous, hairy beneath, sessile or nearly so. Lower stem leaves reduced or absent.

Habitat: Pinelands.

Distribution: Throughout the state.

Flowering time: Summer, fall.

Comment: Stem with dense, short hairs, to 3 ft. (1 m) tall.

Goldenrod
Solidago stricta
Aiton

Family: Asteraceae (aster or daisy).

Flowers: Heads small, of yellow ray and disk florets. Flowers in elongated, slender, wand-like panicles. Bracts smooth, apices blunt or pointed. Stem leaves sessile, abruptly reduced upward.

Leaves: Alternate. Upper leaves lying on the stem. Basal leaves elliptic to oblanceolate, larger, stalked, entire or nearly so, smooth.

Habitat: Wet pinelands, sandy soils, and coastal sites.

Distribution: Throughout the state.

Flowering time: Spring, summer, fall, early winter.

Comment: Stem smooth, slender, to 6 ft. (2 m) tall.

Goldenrod
Solidago odora var. *chapmanii*
(Gray) Cronquist

Family: Asteraceae (aster or daisy).

Flowers: Heads many, of yellow disk and ray florets. Heads borne along 1 side of the floral branches. Bracts smooth, pale yellow, margins entire.

Leaves: Alternate, oblong or elliptic-lanceolate, sessile, margins entire, revolute, dark green on both surfaces.

Habitat: Dry, open woods and pinelands.

Distribution: Throughout the state.

Flowering time: Spring, summer, fall.

Comment: Stem slightly hairy, to 4½ ft. (1.5 m) tall or more. Synonym: *S. chapmanii.*

Goldenrod
Solidago fistulosa
Miller

Family: Asteraceae (aster or daisy).

Flowers: Heads of yellow ray and yellow disk florets in plumelike panicles. Heads borne along 1 side of the floral branches. Floral branches numerous, often recurved. Bracts thin, overlapping.

Leaves: Alternate, lanceolate-ovate to obovate, usually toothed, sessile. Upper and lower surfaces rough. Basal leaves lacking.

Habitat: Dry pinelands and disturbed sites.

Distribution: Throughout the state.

Flowering time: Summer, fall, winter.

Comment: Stem hairy, leafy, to 6 ft. (2 m) tall.

Goldenrod
Solidago canadensis
L.

Family: Asteraceae (aster or daisy).

Flowers: Heads golden-yellow, of yellow ray and disk florets in terminal panicles. Heads borne along 1 side of the floral branches. Bracts smooth, short.

Leaves: Alternate, rough above, hairy below, elliptic to lanceolate, toothed. Veins lateral to the leaf's midrib prominent.

Habitat: Disturbed sites.

Distribution: North Florida.

Flowering time: Fall.

Comment: Stem hairy, to 3 ft. (1 m) tall or more. Synonym: *Solidago altissima.*

Rayless Goldenrod
Bigelowia nudata
(Michaux) DC.

Family: Asteraceae (aster or daisy).

Flowers: Heads of yellow, tubular disk florets in flat-topped corymbs. Ray florets absent. Bracts linear, pointed.

Leaves: Stem leaves alternate, few, linear or spatulate. Basal leaves in rosettes.

Habitat: Swamp margins and moist pinelands.

Distribution: Throughout the state.

Flowering time: All year.

Comment: Stem smooth, slender, to 20 in. (50 cm) tall. Synonym: *Chondrophora nudata.*

Yellowtop
Flaveria linearis
Lagasca y Segura

Family: Asteraceae (aster or daisy).

Flowers: Heads many, small, of several yellow disk florets and 1 tiny ray floret. Heads in spreading, terminal, axillary corymbs. Bracts keeled.

Leaves: Opposite, linear or linear-lanceolate, sessile, entire or slightly toothed.

Habitat: Wet areas, especially coastal areas.

Distribution: Throughout the state.

Flowering time: All year.

Comment: Plant often bushy, to 32 in. (80 cm) tall. Stem smooth, branched, often reddish.

Spiny-leaved Sow Thistle

Sonchus asper
(L.) Hill

Family: Asteraceae (aster or daisy).

Flowers: Heads cylindrical, of yellow ray florets. Disk florets lacking. Heads many, stalked, in terminal corymbs. Bracts lanceolate, smooth.

Leaves: Alternate, lanceolate to oblanceolate, toothed, prickly, curled. Leaf bases with roundish lobes. Upper stem leaves reduced.

Habitat: Disturbed sites and old fields.

Distribution: Throughout the state.

Flowering time: Winter, spring, summer.

Comment: Stem smooth or nearly so, to 6 ft. (2 m) tall or more. Sap milky. Native to Europe.

Common Sow Thistle

Sonchus oleraceus
L.

Family: Asteraceae (aster or daisy).

Flowers: Heads cylindrical, of yellow ray florets. Disk florets lacking. Heads stalked in terminal corymbs. Bracts lanceolate, nonglandular.

Leaves: Alternate, toothed or weak spined; leaf bases with triangular or sharp-pointed lobes, not curled. Upper stem leaves reduced.

Habitat: Disturbed sites.

Distribution: Throughout the state.

Flowering time: Winter, spring, summer.

Comment: Stems smooth, to 3 ft. (1 m) tall or more. Sap milky. Native to Europe.

Common Dandelion
Taraxacum officinale
Weber

Family: Asteraceae (aster or daisy).

Flowers: Head large, solitary, of yellow disk and ray florets. Outer bracts cylindrical, reflexed.

Leaves: Oblanceolate, margins deeply cut, in basal rosettes.

Habitat: Disturbed sites and lawns.

Distribution: Central and north Florida.

Flowering time: All year.

Comment: Stem hollow, sap milky. Native to Eurasia.

Hawk's-beard
Youngia japonica
(L.) DC.

Family: Asteraceae (aster or daisy).

Flowers: Heads several, small, yellow, in corymbs or panicles. Outer short bracts at the base of the main ones.

Leaves: Mostly basal, stalked, lobed; upper leaves alternate, reduced or absent.

Habitat: Old fields, lawns, and other disturbed sites.

Distribution: Throughout the state.

Flowering time: All year.

Comment: Stem to 24 in. (60 cm) tall, branched or single; hairy below, nearly smooth above. Sap milky. Native to eastern Asia. Synonym: *Crepis japonica*.

Creeping Oxeye
Wedelia trilobata
(L.) Hitchcock

Family: Asteraceae (aster or daisy).

Flowers: Heads yellow. Ray florets few, apices toothed. Disk florets with triangular lobes. Bracts lanceolate, overlapping, hairy.

Leaves: Opposite, sessile, toothed, 3–5 lobed.

Habitat: Moist, disturbed sites.

Distribution: Central and south Florida.

Flowering time: All year.

Comment: Stem low-growing, creeping, somewhat fleshy, hairy. Native to the West Indies. Plant often used as an ornamental.

Skunk Daisy
Verbesina encelioides
(Cavanilles) Bentham and Hooker

Family: Asteraceae (aster or daisy).

Flowers: Heads long-stalked, in terminal inflorescence. Ray florets yellow, toothed. Disk florets yellow. Bracts linear, hairy, in 2 rows.

Leaves: Upper leaves alternate, lower ones opposite; stalked, ovate, toothed, hairy-gray on the lower surface.

Habitat: Open, disturbed sites.

Distribution: Central and south Florida.

Flowering time: Spring, summer.

Comment: Stem winged, branched, hairy, to 3 ft. (1 m) tall or more.

Pectis prostrata
Cavanilles

Family: Asteraceae (aster or daisy).

Flowers: Heads small, yellow, tubular, sessile or nearly so. Ray florets 5, disk florets variable. Bracts keeled, smooth.

Leaves: Opposite (at least lower ones), linear to lanceolate, sessile. Leaf apices pointed. Bristles occur at the leaf bases. Lower surface gland-dotted.

Habitat: Open, disturbed sites and pinelands.

Distribution: Central and south Florida.

Flowering time: Summer, fall, winter.

Comment: Plant matted, prostrate, branching from the base. Stem gland-dotted and hairy.

Bear's-foot or Yellow Leafcup
Polymnia uvedalia
(L.) L.

Family: Asteraceae (aster or daisy).

Flowers: Heads of yellow ray florets and yellow disk florets. Ray florets toothed. Heads long-stalked, terminal, axillary. Outer bracts ovate, hairy.

Leaves: Opposite, hairy, clasping, rough above; uppermost leaves alternate, reduced. Maple leaf-shaped with 3–5 lobes. Petiole leafy.

Habitat: Moist, deciduous woods.

Distribution: Central and north Florida.

Flowering time: Summer, fall.

Comment: Plant gets to 9 ft. (3 m) tall. Stem hollow, angled, purplish-green, hairy above, smooth below.

Rosinweed
Silphium compositum
Michaux

Family: Asteraceae (aster or daisy).

Flowers: Heads of yellow disk florets and yellow ray florets. Disk florets sterile, styles undivided. Ray florets fertile, styles divided. Flowers in loose, terminal, branched inflorescence. Achenes flattened, winged, inner faces usually hairy. Involucral bracts overlapping, broad, smooth, margins ciliate.

Leaves: Stem leaves alternate, few, reduced above. Lower leaves long-stalked, smooth, deeply lobed or toothed, margins ciliate.

Habitat: Moist pinelands and disturbed sites.

Distribution: Central and north Florida.

Flowering time: Spring, summer, fall.

Comment: Stem 3–12 ft. (1–4 m) tall, smooth, leafy near the base. Synonyms: *Silphium venosum* and *S. ovalifolium.*

Silphium asteriscus
L.

Family: Asteraceae (aster or daisy).

Flowers: Heads of yellow disk florets and yellow, 3-toothed ray florets. Ray florets fertile. Styles divided. Involucre bracts overlapping, broad, margins purplish and ciliate. Seeds flattened, winged, inner faces usually hairy.

Leaves. Upper stem leaves alternate and sessile; lower ones opposite and stalked. Margins toothed, rough to the touch. Basal leaves often absent at flowering.

Habitat: Open dry woodlands.

Distribution: Central and north Florida.

Flowering time: Spring, summer, fall.

Comment: Stem rough, to 3 ft. (1 m) tall or above. Synonym: *Silphium simpsonii.*

Tridax procumbens
L.

Family: Asteraceae (aster or daisy).

Flowers: Heads small, of yellow ray florets and pale yellow disk florets. Rays few, short, 3-lobed. Heads at the end of a long stalk. Outer bracts green, hairy. Anthers narrow.

Leaves: Opposite, toothed, stalked ovate to ovate-lanceolate.

Habitat: Open, disturbed sites.

Distribution: Central and south Florida.

Flowering time: All year.

Comment: Plant low-growing, branched near the base, hairy. Native to South America.

Green Arum or Arrow Arum
Peltandra virginica
(L.) Schott and Endlicher.

Family: Araceae (arum or calla).

Flowers: Perianth absent. Fleshy stalk (spadix) elongated, surrounded by a green, pointed, convoluted spathe. Male flowers on the upper part of the spadix, female flowers on the lower quarter. Berries green or dark brown.

Leaves: Long-stalked, smooth, arrow-shaped, finely veined, sheathed at the base.

Habitat: Wet woods and swamps.

Distribution: Throughout the state.

Flowering time: Winter, spring, early summer.

Green Dragon
Arisaema dracontium
(L.) Schott

Family: Araceae (arum or calla).

Flowers: Perianth absent. The fleshy stalk (spadix) bears small, sessile flowers. Male flowers usually uppermost. Spadix elongated, lashlike, extending beyond the short, sheathing spathe. Mature red berries occur in clusters.

Leaves: Single leaf divided into several leaflets forming a semicircle.

Habitat: Moist woods.

Distribution: Central and north Florida.

Flowering time: Spring, summer.

Comment: Plant contains calcium oxalate crystals that irritate the mouth when eaten raw. Plant gets to 3 ft. (1 m) tall. Synonym: *Muricauda dracontium.*

Jack-in-the-pulpit or Indian Turnip
Arisaema triphyllum
(L.) Schott

Family: Araceae (arum or calla).

Flowers: Perianth absent. The fleshy stalk (spadix) bears small, sessile flowers. Male flowers usually uppermost. Spadix is surrounded by a green, purplish, or striped spathe that arches over the spadix. Mature red berries occur in clusters.

Leaves: Leaflets of the single, stalked leaf usually 3, ovate.

Habitat: Moist woods.

Distribution: Throughout the state.

Flowering time: Spring, summer.

Comment: Plant contains calcium oxalate crystals that irritate the mouth when eaten raw. Plant gets to 3 ft. (1 m) tall. Synonyms: *Arisaema pusillum* and *A. acuminatum*.

Water-lettuce
Pistia stratiotes
L.

Family: Araceae (arum or calla).

Flowers: Perianth absent. Male and female flowers tiny, located on a small, fleshy stalk (spadix) surrounded by a greenish-white sheath (spathe).

Leaves: Succulent, ribbed, spirally-arranged in rosettes. Petioles broad, blades hairy.

Habitat: Ditches, ponds, streams, and sluggish lakes.

Distribution: Throughout the state.

Flowering time: All year.

Comment: Plant free-floating with elongated, branching roots.

Spider Orchid
Habenaria odontopetala
Reichenback f.

Family: Orchidaceae (orchid).

Flowers: Whitish-green, lip narrowly spatulate, unlobed. Spur slender, to 1 in. (26 mm) long. Lateral sepals winglike, dorsal sepal cup-shaped. Raceme densely flowered, cylindric.

Leaves: Elliptic, lanceolate, smooth.

Habitat: Wet, pine flatwoods, swamps, and hammocks.

Distribution: Central and south Florida.

Flowering time: Fall, winter.

Comment: Stem stout, leafy, smooth, to 24 in. (60 cm) tall. Terrestrial. Synonym: *Habenaria strictissima* var. *odontopetala*.

False Nettle or Bog Hemp
Boehmeria cylindrica
(L.) Swartz

Family: Urticaceae (nettle).

Flowers: Petals lacking. Axillary, spikelike branches bear the spaced clusters (verticils) of tiny, greenish flowers. Male flowers with 4 sepals, 4 stamens. Female flowers with 2–4 sepals, 1 pistil.

Leaves: Opposite, lanceolate to ovate, stalked, toothed, rough, main veins 3.

Habitat: Wet woods, bogs, and marshes.

Distribution: Throughout the state.

Flowering time: Spring, summer, fall.

Comment: Stem to 3 ft. (1 m) tall or more. Plant lacks stinging hairs. Synonyms: *Boehmeria drummondii* and *B. decurrens.*

Stinging Nettle
Urtica chamaedryoides
Pursh

Family: Urticaceae (nettle).

Flowers: Petals lacking. Flowers small, greenish, in axillary clusters. Clusters compact, nearly spherical, greenish-pinkish. Sepals 4. Stamens 4.

Leaves: Opposite, toothed, stalked, reduced upward, hairy.

Habitat: Deciduous woods.

Distribution: Central and north Florida.

Flowering time: Late winter, spring, summer.

Comment: Stem slender, squarish, hollow, to 4½ ft. (1.5 m) tall. Plant bears stinging hairs.

Hastate-leaved Dock
Rumex hastatulus
Baldwin

Family: Polygonaceae (buckwheat or knotweed).

Flowers: Petals lacking. Flowers small, greenish, in terminal panicles. Sepals 6. Flowers change from green to reddish as the fruit ripen. Stamens 6.

Leaves: Alternate, stalked, chiefly basal and lobed.

Habitat: Weedy fields and disturbed sites.

Distribution: Central and north Florida.

Flowering time: Winter, spring.

Comment: Plant grows to 3 ft. (1 m) tall or more, singly or in clumps. Edible, taste pungent. Large amounts of the plant may be toxic from oxalates present.

Curled Dock

Rumex crispus
L.

Family: Polygonaceae (buckwheat or knot-weed).

Flowers: Petals lacking. Flowers small, greenish, in contiguous clusters (verticils). Sepals 6. Sepal-wings entire or wavy. Calyx pedicel about the same length as the sepal-wings. Stamens 6.

Leaves: Alternate, lanceolate, stalked, margins wavy and crisp.

Habitat: Disturbed sites.

Distribution: Central and north Florida.

Flowering time: Spring, summer, fall.

Comment: Stem leafy, to 3 ft. (1 m) tall or more. Native to Europe.

Fiddle Dock

Rumex pulcher
L.

Family: Polygonaceae (buckwheat or knot-weed).

Flowers: Petals lacking. Flowers small, greenish, in well-spaced clusters (verticils). Sepals 6. Sepal-wings serrated or spiny. Calyx pedicel shorter than the sepal-wings. Stamens 6.

Leaves: Alternate, stalked, lanceolate to elliptic. Lower leaves and stem may be densely hairy.

Habitat: Disturbed sites.

Distribution: Throughout the state.

Flowering time: Spring, summer, fall.

Comment: Stem leafy, to 3 ft. (1 m) tall or more. Native to Europe.

Swamp Dock
Rumex verticillatus
L.

Family: Polygonaceae (buckwheat or knotweed).

Flowers: Petals lacking. Flowers small, greenish, in contiguous clusters (verticils). Calyx pedicel longer than the sepal-wings. Sepalwings entire or wavy. Stamens 6.

Leaves: Alternate, lanceolate to elliptic, stalked, tapered at the base, margins flat or slightly undulate.

Habitat: Freshwater swamps and disturbed sites.

Distribution: Throughout the state.

Flowering time: Winter, spring, summer.

Comment: Stem leafy, to 3 ft. (1 m) tall or more. Synonyms: *Rumex floridanus* and *R. fasciculatus*.

Bitter Dock
Rumex obtusifolius
L.

Family: Polygonaceae (buckwheat or knotweed).

Flowers: Petals lacking. Flowers small, greenish, mostly in contiguous clusters (verticils). Sepals 6. Calyx pedicel longer than the sepalwings. Sepal-wings spiny or serrate. Stamens 6.

Leaves: Alternate, lanceolate to elliptic. Basal leaves the larger.

Habitat: Disturbed sites.

Distribution: Central Florida.

Flowering time: Spring, summer, fall.

Comment: Stem leafy, to 3 ft. (1 m) tall or more. Native to Europe.

Mexican Tea
Chenopodium ambrosioides
L.

Family: Chenopodiaceae (goosefoot).

Flowers: Petals lacking. Sepals 5, persisting and enclosing the fruit. Flowers tiny, green, in spikelike clusters. Stamens 5.

Leaves: Alternate, lanceolate to lance-elliptic, toothed, stalked, minutely gland-dotted on lower surface.

Habitat: Disturbed sites.

Distribution: Throughout the state.

Flowering time: Spring, summer, fall.

Comment: Stems grooved, to 3 ft. (1 m) tall or more. Plants have an ill-scented, pungent odor. Introduced from tropical America. Synonym: *Ambrina ambrosioides.*

Lamb's-quarters or Pigweed
Chenopodium album
L.

Family: Chenopodiaceae (goosefoot).

Flowers: Petals lacking. Sepals 5, persisting and enclosing the fruit. Flowers tiny, green, sessile, in spikelike clusters. Pistil 1. Stamens 5.

Leaves: Alternate, stalked, thickish. Larger leaves rhombic-ovate, toothed or shallowly lobed, with 3 main veins. Lower surfaces with whitish flecks (mealy). Upper leaves linear, entire.

Habitat: Disturbed sites.

Distribution: Throughout the state.

Flowering time: Spring, summer, fall.

Comment: Stem branched, smooth, grooved, to 6 ft. (2 m) tall or more. Plants lack an ill-scented, pungent odor. Young plants are cooked and eaten like spinach. Synonyms: *Chenopodium lanceolatum* and *C. berlandieri.*

Perennial Glasswort
Salicornia virginica
L.

Family: Chenopodiaceae (goosefoot).

Flowers: Minute, immerged in the thick upper joints. Petals lacking. Inflorescence a terminal spike of paired cymules. Stamens 1 or 2. Flower spikes become bright red in the fruit.

Leaves: Opposite, small, scalelike, apex rounded.

Habitat: Salt marshes.

Distribution: Throughout the state.

Flowering time: Late winter, spring, summer, fall.

Comment: Stems thick, fleshy, jointed. Main stem lying on the ground with erect branches. Plant has a salty taste. Synonym: *Salicornia perennis.* A similar species, the annual glasswort *(Salicornia bigelovii)* has an erect main stem.

Spiny Amaranth
Amaranthus spinosus
L.

Family: Amaranthaceae (amaranth or pigweed).

Flowers: Petals absent. Flowers green, tiny, in slender spikes. Spikes terminal and axillary, usually nodding. Male flowers chiefly terminal; female flowers basal.

Leaves: Alternate, ovate to rhombic-ovate, entire, long-petioled.

Habitat: Disturbed sites.

Distribution: Throughout the state.

Flowering time: All year.

Comment: Stem smooth, branched, to 3 ft. (1 m) tall, with stiff, axillary spines. Our only spiny amaranth.

Water Hemp

Amaranthus cannabinus
(L.) Sauer

Family: Amaranthaceae (amaranth or pig-weed).

Flowers: Petals lacking. Plant dioecious. Flowers in elongated, terminal and axillary spikelike branches. Male flowers mostly with 5 sepals, usually 5 stamens. Female flowers lack sepals. Style branches 3–5.

Leaves: Alternate, petioles long, lanceolate to lance-ovate, tapering to the apices, largest about ⅝ in. (15 cm) long, strongly veined, entire.

Habitat: Brackish and fresh water swamps and marshes and wet, disturbed sites.

Distribution: Central and south Florida.

Flowering time: All year.

Comment: Stem often robust, branched to 9 ft. (3 m) tall or more. Synonym: *Acnida cannabina*.

Painted-leaf

Poinsettia cyathophora
(Murray) Klotzsch and Garcke

Family: Euphorbiaceae (spurge).

Flowers: Petals lacking. Flowers small, green, in terminal clusters. Floral leaflike bracts green or red at the base. Capsule smooth, ²⁄₁₆ or ³⁄₁₆ in. (4 or 5 mm) long.

Leaves: Alternate, mostly lobed, ovate to oblong.

Habitat: Hammocks, old fields, and disturbed sites.

Distribution: Throughout the state.

Flowering time: All year.

Comment: Stem hairy, to 4½ ft. (1.5 m) tall. Sap milky.

Fiddler's Spurge or Painted-leaf
Poinsettia heterophylla
(L.) Klotzsch and Garcke

Family: Euphorbiaceae (spurge).

Flowers: Petals lacking. Flowers small, green, in terminal clusters. Floral leaflike bracts green or purple-spotted at the base, never red. Capsule smooth, ⁵⁄₁₆ or ³⁄₁₆ in. (4 or 5 mm) long.

Leaves: Alternate, mostly lobed, entire or toothed, lanceolate to oblanceolate.

Habitat: Disturbed sites.

Distribution: Throughout the state.

Flowering time: All year.

Comment: Stem smooth or nearly so, to 3 ft. (1 m) tall. Sap milky.

Poison Ivy
Toxicodendron radicans
(L.) Kuntze

Family: Anacardiaceae (cashew or sumac).

Flowers: Flowers axillary, tiny, petals greenish-white. Sepals 5-parted. Stamens 5. Fruit mainly smooth, white or greenish-white, globose.

Leaves: Alternate, leaflets 3, ovate to elliptic, toothed or entire.

Habitat: Moist woods and disturbed sites.

Distribution: Throughout the state.

Flowering time: Spring, summer.

Comment: Low shrub or climbing vine using aerial roots. Sap may cause severe skin irritation.

Virginia Creeper
Parthenocissus quinquefolia
(L.) Planchon

Family: Vitaceae (grape).

Flowers: Petals 5, tiny, greenish-yellow. Flowers opposite the leaves. Calyx 5-toothed. Stamens 5. Berries blue-black.

Leaves: Alternate, palmately compound, petioles long. Leaflets 5, toothed, elliptic-ovate. Older leaves turn red as in the photograph.

Habitat: Hammocks and wet woods.

Distribution: Throughout the state.

Flowering time: Spring, early summer.

Comment: Vine woody, climbing or creeping with tendrils. Synonym: *Parthenocissus hirsuta.*

Southern Fox Grape, Muscadine, or Scuppernong
Vitis munsoniana
Simpson

Family: Vitaceae (grape).

Flowers: Petals 5, tiny, greenish, fused at the tips. Flowers in short panicles. Calyx cup-shaped, small. Stamens 5. Berries purplish, small, thin-skinned.

Leaves: Alternate, simple, somewhat circular, glossy, coarsely toothed.

Habitat: Hammocks and thickets.

Distribution: Throughout the state.

Flowering time: Spring, early summer.

Comment: Vine woody, climbing or trailing, tendrils unbranched and opposite the leaves. Fruit used for jellies, jam, and wine. Synonym: *Muscadinia munsoniana.*

Calusa Grape
Vitis shuttleworthii
House

Family: Vitaceae (grape).

Flowers: Petals 5, tiny, greenish. Flowers in panicles. Stamens 5.

Leaves: Alternate, simple, somewhat heart-shaped, toothed. Lower surface densely covered with white or rusty hairs. Upper surface brownish-green.

Habitat: Thickets and pinelands.

Distribution: Central and south Florida.

Flowering time: Spring.

Comment: Vine woody, climbing or trailing, tendrils forked and opposite the leaves. Synonym: *Vitis coriacea.*

Summer Grape
Vitis aestivalis
Michaux

Family: Vitaceae (grape).

Flowers: Petals 5, tiny, greenish. Inflorescence elongated. Calyx small. Stamens 5.

Leaves: Alternate, stalked, simple, usually broadly ovate, toothed, shallowly to deeply 3–5 lobed. Lower surface of mature leaves with matted, white to rusty, cobwebby hairs. Hairs deciduous with age.

Habitat: Thickets and woods.

Distribution: Throughout the state.

Flowering time: Spring.

Comment: Vine woody, climbing by forked tendrils that are opposite most leaves. Young branches often hairy. Synonyms: *Vitis rufotomentosa* and *V. simpsonii.*

Pepper Vine

Ampelopsis arborea

(L.) Koehne

Family: Vitaceae (grape).

Flowers: Petals 5, separate, greenish-white. Male and female flowers separate. Calyx saucer-shaped, reduced in size. Flowers tiny, in flattened clusters. Stamens 5. Berry black-purplish, not edible.

Leaves: Alternate, stalked, bipinnately compound. Leaflets toothed or lobed, ovate.

Habitat: Wet thickets and hammocks.

Distribution: Throughout the state.

Flowering time: Spring, summer, fall.

Comment: Shrub erect or woody, climbing vine, stem smooth, tendrils absent.

Marine Vine or Sorrel Vine

Cissus trifoliata

L.

Family: Vitaceae (grape).

Flowers: Petals 4, greenish-yellow. Flowers small, in clusters. Calyx cuplike, lobes 4, short and rounded. Stamens 4. Mature berries black, not edible.

Leaves: Alternate. Leaflets 3, coarsely toothed, fleshy, smooth, obovate or wedge-shaped.

Habitat: Coastal dunes, shell mounds, and hammocks.

Distribution: Throughout the state.

Flowering time: Late spring, summer, fall.

Comment: Vine climbing with tendrils. Stem smooth or warty, somewhat fleshy. Synonym: *Cissus incisa*.

Dangleberry
Gaylussacia tomentosa
(Gray) Small

Family: Ericaceae (heath).

Flowers: Corolla 5-lobed, greenish. Flowers small, bell-shaped, in axillary racemes. Calyx 5-lobed, smooth. Stamens 10. Mature berry blue.

Leaves: Alternate, oval to elliptic, lower surfaces pale. Leaves veiny, deciduous.

Habitat: Dry to moist woods and pinelands.

Distribution: Central and north Florida.

Flowering time: Late winter, spring.

Comment: Stem hairy, to 3 ft. (1 m) tall or more. Small golden dots occur on the leaves, calyx, and stem. Synonyms: *Decachaena tomentosa* and *D. frondosa*.

Asclepias pedicellata
Walter

Family: Asclepiadaceae (milkweed).

Flowers: Corolla deeply lobed, petals 5, greenish-yellow. Corolla lobes not reflexed. Flowers few, in umbels. Stamens 5, attached to the stigma.

Leaves: Opposite, sessile, linear, sparsely haired.

Habitat: Pinelands.

Distribution: Throughout the state.

Flowering time: Spring, summer, fall.

Comment: Stem sparsely haired, to 20 in. (50 cm) tall. Sap milky. Synonym: *Podostigma pedicellata*.

◇   ◇   ◇

Asclepias longifolia
Michaux

Family: Asclepiadaceae (milkweed).

Flowers: Corolla 5-lobed, greenish-white, tips purplish. Lobes reflexed. Flowers in stalked, axillary or terminal umbels. Pedicels hairy. Calyx 5-lobed, lobes short and hairy.

Leaves: Opposite and alternate, sparsely haired, linear to narrowly lanceolate, sessile or nearly so, margins ciliate.

Habitat: Wet flatwoods and meadows.

Distribution: Throughout the state.

Flowering time: Spring, summer.

Comment: Stem slender, leafy, to 28 in. (70 cm) tall, sparsely haired above. Sap milky. Synonyms: *Acerates floridana* and *A. delticola*.

Asclepias viridis
Walter

Family: Asclepiadaceae (milkweed).

Flowers: Petals 5, green, erect and not reflexed. Flowers in terminal umbels. Calyx 5-lobed, lobes lanceolate. Stamens 5, purplish-white.

Leaves: Alternate, short-stalked, hairy, ovate to lanceolate-oblong.

Habitat: Pinelands and disturbed sites.

Distribution: Throughout the state.

Flowering time: Spring, summer.

Comment: Plant erect, to 24 in. (60 cm) tall. Sap milky. Synonym: *Asclepiodora viridis*.

Velvet-leaf Milkweed
Asclepias tomentosa
Elliott

Family: Asclepiadaceae (milkweed).

Flowers: Petals 5, greenish-yellow. Corolla lobes reflexed. Flowers in open, sessile umbels. Stamens 5, attached to the stigma.

Leaves: Opposite, elliptic to oval, soft and downy, short-stalked or sessile.

Habitat: Dry pinelands and dunes.

Distribution: Throughout the state.

Flowering time: Spring, summer.

Comment: Stem usually solitary, hairy, to 24 in. (60 cm) tall.

Common Ragweed
Ambrosia artemisiifolia
L.

Family: Asteraceae (aster or daisy).

Flowers: Heads tiny, cup-shaped, greenish. Male and female flowers separate, but on the same plant. Male flowers, with 5 united petals, are in the upper elongated, axillary, spikelike racemes. Female flowers lack corollas and are clustered in the upper leaf axils.

Leaves: Lower leaves opposite, upper ones alternate. Stalked, deeply divided or lobed.

Habitat: Disturbed sites.

Distribution: Throughout the state.

Flowering time: Summer, fall, early winter.

Comment: Stem hairy, to 6 ft. (2 m) tall, freely branched. Pollen from this odiferous plant is a major source for hayfever for some people. Synonyms: *Ambrosia elatior, A. monophylla,* and *A. glandulosa.*

Iva imbricata
Walter

Family: Asteraceae (aster or daisy).

Flowers: Flowers minute, greenish-white, heads drooping, in leafy racemes. Heads subtended by a bract. Male and female flowers separate, but on the same plant. Male flowers with undivided styles, corollas distinctly 5-lobed. Corolla of female flowers slightly lobed. Stamens 5, separate. Bracts in 2 rows.

Leaves: Fleshy, opposite below, alternate above, entire or shallow-toothed, sessile or nearly so, lanceolate.

Habitat: Coastal dunes and beaches.

Distribution: Throughout the state.

Flowering time: Summer, fall.

Comment: Stem smooth, branched mostly at the base, to 3 ft. (1 m) tall.

Roseling or Pink Spiderwort
Cuthbertia ornata
Small

Family: Commelinaceae (spiderwort or day-flower).

Flowers: Petals 3, pink or rose, margins wavy. Flower clusters subtended by small bracts. Sepals 3. Stamens 6, all fertile, filaments hairy.

Leaves: Alternate, grasslike, few, linear (less than 3 mm wide).

Habitat: Dry pinelands and oak woods.

Distribution: Central and south Florida.

Flowering time: Late winter, spring, summer, fall.

Comment: Plant over 16 in. (40 cm) tall. Solitary or in clusters. Flower stem longer than the leaves. A similar, but less common species, *Cuthbertia graminea*, has flower stems shorter than the leaves.

Rose Pogonia
Pogonia ophioglossoides
(L.) Ker-Gawler

Family: Orchidaceae (orchid).

Flowers: Bloom usually 1, pink or rose pink. Lip flat, crested and fringed with fleshy hairs tipped yellow or brown. Flower fragrant.

Leaves: Single, broad, elliptic, sheathing about midway on the stem.

Habitat: Wet, pine flatwoods and marshes.

Distribution: Central and north Florida.

Flowering time: Spring.

Comment: Stem smooth, to 28 in. (70 cm) tall. Terrestrial.

Dwarf Pawpaw

Asimina pygmaea
(Bartram) Dunal

Family: Annonaceae (custard apple).

Flowers: Petals 6. Outer petals pink with maroon streaks. Inner petals deep maroon. Flowers nodding, axillary, appearing after the leaves emerge and on the growth of the current season. Sepals 3. Stamens many.

Leaves. Alternate, oblanceolate to elliptic-oblong, strongly net-veined, smooth with age.

Habitat: Dry pinelands and sandhills.

Distribution: Throughout the state.

Flowering time: Spring.

Comment: Small shrub, branched or unbranched, to 20 in. (50 cm) tall. Reddish hairs on the leaf petioles and veins of lower leaf surface. Synonym: *Pityothamnus pygmaeus.*

Pink Purslane

Portulaca pilosa
L.

Family: Portulacaceae (purslane).

Flowers: Petals 5, pink. Flowers terminal, less than ⅝ in. (15 mm) wide. Sepals 2. Stamens many.

Leaves: Chiefly alternate, to 3 cm long, thick, linear to spatulate. Hairs occur in the leaf axils.

Habitat: Disturbed sites and sandy pinelands.

Distribution: Throughout the state.

Flowering time: Spring, summer, fall.

Comment: Stem fleshy, creeping, branched.

Pink Sundew
Drosera capillaris
Poiret

Family: Droseraceae (sundew).

Flowers: Petals 5, pink. Flowers small, in 1-sided racemes. Flower nodding, stem smooth, lacking tiny glands and hairs. Sepals 5. Stamens 5.

Leaves: Reddish rosettes. Leaf stalk smooth, nonglandular, slightly longer or equaling the length of the blade. Blades spatulate.

Habitat: Damp pinelands and bogs.

Distribution: Throughout the state.

Flowering time: Spring, summer, fall.

Comment: Carnivorous. Stalked glands on leaves produce a sticky secretion that traps insects which are then digested.

Swamp Rose
Rosa palustris
Marshall

Family: Rosaceae (rose).

Flowers: Petals 5, pale pink. Flowers usually in clusters. Pistils united forming a cap. Sepals 5, bristly, ¾–1⅛ in. (2–3 cm) long. Sepals and hypanthium with stalked glands. Stamens many.

Leaves: Alternate, odd-pinnately compound. Leaflets 5–9, margins toothed, elliptic, terminal leaflet the largest. Narrow, elongated, wing-shaped, hairy stipules occur at the bases of the leafstalks.

Habitat: Wet grounds and swamps.

Distribution: Central and north Florida.

Flowering time: Spring.

Comment: Shrubby plant with down-pointed thorns, stems smooth, to 6 ft. (2 m) tall. Synonyms: *Rosa floridana* and *R. lancifolia*.

Sensitive Briar
Schrankia microphylla
(Dryander ex Smith) Macbride

Family: Fabaceae (bean or pea).

Flowers: Heads stalked, round, pink, of many small, sessile flowers. Stamens usually 10. Pod narrow, 4-sided, downy, prickly, ¼₆ in. (6 or 7 mm) long.

Leaves: Even-bipinnately compound. Leaflets numerous, linear or elliptic, closing when touched. Leaflets with 1 prominent midvein below.

Habitat: Pinelands and dry thickets.

Distribution: Throughout the state.

Flowering time: All year.

Comment: Stem briarlike, trailing, prickly, 3 ft. (1 m) long or more. Synonyms: *Leptoglottis chapmanii* and *L. angustisiliqua.*

Mimosa strigillosa
Torrey and Gray

Family: Fabaceae (bean or pea).

Flowers: Heads stalked, round, rose-pink, of many small, sessile flowers. Heads from the leaf axils. Pod rough, jointed.

Leaves: Even-bipinnately compound. Leaflets numerous, linear, closing when touched.

Habitat: Wet, disturbed sites, stream banks, and pinelands.

Distribution: Central and north Florida.

Flowering time: Spring, summer, fall.

Comment: Stem low-growing, hairy, non-prickly, woody below and herbaceous above.

Dalea feayi
(Chapman) Barneby

Family: Fabaceae (bean or pea).

Flowers: Corolla reduced to 1 petal. Flowers pink, in terminal, stalked, globose, headlike spikes. Calyx 5-lobed, lobes leaflike. Stamens 5, alternating with 4 petaloid, infertile stamens.

Leaves: Alternate, odd-pinnately compound. Leaflet segments 5–9, narrow, gland-dotted.

Habitat: Dry pinelands and sand pine scrub.

Distribution: Throughout the state.

Flowering time: Spring, summer, fall.

Comment: Stem somewhat woody, branched, leafy, to 20 in. (50 cm) tall. Synonym: *Petalostemon feayi.*

Indigofera spicata
Forskal

Family: Fabaceae (bean or pea).

Flowers: Corolla pea-shaped, pinkish. Flowers in spikelike racemes. Lateral petals longer than the lower ones. Calyx 5-lobed. Lower petals (keel) with small, lateral pouches. Stamens 10 (9 united, 1 free), anther tips pointed. Pods hairy, clustered and pointed downward.

Leaves: Alternate, odd-pinnately compound. Leaflets hairy, petioles short.

Habitat: Disturbed sites.

Distribution: Central and south Florida.

Flowering time: Spring, summer, fall.

Comment: Plant low-growing, somewhat cloverlike. Native to Africa. Synonyms: *Indigofera hendecaphylla* or *I. endecaphylla.*

Indigofera miniata
Ortega

Family: Fabaceae (bean or pea).

Flowers: Corolla pea-shaped, salmon-pink to reddish. Flowers axillary. Keel with lateral pouches. Calyx 5-lobed, lobes narrow, bristly, and hairy. Stamens 10 (9 united, 1 free).

Leaves: Alternate, odd-pinnately compound, short-stalked. Leaflets 5–9, linear to oblanceolate, narrowing at the base.

Habitat: Dry pinelands and disturbed sites.

Distribution: Central and south Florida.

Flowering time: Spring, summer, fall.

Comment: Stem prostrate with flattened hairs. Photo is of the variety *leptosepala*.

Tephrosia florida
(Dietrich) Wood

Family: Fabaceae (bean or pea).

Flowers: Corolla pea-shaped, white, pink, or red. Flowers in terminal racemes opposite the leaves. Flower stalk leafless, flattened. Pistil hairy. Calyx 5-lobed. Stamens 10 (9 united, 1 free).

Leaves: Odd-pinnately compound. Leaflets 3–19. Leaf petiole longer than the length of the lowest leaflet. Leaflets entire, oblong or ends squared, shallowly notched, apex spine-tipped, base tapered. Parallel veins prominent on the ventral leaflet surface.

Habitat: Pinelands.

Distribution: Throughout the state.

Flowering time: Spring, summer, fall.

Comment: Stem prostrate, twining, angled, hairy. Flowers white, becoming pink and red. Synonym: *Cracca ambigua*.

Tephrosia angustissima
Shuttleworth ex Chapman

Family: Fabaceae (bean or pea).

Flowers: Corolla pea-shaped, pink-purple, upper petal nearly circular. Flowers in slender racemes opposite to and longer than the adjacent leaves. Pistil smooth. Calyx hairy, 5-lobed, lobes awl-shaped. Stamens 10 (9 united, 1 free).

Leaves: Odd-pinnately compound. Leaflets often 13–17, entire, oblong, spine-tipped. Leaf petiole hairy. Parallel veins and hairs prominent on ventral surfaces of the leaflets. Upper leaflet surfaces nearly hairless.

Habitat: Coastal strands.

Distribution: Coastal counties of central and south Florida and Hendry County. Endemic to Florida.

Flowering time: Spring, summer, fall.

Comment: Stems smooth or hairy with wide-spreading, elongate branches that become prostrate. Synonyms: *Tephrosia curtissii* and *Cracca curtissii.*

Aeschynomene americana
L.

Family: Fabaceae (bean or pea).

Flowers: Corolla pea-shaped, pinkish to yellowish-brown with a yellow center bordered red. Flowers in axillary racemes. Calyx 2-lipped. Pod (loment) of 5–9, smooth segments; upper surface straight, lower surface constricted.

Leaves: Compound. Leaflets 16–56, linear, 3-veined, spine-tipped. Leaflet margins minutely toothed; may be bordered with red. Petiole hairy.

Habitat: Pinelands and disturbed sites.

Distribution: Throughout the state.

Flowering time: Late spring, summer, fall.

Comment: Stem woody, hairy, thornless, to 6 ft. (2 m) tall.

Cranesbill

Geranium carolinianum
L.

Family: Geraniaceae (geranium).

Flowers: Petals usually 5, separate, pale pink, about ⅜ in. (1 cm) long. Flowers stalked, often clustered. Stigmas 5. Sepals 5, separate, spine-tipped. Stamens 10.

Leaves: Palmately 5–9 lobed, deeply clefted, toothed. Leaves below the flowers are opposite.

Habitat: Dry soils, lawns, thin woods, and disturbed sites.

Distribution: Throughout the state.

Flowering time: Winter, spring, fall.

Comment: Stem branched, hairy, to 24 in. (60 cm) tall. Only member of the family in Florida.

Violet Wood Sorrel

Oxalis corymbosa
DC.

Family: Oxalidaceae (wood sorrel).

Flowers: Petals 5, rose-purple to pink, striped. Flowers in umbel-like cymes. Styles 5. Sepals 5, smooth, tips wtih brownish tubercles. Stamens 10, of different lengths.

Leaves: Trifoliate, hairy, smooth, tips with brownish tubercles.

Habitat: Moist disturbed sites.

Distribution: Central and north Florida.

Flowering time: Spring, summer, fall.

Comment: These low-growing plants have a sour, acid taste. Native to tropical America. Synonyms: *Ionoxalis martiana* and *Xanthoxalis martiana.*

Saltmarsh Mallow
Kosteletzkya virginica
(L.) Presl ex Gray

Family: Malvaceae (mallow).

Flowers: Petals pink, lavender to whitish. Corolla hibiscuslike, about 2 in. (5 cm) across. Stigmas 5. Flowers solitary, drooping, in the upper leaf axils or terminal. Bracts 8–10. Calyx 5-lobed. Stamens many, attached to the pistil. Capsules flattened, 5-celled, 1 seed/ cell.

Leaves: Alternate, 3–5 lobed or unlobed, ovate or angled, stalked, hairy, margins undulating or toothed.

Habitat: Swamps and marshes.

Distribution: Throughout the state.

Flowering time: Spring, summer, fall.

Comment: Herb or small shrub, stem hairy, to 3 ft. (1 m) tall or more. Synonyms: *Kosteletzkya althaeifolia* and *K. smilacifolia*.

Hibiscus furcellatus
Desvaux

Family: Malvaceae (mallow).

Flowers: Petals 5, pink or rose with dark centers. Flowers solitary, axillary, to 8 in. (20 cm) across, somewhat nodding. Stigmas 5. Bracts many, linear, apex forked. Sepals 5, triangular, 3-veined, bristly. Stamens many, attached to the pistil. Capsules long as broad or longer, 5-celled, 2 or more seeds/cell.

Leaves: Alternate, heart-shaped, grayish, stalked, velvety, toothed.

Habitat: Marshes, swamps, and other wet areas.

Distribution: Central and south Florida.

Flowering time: All year.

Comment: Plant shrublike, hairy, to 6 ft. (2 m) tall or more.

Swamp Hibiscus

Hibiscus grandiflorus
Michaux

Family: Malvaceae (mallow).

Flowers: Petals 5, pink or rose with dark centers. Flowers solitary, axillary, somewhat nodding. Stigmas 5. Bracts narrow, hairy, apices not forked. Sepals 5, hairy. Stamens many, attached to the pistil. Capsules long as broad or longer, 5-celled, 2 or more seeds/cell.

Leaves: Alternate, green-gray, stalked, velvety above and below, heart-shaped, 3-lobed, toothed.

Habitat: Marshes, swamps, and other wet areas.

Distribution: Throughout the state.

Flowering time: Spring, summer, early fall.

Comment: Plant shrublike, woody or herbaceous, hairy, to 6 ft. (2 m) tall or more.

Caesar-weed

Urena lobata
L.

Family: Malvaceae (mallow).

Flowers: Petals 5, pink, bases united. Flowers small, in leaf axils and clustered in the upper stem branches. Bracts 5. Calyx 5-lobed. Capsules small, spiny, round, usually lobed.

Leaves: Alternate, ovate, shallowly lobed, fine-toothed, hairy.

Habitat: Disturbed sites.

Distribution: Central and south Florida.

Flowering time: All year.

Comment: Branching herb or partly woody shrub, stem hairy, to 9 ft. (3 m) tall.

Southern Gaura
Gaura angustifolia
Michaux

Family: Onagraceae (evening-primrose).

Flowers: Petals 3 or 4, pinkish-white, to ⅛ in. (3 mm) long. Sepals 3 or 4, narrow, to ¼ in. (6 mm) long. Stamens 6–8. Flowers small, on or near the ends of slender, wandlike spikes. Fruit small, nutlike, hairy.

Leaves: Alternate, narrowly lanceolate, sessile, toothed or entire, hairy or smooth. Leaves reduced upward.

Habitat: Dry, disturbed sites, and pinelands.

Distribution: Throughout the state.

Flowering time: All year.

Comment: Stem to 6 ft. (2 m) tall, slender, elongated, hairy, branched. Synonyms: *Guara simulans* and *G. eatonii*.

Showy Primrose
Oenothera speciosa
Nuttall

Family: Onagraceae (evening-primrose).

Flowers: Petals 4, pinkish-white, to 1⅜ in. (3.5 cm) long. Style with 4 stigmas and taller than the stamens. Stamens 8, anthers long. Capsule 4-ribbed.

Leaves: Alternate, linear to elliptic, wider leaves toothed or lobed near the base, axillary.

Habitat: Disturbed sites.

Distribution: Central and north Florida.

Flowering time: Spring, summer, fall.

Comment: Stem erect to prostrate. Synonym: *Hartmannia speciosa*.

Fetterbush or Shiny Lyonia
Lyonia lucida
(Lamarck) K. Koch

Family: Ericaceae (heath).

Flowers: Corolla 5-lobed, pink to red (rarely white), urn-shaped. Flowers axillary, in umbel-like clusters. Calyx 5-lobed, lobes lanceolate, to ³⁄₁₆ in. (5 mm) long. Stamens 10, filaments hairy.

Leaves: Alternate, shiny, ovate, obovate to elliptic, entire. The evergreen leaves have a lateral vein that parallels the leaf margin.

Habitat: Pinelands.

Distribution: Throughout the state.

Flowering time: Winter, spring, summer.

Comment: Shrub, low-growing or to 9 ft. (3 m) tall. Upper stem smooth. Synonym: *Desmothamnus lucidus.*

Pinxter Azalea or Wild Azalea
Rhododendron canescens
(Michaux) Sweet

Family: Ericaceae (heath).

Flowers: Corolla 5-lobed, pink to whitish pink. Corolla tube on outside glandular and finely haired. Calyx 5-lobed, lobes ciliate, not glandular. Stamens 5, elongated. Fruit a dry capsule.

Leaves: Alternate, elliptic to oblanceolate, entire or slightly toothed. Petioles hairy.

Habitat: Moist woods and along streams.

Distribution: Central and North Florida.

Flowering time: Spring.

Comment: Woody bush to 15 ft. (5 m) tall, young twigs densely haired. Flowers fragrant, emerging before or as the leaves appear. Synonym: *Azalea canescens.*

Water Pimpernel
Samolus ebracteatus
HBK.

Family: Primulaceae (primrose).

Flowers: Corolla 5-lobed, pinkish-white. Bases of lobes glandular and hairy. Calyx 5-lobed, lobes triangular and glandular. Terminal racemes not leafy. Stamens 5, attached to upper corolla tube and opposite the petals. Infertile stamens lacking.

Leaves: Basal leaves often absent at flowering time. Stem leaves alternate, oblanceolate, obovate, entire, thickish, smooth. Lower midvein often reddish-purple. Lower leaf petioles winged.

Habitat: Wet brackish and fresh water areas, especially of coastal sites.

Distribution: Throughout the state.

Flowering time: All year.

Comment: Stem smooth, reddish-purple, branched, to 14 in. (35 cm) tall, upper part glandular. Synonym: *Samodia ebracteata.*

Sabatia grandiflora
(Gray) Small

Family: Gentianaceae (gentian).

Flowers: Corolla 5-lobed, rose, eye green-yellow. Style bilobed. Calyx 5-lobed, lobes narrow and shorter than the corolla lobes. Stamens 5.

Leaves: Opposite, thick, linear, entire, sessile; midvein obscure. Lower leaves the larger.

Habitat: Wet pinelands.

Distribution: Throughout the state.

Flowering time: All year.

Comment: Stem smooth, to 3 ft. (1 m) tall or more, branched.

Sabatia stellaris
Pursh

Family: Gentianaceae (gentian).

Flowers: Petals 5, pink or pale rose, eye yellow bordered by red and forming a star-shaped pattern. Floral branches alternate. Style bilobed. Calyx 5-lobed, lobes linear. Stamens 5.

Leaves: Opposite, narrowly elliptic, thin, smooth, entire, sessile, midvein prominent.

Habitat: Salt or brackish marshes and dunes. Rarely inland.

Distribution: Central and north Florida.

Flowering time: Spring, summer, fall.

Comment: Stem branched, smooth, to 24 in. (60 cm) tall.

Sabatia bartramii
Wilbur

Family: Gentianaceae (gentian).

Flowers: Petals 8–12, pink, eye yellow bordered by red and forming a star-shaped pattern. Style bilobed. Sepal lobes narrow, 8–12. Stamens 5.

Leaves: Basal leaves spatulate. Stem leaves opposite, smooth, linear, entire, sessile, succulent, about 1 in. (25 mm) long.

Habitat: Wet pinelands, margins of ponds, and ditches.

Distribution: Throughout the state.

Flowering time: Summer, fall.

Comment: Stem branched, smooth, to 3 ft. (1 m) tall.

Swamp Milkweed
Asclepias incarnata
L.

Family: Asclepiadaceae (milkweed).

Flowers: Corolla deeply lobed, petals 5, pink to rose-purple. Corolla lobes reflexed. Flowers in umbels; inflorescence branches often paired. Stamens 5, attached to the stigma.

Leaves: Opposite, stalked, narrowly oblong to linear-lanceolate. Leaves hairy below.

Habitat: Swamps and wet woods.

Distribution: Central and south Florida.

Flowering time: Summer, fall.

Comment: Stem leafy, to 3 ft. (1 m) tall or more, usually branched above. Sap milky.

Annual Garden Phlox
Phlox drummondii
Hooker

Family: Polemoniaceae (phlox).

Flowers: Corolla tubular, 5-lobed, pink, lavender, magenta, or white. Flowers in terminal clusters. Style 3-parted. Calyx 5-lobed, lobes lanceolate, hairy. Stamens 5.

Leaves: Upper leaves alternate, elliptic, lanceolate, or oblanceolate, spine-tipped. Lower leaves opposite. Leaf surfaces hairy.

Habitat: Dry, sandy soils of open, disturbed sites.

Distribution: Throughout the state.

Flowering time: Winter, spring, summer.

Comment: Stem to 20 in. (50 cm) tall, glandular-hairy, usually branched. Often occurs in large masses. Escapee from cultivation. Native to Texas.

Beautybush or French Mulberry
Callicarpa americana
L.

Family: Verbenaceae (vervain).

Flowers: Petals usually 4, united, small, pinkish to bluish. Flowers in axillary clusters. Calyx usually 4, united, shallowly toothed. Stamens 4. Berries reddish-purple in axillary clusters on the branches.

Leaves: Opposite, ovate, lanceolate to elliptic, simple, finely toothed, stalked, base narrow, whitish and hairy below.

Habitat: Woods and thickets.

Distribution: Throughout the state.

Flowering time: Spring, summer, fall.

Comment: Stem branched, woody, hairs star-shaped. The shrub gets to 6 ft. (2 m) tall or more. Fruit eaten by birds, especially the northern mockingbird.

Hedge Nettle
Stachys floridana
Shuttleworth ex Bentham

Family: Lamiaceae (mint).

Flowers: Corolla 2-lipped, pink or pale purple with dark dots. Upper lip small, hoodlike; lower lip the larger, 3-lobed. Flowers whorled in terminal racemes. Style 2-lobed. Calyx 5-lobed, lobes spine-tipped. Stamens 4, arched under the upper lip.

Leaves: Opposite, lanceolate, stalked, toothed.

Habitat: Open woods and disturbed sites.

Distribution: Central and north Florida.

Flowering time: All year.

Comment: Stem square, branched, hairy or smooth, to 20 in. (50 cm) tall.

Wood Sage or Wood Germander
Teucrium canadense
L.

Family: Lamiaceae (mint).

Flowers: Corolla tubular, pale pink-purple. Lip 5-lobed, lower lip the larger and dipper-like. Flowers in terminal, spikelike racemes. Style 2-lobed. Calyx 5-lobed, lower 2 lobes pointed. Stamens 4, arched upward.

Leaves: Opposite, toothed, stalked, elliptic or lanceolate. Lower surface paler than the upper. Basal leaves absent.

Habitat: Wet thickets, hammocks.

Distribution: Throughout the state.

Flowering time: All year.

Comment: Stem square, leafy, hairy, to 3 ft. (1 m) tall or more. Synonym: *Teucrium nashii.*

Dicerandra linearifolia
(Elliott) Bentham

Family: Lamiaceae (mint).

Flowers: Corolla rose or pink-purple (sometimes white), spotted and streaked inside. Lower lip 3-lobed, upper lip 2-lobed. Flowers aromatic, stalked, clustered along the upper branches. Style 2-branched. Calyx 2-lipped, green, tinged pinkish. Upper lip entire, lower lip of 2 teeth. Stamens 4, longer than the corolla. Anthers bear pointed horns.

Leaves: Opposite, entire, linear, glandular.

Habitat: Sandhills, open woods, and scrub.

Distribution: Central and north Florida.

Flowering time: Summer, fall.

Comment: Stem square, to 20 in. (50 cm) tall, hairy.

False Dragonhead
Physostegia purpurea
(Walter) Blake

Family: Lamiaceae (mint).

Flowers: Corolla 2-lipped, pink to rose purple, streaked and spotted. Flowers in leafless, terminal, spikelike racemes. Lower lip 3-lobed. Style 2-lobed. Calyx 5-lobed, hairy. Stamens 4, arched under the upper lip.

Leaves: Opposite, stalked or sessile, toothed or nearly so, lanceolate to oblanceolate, reduced upward.

Habitat: Damp pinelands and borders of marshes and swamps.

Distribution: Throughout the state.

Flowering time: Spring, summer, fall.

Comment: Stem smooth, square, to 3 ft. (1 m) tall. These mints are also called "obedient plants" because an individual flower stays put when turned. Synonym: *Dracocephalum denticulata*.

Beardtongue
Penstemon australis
Small

Family: Scrophulariaceae (snapdragon or figwort).

Flowers: Corolla 5-lobed, pink to red-purple with red-purple lines within the flower. Flowers terminal. Style 1. Sepals 5. Fertile stamens 4; 1 yellow, hairy infertile stamen (staminode).

Leaves: Stem leaves opposite, narrowly lanceolate, toothed or entire. Basal leaves stalked, oblanceolate, in rosettes. Uppermost leaves reduced.

Habitat: Dry pinelands.

Distribution: Central and north Florida.

Flowering time: Spring.

Comment: Stem to 32 in. (80 cm) tall, unbranched above, gray-downy.

Climbing Aster
Aster carolinianus
Walter

Family: Asteraceae (aster or daisy).

Flowers: Heads of pink or pale purple ray florets and yellow to reddish disk florets. Bracts hairy, overlapping, spatulate to linear, whitish with reflexed green tips.

Leaves: Alternate, elliptic to lanceolate, entire, apex tapered, hairy, clasping. Leaves smooth or rough on both surfaces.

Habitat: Swamps, wet hammocks, and other wet areas.

Distribution: Throughout the state.

Flowering time: All year.

Comment: Stem woody, hairy, vinelike, clambering or sprawling, branching.

Paint Brush
Carphephorus corymbosus
(Nuttall) Torrey and Gray

Family: Asteraceae (aster or daisy).

Flowers: Heads of pink or bright lilac disk florets in flattened, terminal corymbs. Ray florets lacking. Bracts ovate, green, margins white, tips blunt.

Leaves: Stem leaves alternate, elliptic, chiefly entire, sessile, reduced upward. Basal leaves spatulate.

Habitat: Dry pinelands.

Distribution: Throughout the state.

Flowering time: Summer, fall.

Comment: Stem hairy, to 3 ft. (1 m) tall or more.

Joe-pye-weed
Eupatoriadelphus fistulosus
(Barratt) King and Robins

Family: Asteraceae (aster or daisy).

Flowers: Heads of 5–7, pinkish disk florets. Ray florets lacking. Inflorescence axillary, branched, terminal.

Leaves: Whorls of 4–7 leaves, margins toothed or scalloped, stalked, tips pointed.

Habitat: Moist meadows and woods.

Distribution: Central and north Florida.

Flowering time: Late spring, summer, fall.

Comment: Stem hollow, to 6 ft. (2 m) tall or more. Synonym: *Eupatorium fistulosum.*

Pluchea rosea
Godfrey

Family: Asteraceae (aster or daisy).

Flowers: Heads sessile, of tubular, pinkish to rose florets. Ray florets lacking. Heads hairy, in terminal clusters.

Leaves: Alternate, oblong to obovate, sessile-clasping, hairy, toothed, thickish.

Habitat: Wet or dry pinelands and disturbed sites.

Distribution: Throughout the state.

Flowering time: Spring, summer, fall.

Comment: Stem to 3 ft. (1 m) or more. Plant odiferous.

Palafoxia integrifolia
(Nuttall) Torrey and Gray

Family: Asteraceae (aster or daisy).

Flowers: Heads of tubular, pink-whitish florets. Ray florets lacking. Heads stalked, in terminal, branching corymbs. Bracts broad, sparsely hairy, margins entire and white-pinkish.

Leaves: Alternate, entire, hairy, linear-lanceolate. Lower leaves linear.

Habitat: Dry pinelands.

Distribution: Throughout the state.

Flowering time: Fall.

Comment: Upper stem hairy and herbaceous; lower woody. Plant slender, to 3 ft. (1 m) or more tall, branching. Synonym: *Polypteris integrifolia.*

Day-flower
Commelina erecta
L.

Family: Commelinaceae (spiderwort or day-flower).

Flowers: Petals 3 (2 lateral blues; 1 smaller white). Flowers ephemeral, in terminal clusters, enclosed by a sticky, tubular sheath. Sepals 3, greenish, equal. Stamens 6 (3 fertile, 3 unfertile).

Leaves: Alternate, lanceolate or elliptic, succulent.

Habitat: Dry, sandy soils and cultivated sites.

Distribution: Throughout the state.

Flowering time: Late winter, spring, summer, fall.

Comment: Stem knotty, erect or on or near the ground, to 24 in. (60 cm) tall. Seeds eaten by doves, quail, and songbirds. Synonyms: *Commelina angustifolia* and *C. crispa.*

Day-flower
Commelina diffusa
Burman f.

Family: Commelinaceae (spiderwort or day-flower).

Flowers: Petals 3, blue, nearly equal in size. Flowers ephemeral, enclosed by a tubular sheath. Sepals 3, greenish, unequal. Stamens 6 (3 fertile, 3 unfertile).

Leaves: Alternate, lanceolate, succulent.

Habitat: Moist, sandy soils, yards, and cultivated sites.

Distribution: Throughout the state.

Flowering time: All year.

Comment: Stem creeping, smooth, mat-forming. Plant roots at the stem nodes. Synonym: *Commelina longicaulis.*

Spiderwort
Tradescantia ohiensis
Rafinesque

Family: Commelinaceae (spiderwort or day-flower).

Flowers: Petals 3, symmetrical, blue-violet (rarely white). Flowers ephemeral, in drooping, umbel-like clusters. Clusters subtended by 1–3, leaflike bracts. Sepals 3, with tufts of hairs at the apices. Stamens 6, all fertile, filaments hairy.

Leaves: Linear or lanceolate, smooth, folded lengthwise.

Habitat: Moist roadsides and meadows. Often cultivated in lawns.

Distribution: Throughout the state.

Flowering time: All year.

Comment: Stem smooth, to 25⅝ in. (65 cm) tall or more. John Tradescant, for whom the genus was named, was a botanical explorer and gardener to Queen Henrietta Maria of England. Synonyms: *Tradescantia reflexa* and *T. incarnata*.

Pickerelweed
Pontederia cordata
L.

Family: Pontederiaceae (pickerelweed).

Flowers: Corolla 2-lipped, purple-blue (rarely white). Upper lip of 3 fused lobes; lower lip of 3 separate lobes. Flowers in a hairy spike. Stamens 6 (3 long, 3 short).

Leaves: Mostly basal, long-stalked, arrow- to lance-shaped, broadest near the base.

Habitat: Edges of ponds, ditches, and other shallow, wet areas.

Distribution: Throughout the state.

Flowering time: Spring, summer, fall.

Comment: Plant attached to the soil, often colonial. Leaves and stems edible. Stem soft, to 3 ft. (1 m) tall. Synonym: *Pontederia lanceolata*.

Water Hyacinth

Eichhornia crassipes
(Martius) Solms

Family: Pontederiaceae (pickerelweed).

Flowers: Corolla 2-lipped, tubular, pale purple. Upper lobes yellow-spotted. Flowers occur in spikes. Stamens 6, filaments curved.

Leaves: Basal, ovate or elliptic. Leaves usually with short, inflated stalks.

Habitat: Ditches, marshes, and lakes.

Distribution: Throughout the state.

Flowering time: Spring, summer, fall.

Comment: Plant may be rooted in the mud, but usually floating. Often growing in large masses. Native to tropical America. Synonym: *Piaropus crassipes.*

Prairie Iris

Iris hexagona
Walter

Family: Iridaceae (iris).

Flowers: Petals 3, violet-blue, variegated with white and green toward the base. Sepals 3 (outermost and drooping) bearing a furry, yellow ridge (the beard). Sepals larger than the petals. Styles 3, flat, petal-like. Stamens 3.

Leaves: Yellowish-green, sword-shaped, bases sheathed.

Habitat: Low grounds and around ditches.

Distribution: Throughout the state.

Flowering time: Spring.

Comment: Stem leafy, to 3 ft. (1 m) tall or more. Synonyms: *Iris savannarum* and *I. albispiritus.*

Celestial Lily or Fall-flowering Ixia
Nemastylis floridana
Small

Family: Iridaceae (iris).

Flowers: Perianth 6-parted, violet-blue. Petals and sepals similar. Style short, branched into 6 threads. Stamens 3, bright yellow.

Leaves: Few, linear, bases sheathing, plaited lengthwise.

Habitat: Grassy openings of marshes, low flatwoods, and hammocks.

Distribution: Central Florida. Endemic and localized to a few eastern counties of peninsular Florida.

Flowering time: Fall.

Comment: The blue color in this flower does not photograph well. Stem slender, to 32 in. (80 cm) tall. Flower opens from about 4 to 6 PM.

Blue-eyed Grass
Sisyrinchium rosulatum
Bicknell

Family: Iridaceae (iris).

Flowers: Perianth 6-parted, pale blue-purple to whitish with a yellow eye-ring circled with rose-purple. Flowers small. Flower stalk has a swelling below the perianth. Stamens 3, united to the style.

Leaves: Narrow, grasslike.

Habitat: Moist pinelands, roadsides, and lawns.

Distribution: Central and north Florida.

Flowering time: Late winter, spring, summer.

Comment: Flower stem and leaves spreading on or near the ground. Native to South America.

Blue-eyed Grass

Sisyrinchium atlanticum
Bicknell

Family: Iridaceae (iris).

Flowers: Perianth 6-parted, bluish-purple with a yellow center. Flower stalk has a swelling below the perianth. Stamens 3, united to the style.

Leaves: 2–4 mm wide, grasslike; shorter than or equal to the flower stem.

Habitat: Wet flatwoods, marshes, and other wet areas.

Distribution: Throughout the state.

Flowering time: Spring, summer.

Comment: Plant gets to 20 in. (50 cm) tall. Flower stem stiff, wing-edged, usually bearing 2 sheaths.

Grass-pink

Calopogon tuberosus
(L.) BSP.

Family: Orchidaceae (orchid).

Flowers: Petals 3, purplish-pink to magenta. Flowers in terminal racemes. Lip fan-shaped, bearing cream-colored hairs. Sepals 3, petal-like.

Leaves: Linear, over ³⁄₁₆ in. (5 mm) wide, sheathing near the base.

Habitat: Swamps, bogs, and other wet, acid soils.

Distribution: Central and north Florida.

Flowering time: Spring, summer.

Comment: Stem erect, slender, smooth. Terrestrial. Synonyms: *Calopogon pulchellus, Limodorum tuberosum,* and *L. simpsonii.*

Grass-pink
Calopogon multiflorus
Lindley

Family: Orchidaceae (orchid).

Flowers: Petals 3, purplish-pink to magenta. Petals widest above the middle. Flowers many, in terminal racemes. Flowers open almost together in groups. Lip clawed with long, yellow hairs near the base.

Leaves: Leaves 1 or 2, less than 3/16 in. (5 mm) wide, sheathing the stem.

Habitat: Low grounds and wet, pine flatwoods.

Distribution: Throughout the state.

Flowering time: Winter, spring, summer.

Comment: Stem slender, smooth, to 16 in. (40 cm) tall. Terrestrial. Synonyms: *Limodorum pinetorum* and *L. multiflorum*.

Sea Purslane
Sesuvium portulacastrum
L.

Family: Aizoaceae (ice plant or carpetweed).

Flowers: Petals lacking. Sepals 5-pointed, purplish-pink within and green on the outside. Flowers solitary, on axillary pinkish pedicels (3 mm long or more). Stamens many.

Leaves: Opposite, fleshy, linear.

Habitat: Salt flats and dunes.

Distribution: Throughout the state.

Flowering time: All year.

Comment: Stem fleshy, reddish, jointed, creeping. Plant has a salty taste.

Clematis reticulata
Walter

Family: Ranunculaceae (buttercup or crowfoot).

Flowers: Petals lacking. Sepals 4, purplish, ⅝–1 in. (15–25 mm) long. Flowers solitary, bell-shaped, nodding, stalked, terminal. Style plumelike. Stamens many.

Leaves: Opposite, pinnately compound. Leaflets usually 3–9, leathery, ovate or elliptic, veins netted and raised.

Habitat: Pinelands.

Distribution: Central and north Florida.

Flowering time: Spring, summer.

Comment: Vine herbaceous, sprawling or weakly ascending, stem many-angled. Synonyms: *Viorna subreticulata* and *V. reticulata*.

Leather Flower
Clematis crispa
L.

Family: Ranunculaceae (buttercup or crowfoot).

Flowers: Petals lacking. Sepals 4, bluish-purple. Flowers solitary, stalked, bell-shaped, nodding. Sepal margins thin. Stamens many.

Leaves: Opposite, pinnately compound, leaflets usually 3–5, smooth, stalked, thin, entire, linear to ovate.

Habitat: Wet marshes and woods.

Distribution: Central and north Florida.

Flowering time: Spring, summer.

Comment: Vine smooth, twining, stem many-angled. Synonyms: *Viorna crispa* and *V. obliqua*.

Pine-hyacinth
Clematis baldwinii
Torrey and Gray

Family: Ranunculaceae (buttercup or crow-foot).

Flowers: Petals lacking. Sepals 4, pale bluish-purple to pinkish. Flowers bell-shaped, nodding, solitary, stalked. Stamens many.

Leaves: Opposite, lanceolate to elliptic, lobed or unlobed, smooth, stalked, entire.

Habitat: Pinelands.

Distribution: Central and south Florida.

Flowering time: All year.

Comment: Erect herb, to 20 in. (50 cm) tall. Synonym: *Viorna baldwinii.*

Scrub Lupine
Lupinus aridorum
McFarlin ex Beckner

Family: Fabaceae (bean or pea).

Flowers: Corolla pea-shaped, purplish with a deep reddish-purple spot. Flowers stalked, in terminal spikes. Calyx 2-lipped, hairy. Stamens united as 1 group, of 2 lengths. Pod hairy, flattened, ¾ or 1⅛ in. (2 or 3 cm) long.

Leaves: Unifoliate, silky-haired, stalked, entire, ovate, stipules small to elliptic.

Habitat: White sand scrubs.

Distribution: Species localized in Polk and Orange counties of central Florida.

Flowering time: Spring.

Comment: Woody-branched herbs with hairy, erect or reclining stems, to 16 in. (40 cm) tall or more.

Sky-blue Lupine
Lupinus diffusus
Nuttall

Family: Fabaceae (bean or pea).

Flowers: Corolla blue (of varying shades), pea-shaped, upper petal with a creamy-white, central spot. Flowers stalked, in terminal spikes. Calyx 2-lipped, hairy. Stamens united as 1 group, of 2 lengths. Pod hairy, somewhat flattened, 1⅛ or 1½ in. (3 or 4 cm) long.

Leaves: Unifoliate, silky-haired, stalked, entire, ovate to elliptic.

Habitat: Sandhills and sand pine scrub.

Distribution: Throughout the state.

Flowering time: Mid-winter, spring.

Comment: Woody-branched herbs with hairy, erect or reclining stems, to 16 in. (40 cm) tall or more.

Lady Lupine
Lupinus villosus
Willdenow

Family: Fabaceae (bean or pea).

Flowers: Corolla pea-shaped, pink to purplish with a deep reddish-purple spot on the upper petal. Flowers stalked, in terminal, hairy spikes. Calyx 2-lipped, hairy. Stamens 10, united, of 2 lengths. Pod covered with white, shaggy hairs.

Leaves: Alternate, unifoliate, hairy, elliptic or oval. Stipules large.

Habitat: Disturbed sites, sandhills, scrub, and open woods.

Distribution: Central and north Florida.

Flowering time: Spring.

Comment: Stem woody, erect or branches reclining, to 20 in. (50 cm) tall. Stem and leaf petioles covered wtih long, shaggy hairs.

Butterfly-pea
Clitoria mariana
L.

Family: Fabaceae (bean or pea).

Flowers: Corolla pale purple with magenta lines and a yellow space on the largest petal. Upper petal spurless. Keel uppermost. Calyx tube longer than the lobes. Stamens 10, filaments united into a tube. Pod flattened, 1⅛–2⅜ in. (3–6 cm) long; seeds sticky.

Leaves: Leaflets 3, entire, mostly ovate to ovate-lanceolate, smooth or nearly so.

Habitat: Dry flatwoods and sandhills.

Distribution: Central and north Florida.

Flowering time: Spring, summer.

Comment: Vine herbaceous, stem to 3 ft. (1 m) long, trailing or twining using tendrils. Synonym: *Martiusia mariana.*

Butterfly-pea
Centrosema virginianum
(L.) Bentham

Family: Fabaceae (bean or pea).

Flowers: Corolla pale bluish to pinkish, center white. Keel uppermost. Blunt spur near base of the largest petal on its ventral surface. Calyx 2-lipped, 5-lobed; lateral lobes of the lower calyx lip nearly equaling the median one. Stamens 10 (9 united, 1 free). Pod 2¾–5½ in. (7–14 cm) long, linear, flattened, with an elongated terminal tip.

Leaves: Leaflets 3, margins entire, stalked, ovate, oblong to elliptic.

Habitat: Pinelands and open clearings.

Distribution: Throughout the state.

Flowering time: All year.

Comment: Vine herbaceous, hairy, twining or climbing, to 1.5 mm long. Synonym: *Bradburya virginiana.* A similar species, *Centrosema arenicolum,* has lateral lobes of the lower calyx-lip much shorter than the median one.

Galactia regularis
(L.) BSP.

Family: Fabaceae (bean or pea).

Flowers: Corolla pea-shaped, purplish-red with a yellowish, medial spot. Flowers few, in axillary racemes. Upper petal ⅜–¾ in. (10–18 mm) long. Lower petals (keel) ⅜ in. (10 mm) or longer. Calyx 4-lobed, nearly smooth, upper 2 lobes fused. Stamens 10 (9 united, 1 free). Pod to 5 cm long, compressed, densely hairy.

Leaves: Alternate. Leaflets 3, stalked, ovate, oblong to elliptic, entire. Leaflets pale green and hairy below, nearly smooth above.

Habitat: Pinelands, hammock edges, and sandhills.

Distribution: Throughout the state.

Flowering time: All year.

Comment: Vine hairy to nearly smooth, prostrate, trailing; weakly climbing in some individuals.

Galactia volubilis
(L.) Britton

Family: Fabaceae (bean or pea).

Flowers: Corolla pea-shaped, purplish-rose. Flowers few, in axillary racemes. Upper petal ¼–½ in. (7–12 mm) long. Lower petals (keel) less than ⅜ in. (10 mm) long. Calyx 4-lobed, hairy, upper 2 lobes fused. Stamens 10 (9 united, 1 free). Pod to ¼ in. (6 mm) long, compressed, hairy, tip narrow.

Leaves: Alternate. Leaflets 3, stalked, oblong, elliptic, or ovate, spine-tipped, entire. Smooth or nearly so above, hairy below.

Habitat: Dry pinelands.

Distribution: Throughout the state.

Flowering time: All year.

Comment: Vine hairy, much branched, vigorously trailing and climbing.

Sand Vetch
Vicia acutifolia
Elliott

Family: Fabaceae (bean or pea).

Flowers: Corolla pale blue or whitish. Upper petal purple-tipped. The 4–10, small flowers are in axillary racemes. Style apex hairy. Stamens 10 (9 united, 1 free). Pod narrow, flattened, short-haired, 1- to 3-seeded.

Leaves: Even-pinnately compound. Leaflets 2–4 (often 4), linear or elliptic, ⅝ in. (1.5 cm) long or less. Tendril terminating the leaf.

Habitat: Along ditches and other moist areas.

Distribution: Throughout the state.

Flowering time: All year.

Comment: Vine herbaceous, climbing, twining, or sprawling, hairy to nearly smooth, to 3 ft. (1 m) long or more.

Bastard Indigo
Amorpha fruticosa
L.

Family: Fabaceae (bean or pea).

Flowers: Corolla violet-purple, with 1 petal. Flowers many, in elongated axillary or terminal spikelike racemes. Calyx 5-lobed. Stamens 10, orangish. Pod 1 or 2 seeded, glandular, smooth.

Leaves: Alternate, odd-pinnately compound. Leaflets entire, opposite, stalked, oblong to elliptic. Midvein of each leaflet extends as a short, abrupt, point.

Habitat: Streams, river banks, and open, wet woods.

Distribution: Central and north Florida.

Flowering time: Spring, summer.

Comment: Shrub woody, bushy, to 12½ ft. (4 m) tall.

Florida Beggarweed

Desmodium tortuosum
(Swartz) DC.

Family: Fabaceae (bean or pea).

Flowers: Corolla small, pea-shaped, purplish. Inflorescence terminal and axillary. Calyx 2-lipped; lower lip 3-toothed. Stamens 10 (9 united, 1 free). Pod a hairy, sticktight (loment) with nearly equal upper and lower constrictions (usually 5 or 6, ovoid segments).

Leaves: Leaflets 3, entire, spine-tipped, rough to the touch. Terminal leaflets rhombic; lateral leaflets ovate to oblong.

Habitat: Disturbed sites and hammocks.

Distribution: Throughout the state.

Flowering time: All year.

Comment: Plant to 3 ft. (1 m) tall or more, arising from a taproot. Branches wide-spreading. Introduced as a forage plant. Synonym: *Meibomia purpurea.*

Beggarweed

Desmodium viridiflorum
(L.) DC.

Family: Fabaceae (bean or pea).

Flowers: Corolla small, pea-shapred, purplish. Inflorescence terminal and axillary. Calyx 2-lipped; lower lip 3-toothed. Stamens 10 (9 united, 1 free). Pod a sticktight (loment) with 3–7 rhombic segments; lower constrictions deeper than the upper ones.

Leaves: Leaflets 3, entire, rhombic or triangular, less than 3 times longer than wide. Upper surfaces of leaves rough; lower surfaces velvety.

Habitat: Disturbed sites and hammocks.

Distribution: Throughout the state.

Flowering time: Summer, fall.

Comment: Stem slender, hairy, to 6 ft. (2 m) tall. Plants valuable forage and soil builders. Fruit eaten by birds. Synonym: *Meibomia viridiflora.*

Beggarweed
Desmodium tenuifolium
Torrey and Gray

Family: Fabaceae (bean or pea).

Flowers: Corolla small, pea-shaped, purplish. Inflorescence terminal and axillary. Calyx 2-lipped; lower lip 3-toothed. Stamens 10 (9 united, 1 free). Pod a sticktight (loment) of 1–4, nearly equal segments with constrictions on both upper and lower surfaces.

Leaves: Leaflets 3, entire, linear to linear-lanceolate, longer than wide.

Habitat: Sandhills.

Distribution: Central and north Florida.

Flowering time: Spring, summer, fall.

Comment: Stem to 3 ft. (1 m) tall or more, branched, hairy. Synonym: *Meibomia tenuifolia*.

Beggarweed
Desmodium incanum
DC.

Family: Fabaceae (bean or pea).

Flowers: Corolla small, pea-shaped, purple. Inflorescence terminal and axillary. Calyx 2-lipped; lower lip 3-toothed. Stamens 10 (9 united, 1 free). Pod a hairy sticktight (loment) of 4 or 6 segments. Upper surface of loment straight, lower surface constricted.

Leaves: Leaflets 3, entire, elliptic, ¾–2¾ in. (2–7 cm) long, smooth above and hairy especially on the flower leaf veins.

Habitat: Disturbed sites.

Distribution: Throughout the state.

Flowering time: All year.

Comment: Stem horizontal, rooting at the nodes and giving rise to a new plant. This beggarweed is often low-growing, but may get to 3 ft. (1 m) tall. Synonyms: *Desmodium canum* and *Meibomia cana*.

Beggarweed
Desmodium triflorum
(L.) DC.

Family: Fabaceae (bean or pea).

Flowers: Corolla small, pea-shaped, purple. Flowers in axillary clusters. Calyx hairy, 2-lipped; lower lip 3-toothed. Stamens 10 (9 united, 1 free). Pod (loment) hairy, small, 3–5 segments, lower edge constricted.

Leaves: Leaflets 3, entire, ovoid to wedge-shaped, small, margins and petiole hairy, surfaces sparsely hairy.

Habitat: Disturbed sites.

Distribution: Central and south Florida.

Flowering time: All year.

Comment: Stem prostrate, hairy. Native to the Old World. Synonym: *Sagotia triflora*.

Seaside Bean
Canavalia rosea
(Swartz) DC.

Family: Fabaceae (bean or pea).

Flowers: Corolla purple-pink, pea-shaped. Flowers in long-stalked racemes. Calyx 2-lipped: upper lip the broadest and longest. Stamens 10 (9 united, 1 free). Pod thick, large, ribbed on each side of the upper suture.

Leaves: Leaflets 3, obovate or oval, thick, entire.

Habitat: Coastal beaches and dunes.

Distribution: Central and south Florida.

Flowering time: All year.

Comment: Vine fleshy, prostrate, trailing, several meters long. Synonym: *Canavalia maritima*.

False Moneywort
Alysicarpus ovalifolus
(Schum. and Thonn.) J. Leonard.

Family: Fabaceae (bean or pea).

Flowers: Corolla pea-shaped, purplish-pink. Flowers ³⁄₁₆–⁵⁄₁₆ in. (5–7 mm) long, paired, stalked, axillary and terminal. Calyx 2-lipped. Stamens 10 (9 united, 1 free). Pod erect, a cylindical loment about 2 cm long.

Leaves: Alternate, unifoliate, tips sharp-pointed, sparsely haired, lanceolate, oval or linear on the same plant. Stipules with striations.

Habitat: Open, disturbed sites.

Distribution: Throughout the state.

Flowering time: Summer, fall.

Comment: Stem sparsely haired, branched, to 3 ft. (1 m) tall. Native to the Old World.

Wild Bean
Phaseolus polystachios
(L.) BSP.

Family: Fabaceae (bean or pea).

Flowers: Corolla pea-shaped, rose-purple to pinkish. Flowers long-stalked, axillary. Upper petal to ⅜ in. (1 cm) long. Calyx 2.5–3.0 mm long, lobes 5, hairy. Keel spirally twisted. Style hairy. Stamens 10 (9 united, 1 free). Pod oblong.

Leaves: Alternate, stalked, leaflets 3. Leaflets broadly ovate, base round, hairs hooked.

Habitat: Thickets, woods.

Distribution: Central and north Florida.

Flowering time: Summer, fall.

Comment: Stem climbing, twining, hairy.

Sand Bean
Strophostyles helvola
(L.) Elliott

Family: Fabaceae (bean or pea).

Flowers: Corolla pea-shaped, pale purple fading to green. Flowers few at the end of a long stalk. Style strongly incurved, dark. Bracts below flowers lanceolate, equaling or exceeding the calyx tube. Stamens 10 (9 united, 1 free). Seeds woolly.

Leaves: Usually trifoliate, stalked. Leaflets ovate to rhombic-ovate, basally lobed, margins entire.

Habitat: Open woods, fields, beaches, and salt marsh and pond margins.

Distribution: Central and north Florida.

Flowering time: Spring, summer, fall.

Comment: Trailing vine, smooth or hairy.

Polygala grandiflora
Walter

Family: Polygalaceae (milkwort).

Flowers: Corolla rose-purple. Flowers in loose racemes. Lateral sepals 2, pink, winglike or broadly egg-shaped. Stamens 8.

Leaves: Alternate, linear to lanceolate, entire.

Habitat: Dry grounds.

Distribution: Throughout the state.

Flowering time: All year.

Comment: Stem hairy or smooth, to 20 in. (50 cm) tall. Synonyms: *Asemeia leiodes* and *A. cumulicola.*

Drumheads
Polygala cruciata
L.

Family: Polygalaceae (milkwort).

Flowers: Heads pink-purple, compact, cylindrical, ⅝ in. (1.5 cm) wide. Corolla small, fringed. Sepals greenish-pink, triangular-ovate. Stamens 8.

Leaves: Usually in whorls of 4. Lower leaves spatulate, upper ones linear or oblanceolate.

Habitat: Wet pinelands.

Distribution: Throughout the state.

Flowering time: Spring, summer, fall.

Comment: Stem angled, branched, smooth or nearly so, to 14¼ in. (36 cm) tall. Synonym: *Polygala ramosior.*

Lewton's Milkwort
Polygala lewtonii
Small

Family: Polygalaceae (milkwort).

Flowers: Corolla 3-lobed, purplish-pink. Largest petal forms a keel that terminates in many fingerlike projections. Flowers in racemes. Three bracts occur at the pedicel bases. Sepals 5; three are green and 2 are winglike, ovoid, and pink-purple. Stamens 8.

Leaves: Alternate, spatulate, succulent, overlapping, gland-dotted, smooth or nearly so, spine-tipped, more than 2 mm wide.

Habitat: Dry oak woods and scrub.

Distribution: Central Florida Ridge.

Flowering time: Spring, summer.

Comment: One or more stems grow from a central crown. Stems erect, succulent, 4-angled, smooth or nearly so, to 8 in. (20 cm) tall.

Polygala polygama
Walter

Family: Polygalaceae (milkwort).

Flowers: Corolla 3-lobed, purple-pink or white, lower petal fringed. Flowers not crowded in slender, terminal racemes. Sepals 5, smaller ones green with pink-white margins. The larger sepals are elliptic and pink. Stamens 8.

Leaves: Alternate, smooth, linear, oblong or lanceolate. Apices sharp-tipped. Lower leaves the larger.

Habitat: Dry pinelands and coastal dunes.

Distribution: Throughout the state.

Flowering time: Spring, summer.

Comment: Stems smooth, clustered, uniformly leafy, to 20 in. (50 cm) tall. Synonym: *Polygala aboriginum.*

Viola septemloba
Le Conte

Family: Violaceae (violet).

Flowers: Petals 5, pale to dark violet. Flowers solitary, stalked, spurred petal bearded. Sepals 5. Stamens 5.

Leaves: Basal, shaped varied, but usually dissected into several lobes.

Habitat: Damp pinelands.

Distribution: Central and north Florida.

Flowering time: Winter, spring.

Florida Violet
Viola affinis
Le Conte

Family: Violaceae (violet).

Flowers: Petals 5, bluish-purple to pale blue. Flowers solitary, stalked, spurred petal bearded. Sepals 5. Stamens 5.

Leaves: Basal, mainly smooth, triangular-ovate, shallowly toothed, but not dissected.

Habitat: Damp areas.

Distribution: Throughout the state.

Flowering time: Winter, spring.

Comment: Synonym: *Viola floridana*.

Passion-flower or Maypop
Passiflora incarnata
L.

Family: Passifloraceae (passion flower).

Flowers: Petals 5, bluish or lavender. Flowers with a fringed corona of blue-purple. Sepals 5, petal-like, whitish above and green below. A spinelike appendage occurs on the back of each sepal. Stamens 5, elevated. Berry round, green (yellowish at maturity), pulpy inside, edible.

Leaves: Alternate, finely toothed, 3-lobed.

Habitat: Open, dry woods, old fields, and disturbed sites.

Distribution: Throughout the state.

Flowering time: Spring, summer, fall.

Comment: Vine prostate, erect or climbing using tendrils.

Loosestrife
Lythrum alatum
Pursh

Family: Lythraceae (loosestrife).

Flowers: Petals 6, violet. Flowers small, bluish-pink, axillary or terminal, in spikelike racemes. Calyx 6-lobed, tube smooth, ribbed. Stamens 6.

Leaves: Mostly alternate, elliptic or lanceolate, base narrow.

Habitat: Open, wet areas.

Distribution: Throughout the state.

Flowering time: Spring, summer, fall.

Comment: Stem 4-angled, leafy, branched, smooth, to 3 ft. (1 m) tall or more. Synonym: *Lythrum lanceolatum.*

Cuphea carthagenensis
(Jacquin) Macbride

Family: Lythraceae (loosestrife).

Flowers: Petals 6, pink-purplish; 2 petals above, 4 below. Flowers tiny, axillary. Calyx 6-lobed, pale green, hairy. Stamens 11 or 12, attached to the upper inside of floral tube.

Leaves: Opposite, ovate, stalked, toothed, rough on both surfaces.

Habitat: Wet, disturbed sites.

Distribution: Throughout the state.

Flowering time: Spring, summer, fall.

Comment: Leaves and stem sticky. Stem hairy, branched, to 20 in. (50 cm) tall. Synonym: *Parsonsia balsamona.*

Pale Meadow Beauty
Rhexia mariana
L.

Family: Melastomataceae (meadow beauty).

Flowers: Petals 4, lopsided, to 1 in. (25 mm) long, purplish-red to pale purple (may be white). Sepals 4, lobes linear. Stamens 8, anthers curved, over 5 mm long. Floral tube with gland-tipped hairs, to ⅜ in. (1 cm) long. Capsule urn-shaped, hairy or smooth.

Leaves: Opposite, elliptic, lanceolate to ovate, hairy, margins fine-toothed, 3-veined.

Habitat: Wet areas.

Distribution: Throughout the state.

Flowering time: Spring, summer, fall.

Comment: Stem to 32 in. (80 cm) tall, hairy. Synonyms: *Rhexia lanceolata* and *R. delicatula*.

Rhexia alifanus
Walter

Family: Melastomataceae (meadow beauty).

Flowers: Petals 4, to ⅞ in. (22 mm) long, bright purple to rose. Sepals 4, triangular. Stamens 8, anthers curved over 3⁄16 in. (5 mm) long. Capsule urn-shaped, with gland-tipped hairs.

Leaves: Opposite, lanceolate or narrowly elliptic, smooth, 3-veined, margins entire.

Habitat: Wet areas.

Distribution: Central and north Florida.

Flowering time: Spring, summer.

Comment: Stem round, smooth, to 3 ft. (1 m) tall.

Nuttall's Rhexia
Rhexia nuttallii
C. M. James

Family: Melastomataceae (meadow beauty).

Flowers: Petals 4, purplish-pink, with gland-tipped hairs. Sepals 4, triangular. Stamens 8, anthers nearly straight, ca. 2 mm long. Floral tube with gland-tipped hairs. Capsule urn-shaped, smooth.

Leaves: Opposite, ovate, 3-veined, smooth, margins with glands.

Habitat: Low, sandy pinelands.

Distribution: Throughout the state.

Flowering time: Spring, summer, fall.

Comment: Stem square, smooth, un-branched, to 14 in. (35 cm) tall (sometimes prostrate). Stem and lower surfaces of leaves often lavender. Nuttall, an early nineteenth-century English explorer, named many plants. Synonym: *Rhexia serrulata.*

Rhexia nashii
Small

Family: Melastomataceae (meadow beauty).

Flowers: Petals 4, magenta or pale purple. Sepals 4, triangular. Stamens 8, anthers curved, over 2 mm long. Floral tube over ⅜ in. (1 cm) long, virtually smooth. Capsule urn-shaped, smooth.

Leaves: Opposite, lanceolate, ovate-lanceolate or elliptic, 3-veined, sessile or nearly so, hairy, margins minutely toothed.

Habitat: Wet pinelands.

Distribution: Throughout the state.

Flowering time: Spring, summer, fall.

Comment: Stem hairy, branched, to 32 in. (80 cm) tall.

Corn Snakeroot
Eryngium aquaticum
L.

Family: Apiaceae (celery).

Flowers: Heads terminal, of many small blue flowers. The dense, globose heads are subtended by 3-toothed bracts nearly as long as the heads.

Leaves: Alternate, smooth, linear, margins toothed or entire, spineless.

Habitat: Marshes and wet pinelands.

Distribution: Central and north Florida.

Flowering time: Summer, fall.

Comment: Stem solitary, branched above, smooth or nearly so, to 3 ft. (1 m) tall. Synonyms: *Eryngium virginianum* and *E. floridanum.*

Eryngium baldwinii
Sprengel

Family: Apiaceae (celery).

Flowers: Heads dense, ovoid, bluish-purple. Heads less than 3/16 in. (5 mm) long, solitary, arising from the leaf axils. The many, tiny flowers in the heads have 5 petals and 5 stamens. Involucre bracts short, not extending or barely so beyond the base of the head.

Leaves: Alternate, margins toothed, elliptic to elliptic-ovate.

Habitat: Moist pinelands and disturbed sites.

Distribution: Throughout the state.

Flowering time: All year.

Comment: Stem prostrate, slender, creeping.

Seaside Gentian
Eustoma exaltatum
(L.) Grisebach

Family: Gentianaceae (gentian).

Flowers: Corolla 5-lobed, tubular, lavender or purple, center dark. Style bilobed. Calyx 5-lobed, lobes narrow and long. Stamens 5.

Leaves: Opposite, elliptic to lanceolate, fleshy, grayish-green, clasping.

Habitat: Coastal dunes, wet marshes, and disturbed sites.

Distribution: Central and south Florida.

Flowering time: Spring, summer, fall.

Comment: Stem smooth, to 3 ft. (1 m) tall.

Asclepias humistrata
Walter

Family: Asclepiadaceae (milkweed).

Flowers: Corolla deeply lobed, petals 5, pale purple or ashy. Corolla lobes reflexed. Flowers in umbels. Stamens 5, attached to the stigma.

Leaves: Opposite, broad, ovate, sessile-clasping. Leaves pale green with pink-purple veins.

Habitat: Sandy soils of pinelands and scrub.

Distribution: Throughout the state.

Flowering time: Spring, summer.

Comment: Stem erect or lying on or near the ground, essentially smooth, to 28 in. (70 cm) tall. Sap milky.

Glades Morning-glory
Ipomoea sagittata
Poiret

Family: Convolvulaceae (morning-glory).

Flowers: Corolla funnel-shaped, rose-purple, throat darker. Pedicels smooth. Style 1. Sepals 5, separate, smooth. Stamens 5.

Leaves: Alternate, narrowly arrow-shaped, smooth.

Habitat: Wet areas often near the coast.

Distribution: Throughout the state.

Flowering time: Spring, summer, fall.

Comment: Stem smooth, twining or trailing.

Morning-glory
Ipomoea cordatotriloba
Dennstedt

Family: Convolvulaceae (morning-glory).

Flowers: Corolla funnel-shaped, purplish-pink (rarely white). Pedicels smooth. Sepals 5, separate, pointed, base hairy. Stamens 5.

Leaves: Alternate, hairy, ovate, unlobed or with 2 basal lobes.

Habitat: Disturbed sites and thickets.

Distribution: Throughout the state.

Flowering time: All year.

Comment: Vine twining or trailing, sparsely haired. Synonym: *Ipomea trichocarpa*.

Bush Morning-glory
Ipomoea cairica
(L.) Sweet

Family: Convolvulaceae (morning-glory).

Flowers: Corolla funnel-shaped, pink-purplish, throat darker. Style 1. Sepals 5, separate, blunt. Stamens 5.

Leaves: Alternate, palmate, somewhat circular with 5–7 segments, lanceolate to triangular-lanceolate.

Habitat: Disturbed sites and roadsides.

Distribution: Throughout the state.

Flowering time: All year.

Comment: Vine twining or trailing. Native to Africa.

Railroad-vine
Ipomoea pes-caprae
(L.) R. Brown

Family: Convolvulaceae (morning-glory).

Flowers: Corolla funnel-shaped, lavender, center darker. Style 1. Sepals 5, separate, ovate, unequal. Stamens 5.

Leaves: Alternate, smooth, entire, succulent, long-stalked. Leaves notched at apex, large, ovoid or kidney-shaped.

Habitat: Coastal beaches and dunes.

Distribution: Throughout the state.

Flowering time: All year.

Comment: Stem ropelike, long, smooth, creeping, rooting at the nodes.

Morning-glory
Ipomoea indica
(Burman f.) Merriam

Family: Convolvulaceae (morning-glory).

Flowers: Corolla tubular, purple or pink-purple with pinkish stripes. Flower stalks hairy. Style 1. Sepals 5, separate, tapered, with soft, grayish hairs. Stamens 5.

Leaves: Alternate, unlobed or 3-lobed, hairy.

Habitat: Disturbed sites and thickets.

Distribution: Central and north Florida.

Flowering time: All year.

Comment: Stem hairy, twining, climbing. Synonyms: *Ipomoea acuminata* and *Pharbitis cathartica*.

Morning-glory
Ipomoea macrorhiza
Michaux

Family: Convolvulaceae (morning-glory).

Flowers: Corolla tubular, pale blue to white, throat purplish inside. Style 1, bilobed. Bracts 3. Sepals 3, hairy. Stamens 5, anthers ⁵⁄₁₆ in. (8 mm) long.

Leaves: Alternate, triangular, ovate or 3-lobed, hairy below.

Habitat: Thickets and middens.

Distribution: Central and north Florida.

Flowering time: Summer, fall.

Comment: Plant hairy, trailing. Rare in scattered localities. Blooms at night or early morning. Probably native to tropical America.

Florida Bonamia or Scrub Morning-glory

Bonamia grandiflora
(Gray) Heller

Family: Convolvulaceae (morning-glory).

Flowers: Corolla funnel-shaped, blue or blue-purple, throat white. Outer corolla hairy. Flowers more than ¾ in. (2 cm) wide. Styles 2. Sepals 5, lanceolate to oblong, hairy. Stamens 5.

Leaves: Alternate, ovate, sessile.

Habitat: Sand pine scrub.

Distribution: Central Florida Ridge.

Flowering time: Spring, summer, fall.

Comment: Stem trailing, prostrate, hairy, 3 ft. (1 m) or more in length. Species rare.

Trailing Phlox

Phlox nivalis
Lodd

Family: Polemoniaceae (phlox).

Flowers: Corolla tubular, 5-lobed, pale purple or violet usually with a dark center. Style 3-parted. Calyx 5-lobed, hairy, lobes lanceolate. Stamens 5.

Leaves: Upper leaves opposite, not spine-tipped, linear to lanceolate, margins ciliate.

Habitat: Pinelands and open fields.

Distribution: Central and north Florida.

Flowering time: Spring, early summer.

Comment: Stem semiwoody, low-growing, floral branches erect.

Sky Flower

Hydrolea corymbosa
Macbride ex Elliott

Family: Hydrophyllaceae (waterleaf).

Flowers: Corolla 5-parted, azure-blue. Flowers in terminal clusters. Styles 2. Calyx 5-lobed, lobes hairy. Stamens 5, filaments long.

Leaves: Alternate, stalked, elliptic or lanceolate, entire, narrowly tipped.

Habitat: Swamps and roadside ditches.

Distribution: Throughout the state.

Flowering time: Summer, fall.

Comment: Stem to 24 in. (60 cm) tall; upper part hairy, lower part smooth. Synonym: *Nama corymbosum.* The blue color of this flower does not photograph well.

Verbena brasiliensis
Velozo

Family: Verbenaceae (vervain).

Flowers: Corolla tubular, hairy, bluish-purple. Flowers small, loosely arranged (except lower ones) on terminal, slender spikes. Calyx 5-lobed, hairy. Stamens 4.

Leaves: Opposite, simple, rough, elliptic, sharp-toothed, bases tapered. Central stem leaves not clasping.

Habitat: Open, disturbed sites.

Distribution: Central and north Florida.

Flowering time: Spring, summer, fall.

Comment: Stem square, branched, rough especially on the stem angles. Plant may grow over 6 ft. (2 m) tall.

Harsh Vervain
Verbena scabra
Vahl

Family: Verbenaceae (vervain).

Flowers: Corolla tubular, small, smooth, pink to lavender. Flowers loosely arranged on axillary, filiform spikes. Calyx 5-lobed, hairy. Stamens 4.

Leaves: Opposite, stalked, coarsely toothed, ovate.

Habitat: Moist pinelands and disturbed sites.

Distribution: Throughout the state.

Flowering time: Spring, summer, fall.

Comment: Stem branched, spreading to ascending, to 3 ft. (1 m) tall or more. Both stem and leaf blade (especially upper surface) very rough.

Verbena officinalis
(L.) Small

Family: Verbenaceae (vervain).

Flowers: Corolla 5-lobed, pale purple. Flowers small, in elongated, slender, terminal and axillary spikes. Calyx hairy, 2-lipped, lobes pointed. Stamens 4, attached to the corolla tube.

Leaves: Opposite, deeply dissected, hairy especially below.

Habitat: Disturbed sites and open woods.

Distribution: Central and north Florida.

Flowering time: Spring, summer, fall.

Comment: Stem hairy, branched above, main branches opposite. Synonym: *Verbena halei.*

Blue Porterweed
Stachytarpheta jamaicensis
(L.) Vahl

Family: Verbenaceae (vervain).

Flowers: Corolla tubular, 5-lobed, blue-violet with a white eye. Flowers sessile on elongated, narrow spikes. Flowers bloom few at a time. Calyx 5-lobed, unequal. Fertile stamens 2.

Leaves: Opposite, toothed, ovate, lanceolate or elliptic.

Habitat: Disturbed sites and coastal dunes.

Distribution: Central and south Florida.

Flowering time: All year.

Comment: Stem branched, smooth, 4-angled, to 3 ft. (1 m) tall or more. Synonym: *Valerianoides jamaicensis.*

Glandularia maritima
(Small) Small

Family: Verbenaceae (vervain).

Flowers: Corolla tubular, 5-lobed, purplish-pink. Flowers in flat-topped spikes. Style 2-branched. Calyx 5-lobed, glandular. Calyx lobes not bristle-tipped. Stamens 4.

Leaves: Opposite, toothed or lobed, ovate to wedge-shaped, somewhat succulent.

Habitat: Pinelands and coastal dunes.

Distribution: Central and south Florida.

Flowering time: All year.

Comment: Stem branched, square, sparsely haired, spreading, to 3 ft. (1 m) long. Synonym: *Verbena maritima.*

Glandularia tampensis
(Nash) Small

Family: Verbenaceae (vervain).

Flowers: Corolla tubular, 5-lobed, purplish-pink. Flowers in flat-topped spikes. Style 2-branched. Calyx 5-lobed, nonglandular, hairy. Larger calyx lobes bristle-tipped. Stamens 4.

Leaves: Opposite, deeply and sharply toothed, lanceolate, elliptic, papery.

Habitat: Pinelands and coastal dunes.

Distribution: Central and south Florida.

Flowering time: Spring, summer, fall.

Comment: Stem branched, often erect, sparsely haired, to 24 in. (60 cm) tall. Synonym: *Verbena tampensis*.

Moss Verbena
Glandularia pulchella
(Sweet) Troncoso

Family: Verbenaceae (vervain).

Flowers: Corolla 5-lobed, lavender, purple, pink, or white. Tips of petals lobed. Flowers in spikelike clusters. Stamens 4, attached to the corolla tube. Calyx 5-lobed, lobes short and pointed.

Leaves: Opposite, deeply and narrowly dissected, hairy.

Habitat: Disturbed sites.

Distribution: Throughout the state.

Flowering time: All year.

Comment: Stems square, creeping or prostrate with tips ascending, to 12 in. (30 cm) long. Native to South America. Synonyms: *Verbena tenuisecta* and *Glandularia tenuisecta*.

Pennyroyal
Piloblephis rigida
(Bartram ex Bentham) Rafinesque

Family: Lamiaceae (mint).

Flowers: Corolla 2-lipped, pale purple, dotted purple on the lower, 3-lobed lip. Heads dense, oblong, fragrant. Style 2-lobed. Calyx 5-lobed. Stamens 4.

Leaves: Opposite, numerous, thick, entire, needlelike, evergreen.

Habitat: Pinelands.

Distribution: Central and south Florida. Endemic.

Flowering time: All year.

Comment: Stem somewhat woody, leafy, branched, to 28 in. (70 cm) long or more (usually less). A delightful tea can be brewed from this mint. Synonyms: *Satureja rigida* and *Pycnothymus rigidus*.

Rough Skullcap
Scutellaria integrifolia
L.

Family: Lamiaceae (mint).

Flowers: Corolla blue to pale violet, 2-lipped, nonaromatic. Upper lip hoodlike, 3-lobed. Flowers in terminal, spikelike racemes. Style 2-lobed. Calyx 2-lipped, upper lip crested. Stamens 4, located in the hooded lip.

Leaves: Opposite, margins not revolute, stalked or sessile. Lower leaves toothed, triangular-ovate, rough. Stem leaves below inflorescence narrow, entire.

Habitat: Dry pinelands.

Distribution: Central and north Florida.

Flowering time: Spring, summer, fall.

Comment: Stem square, often branched, hairy, to 30 in. (75 cm) tall (usually less).

Skullcap

Scutellaria arenicola
Small

Family: Lamiaceae (mint).

Flowers: Corolla blue or pale violet, 2-lipped, nonaromatic. Upper lip hoodlike, 3-lobed. Flowers in terminal, spikelike racemes. Calyx 2-lipped, upper lip crested. Stamens 4, located in the hooded lip.

Leaves: Opposite, stalked or sessile. Most leaves in the inflorescence are entire, small, sessile or nearly so. Leaves below the inflorescence are larger, elliptic, and toothed.

Habitat: Dry pinelands.

Distribution: Central Florida.

Flowering time: Spring, summer.

Comment: Stem square, branched, hairy, to 30 in. (75 cm) tall (usually less).

Blue Curls

Trichostema dichotomum
L.

Family: Lamiaceae (mint).

Flowers: Corolla 5-lobed, 2-lipped, bluish-purplish. Lower lip spotted, narrow, drooping. Flowers axillary, near the terminal branches. Style 2-lobed. Calyx 2-lipped, lower lip the longest, 3-toothed; upper lip of 2, shorter teeth. Stamens 4, long-curled.

Leaves: Opposite, entire or toothed, elliptic to lanceolate, over 5 mm wide.

Habitat: Dry pinelands and thickets.

Distribution: Throughout the state.

Flowering time: Summer, fall.

Comment: Stem hairy, to 32 in. (80 cm) tall, branches opposite, base often woody. Synonym: *Trichostema suffrutescens.*

Lyre-leaved Sage
Salvia lyrata
L.

Family: Lamiaceae (mint).

Flowers: Corolla violet, tubular, 2-lipped. Flowers in whorls on the stem. Style 2-lobed. Calyx 2-lipped, hairy, bluish-purple, spine-tipped. Upper lip 3-lobed, lower lip 2-lobed. Fertile stamens 2.

Leaves: Mostly in basal rosettes. Stem leaves absent or few, opposite, elliptic, unlobed or lobed, mostly sessile. Basal leaves broadened upward, stalked, margins toothed, entire or lobed.

Habitat: Roadsides, thickets, and disturbed sites.

Distribution: Throughout the state.

Flowering time: All year.

Comment: Stem square, hairy, to 24 in. (60 cm) tall. Some individuals have varying amounts of purple mixed with green in the stem and leaves.

Blue Sage
Salvia azurea
Lamarck

Family: Lamiaceae (mint).

Flowers: Corolla 2-lipped, blue or white. Lower lip broad, notched. Flowers in terminal, spikelike clusters. Style 2-lobed. Calyx 2-lipped; upper lip entire, the lower 2-toothed. Fertile stamens 2.

Leaves: Opposite, entire or toothed. Upper leaves linear to lanceolate. Basal leaves absent.

Habitat: Dry woods and pinelands.

Distribution: Central and north Florida.

Flowering time: Summer, fall, early winter.

Comment: Stem slender, branches few, hairy, leafy, to 3 ft. (1 m) tall or more.

Salvia riparia
HBK.

Family: Lamiaceae (mint).

Flowers: Corolla 2-lipped, purplish-blue. Racemes spicate, elongated and slender. Flowers widely scattered along the rachis. Calyx 2-lipped, glandular-hairy, lower lobes awn-tipped. Mature calyx over 3/16 in. (5 mm) long. Fertile stamens 2.

Leaves: Opposite, ovate, stalked, toothed, blades slightly extending onto the petioles.

Habitat: Woods and thickets.

Distribution: Central Florida.

Flowering time: Spring, summer, fall.

Comment: Stem square, hairy. Synonym: *Salvia privoides*.

Dicerandra densiflora
Bentham

Family: Lamiaceae (mint).

Flowers: Corolla pink-purple (sometimes white), spotted inside. Lower lip 3-lobed, upper lip 2-lobed. Flowers aromatic, sessile or nearly so, crowded in the leaf axils. Style 2-branched. Calyx 2-lipped, green, tinged pinkish. Upper lip entire, lower lip of 2 teeth. Stamens 4, longer than the corolla. Anther horns blunt.

Leaves: Opposite, entire, linear, glandular.

Habitat: Disturbed, moist sites.

Distribution: Central and north Florida.

Flowering time: Summer, fall.

Comment: Stem square, to 20 in. (50 cm) tall, hairy.

Micromeria brownei
(Swartz) Bentham

Family: Lamiaceae (mint).

Flowers: Corolla 2-lipped, pale lavender. Flowers small, solitary or in pairs from the leaf axils. Upper lip 2-parted, lower 3-parted. Calyx tubular; teeth acute, nearly equal in size. Stamens 4.

Leaves: Opposite, stalked, broadest at base, apex toothed.

Habitat: Swamps, ditches, and moist woods.

Distribution: Central and north Florida.

Flowering time: All year.

Comment: Stem square, creeping or erect. Plant fragrant. Synonym: *Micromeria pilosiuscula.*

Buttermint
Hyptis mutabilis
(Richard) Briquet

Family: Lamiaceae (mint).

Flowers: Corolla 2-lipped, pale lavender to purple. Flowers small, in separated, sessile clusters (verticils) on axillary, terminal spikes. Calyx 5-lobed, tubular, about ⁵⁄₁₆ in. (7 mm) long. Stamens 4.

Leaves: Opposite, stalked, ovate, toothed. Lower leaves the larger.

Habitat: Moist, open areas.

Distribution: Throughout the state.

Flowering time: All year.

Comment: Stem square, branched, somewhat woody, hairy, rough. Plant odiferous, gets to 6 ft. (2 m) tall or more. Native to tropical America.

Conradina grandiflora
Small

Family: Lamiaceae (mint).

Flowers: Corolla 2-lipped, pale bluish-purple; upper lip erect, lower lip 3-lobed, spotted. Flowers in axillary cymes. Calyx hairy, 2-lipped; upper lip with 3 short lobes, lower lip with 2 longer lobes. Stamens 4, lying below the upper lip.

Leaves: Opposite, narrow, clustered, entire, margins turned down. Midrib of lower leaf surface smooth or nearly so.

Habitat: Pinelands.

Distribution: Central and south Florida.

Flowering time: All year.

Comment: Plant aromatic, bushy-branched, stem woody.

Conradina canescens
(Torrey and Gray) Gray

Family: Lamiaceae (mint).

Flowers: Corolla 2-lipped, purplish; upper lip erect, lower lip 3-lobed, spotted. Flowers in axillary cymes. Calyx 2-lipped, tube very hairy; upper lip 3-lobed, lower lip with 2 longer lobes. Stamens 4, lying below the upper lip.

Leaves: Opposite, narrow, clustered, entire, margins turned down. Lower leaf surfaces bearing flattened hairs.

Habitat: Sand pine scrub.

Distribution: Central and north Florida.

Flowering time: Spring, summer, fall.

Comment: Plant aromatic, bushy-branched, stem woody. Synonym: *Conradina puberula*.

Calamintha ashei
(Weatherby) Shinners

Family: Lamiaceae (mint).

Flowers: Corolla outside hairy, 2-lipped, pink-purple. Lower lip spotted, 3-lobed, middle lobe the larger. Corolla tube straight. Calyx 2-lipped, ¼–⁵⁄₁₆ in. (6–8 mm) long. Upper lip lobes fused. Stamens 4, lying below the upper lip.

Leaves: Opposite, narrow, clustered, entire, margins strongly turned down. Lower surfaces of leaves bearing erect hairs.

Habitat: Dry pinelands and sand pine scrub.

Distribution: Central Florida.

Flowering time: Spring, summer, fall.

Comment: Plant aromatic, bushy-branched, stem woody, to 20 in. (50 cm) tall. Synonym: *Clinopodium ashei.*

Christmasberry
Lycium carolinianum
Walter

Family: Solanaceae (nightshade).

Flowers: Corolla lavender or white, 5-lobed, lobes longer than the tube. Calyx 5-lobed. Stamens 5. Berry elliptic, bright red.

Leaves: Alternate, succulent, narrow, clustered, sessile.

Habitat: Coastal marshes.

Distribution: Throughout the state.

Flowering time: All year.

Comment: Shrub thorny, to 6 ft. (2 m) tall.

Agalinis fasciculata
(Elliott) Rafinesque

Family: Scrophulariaceae (snapdragon or fig-wort).

Flowers: Corolla bell-shaped, 5-lobed, rose-purple. Outer corolla hairy. Inner bases of upper 2 corolla lobes hairy. Throat inside hairy, lined with yellow lines and purplish dots. Flower pedicels stout, shorter than the calyx tube. Calyx 5-lobed. Stamens 4, bases hairy.

Leaves: Opposite, linear, rough, well-developed fascicles in axils of main leaves.

Habitat: Open, moist fields and disturbed sites.

Distribution: Throughout the state.

Flowering time: Summer, fall.

Comment: Stem rough, branched, to 3 ft. (1 m) tall or more, branches angled. Parasitic on nearby plants. Plant blackens when dried. Synonym: *Gerardia fasciculata*.

False Foxglove
Agalinis purpurea
(L.) Pennell

Family: Scrophulariaceae (snapdragon or fig-wort).

Flowers: Corolla bell-shaped, 5-lobed, rose-purple. Outer corolla hairy. Inner bases of upper 2 corolla lobes hairy. Throat inside hairy with yellow lines and purplish dots. Flower pedicels stout, shorter than the calyx tube. Calyx 5-lobed. Stamens 4, bases hairy.

Leaves: Mostly opposite, entire, linear to linear-lanceolate, rough above. Fascicles in main leaf axils lacking or reduced.

Habitat: Moist pinelands and meadows.

Distribution: Throughout the state.

Flowering time: Summer, fall.

Comment: Stem wiry, smooth or faintly rough, branched above, to 3 ft. (1 m) tall. Parasitic on nearby plants. Plant blackens when dried. Synonym: *Gerardia purpurea*.

Agalinis setacea
(J. F. Gmelin) Rafinesque

Family: Scrophulariaceae (snapdragon or fig-wort).

Flowers: Corolla bell-shaped, 5-lobed, rose-purple. Outer corolla hairy. Inner bases of upper 2 corolla lobes hairy. Lobes about equal in size. Corolla throat inside hairy, lined with yellow lines and purplish dots. Flower pedicel slender, much longer than the calyx. Calyx 5-lobed, lobes awl-shaped, less than 1 mm long. Stamens 4, bases hairy.

Leaves: Mostly opposite, linear to filiform.

Habitat: Dry pinelands.

Distribution: Central and north Florida.

Flowering time: Summer, fall.

Comment: Stem smooth or nearly so, slender, branched, to 28 in. (70 cm) tall. Parasitic on nearby plants. Plant darkens when dried. Synonyms: *Agalinis laxa, A. plukenetii,* and *Gerardia setacea.*

Blue Toadflax
Linaria canadensis
(L.) Dumont

Family: Scrophulariaceae (snapdragon or fig-wort).

Flowers: Corolla 2-lipped, petals 5, bluish-whitish. Lower lip with 2, whitish edges; base spurred 3/16–3/8 in. (5–9 mm) long. Flowers in terminal racemes. Calyx 5-parted. Stamens 4.

Leaves: Main stem leaves usually alternate, linear. Basal leaves opposite, in rosettes. Upper stem usually leafless.

Habitat: Disturbed sites.

Distribution: Throughout the state.

Flowering time: Winter, spring.

Comment: Stem slender, smooth, to 20 in. (50 cm) tall.

False Pimpernel

Lindernia grandiflora
Nuttall

Family: Scrophulariaceae (snapdragon or fig-wort).

Flowers: Corolla 2-lipped, pale blue, mottled blue inside, throat inside has 2 hairy, yellow ridges. Lower lip 3-lobed, longer than the upper, notched lip. Flowers small, solitary, stalked. Sepals 5, linear. Fertile stamens 2. Lower stamens partially fused to the yellow ridges.

Leaves: Opposite, small, ovoid, entire or toothed, petioles slender.

Habitat: Moist, sandy soils, fields, along roads, and ditches.

Distribution: Central and south Florida.

Flowering time: All year.

Comment: Stems slender, smooth, low-growing, often mat-forming. Synonym: *Ilysanthes grandiflora*.

Blue Hyssop

Bacopa caroliniana
(Walter) Robinson

Family: Scrophulariaceae (snapdragon or fig-wort).

Flowers: Corolla blue, tubular, lobes 5 (4). Flowers solitary, axillary, pedicels hairy. Sepals 5, unequal. Stamens 4.

Leaves: Opposite, entire, ovate to elliptic, clasping, thick. Main veins 3–7, palmate.

Habitat: Shallow water of ditches, ponds, and swamps.

Distribution: Throughout the state.

Flowering time: All year.

Comment: Stem succulent, hairy, creeping or floating. Plant has a strong lemonlike odor. Synonym: *Hydrotrida caroliniana*.

Blue Butterwort
Pinguicula caerulea
Walter

Family: Lentibulariaceae (bladderwort).

Flowers: Corolla 2-lipped, lobes 5, blue or lavender, veiny. Flower solitary on a slender stalk. Lower lip spurred. Calyx 5-lobed. Stamens 2. Fruit a capsule.

Leaves: Pale green, oblong, in basal rosettes. Leaves rolled inward from the edge; greasy.

Habitat: Moist, acid pinelands.

Distribution: Central and north Florida.

Flowering time: Winter, spring.

Comment: Carnivorous. Habits similar to that of the yellow butterwort. Stem leafless, to 12 in. (30 cm) tall. Terrestrial.

Small Butterwort
Pinguicula pumila
Michaux

Family: Lentibulariaceae (bladderwort).

Flowers: Corolla 2-lipped, lobes 5, pale purple, lavender or whitish. Corolla lobes shallowly notched. Flower solitary, less than 1⅛ in. (3 cm) across. Lower lip spurred. Calyx 5-lobed. Stamens 2. Fruit a capsule.

Leaves: Small, succulent, ovate or elliptic, in basal rosettes.

Habitat: Moist, acid pinelands.

Distribution: Throughout the state.

Flowering time: Winter, spring.

Comment: Carnivorous. Habits similar to that of other butterworts. More than 1 flowering stem may be present. Plant gets to 8 in. (20 cm) tall. Terrestrial.

Blue Twinflower
Dyschoriste oblongifolia
(Michaux) Kuntze

Family: Acanthaceae (acanthus).

Flowers: Corolla funnelform, 5-lobed, bluish-purple with dark dots. Flowers axillary, dotted in the lower petal. Calyx 5-lobed, hairy, lobes slender, spine-tipped. Stamens 4.

Leaves: Opposite, entire, oval, obovate or oblong, sessile or nearly so.

Habitat: Dry pinelands and sandhills.

Distribution: Throughout the state.

Flowering time: Spring, summer, fall.

Comment: Stem hairy, branches opposite, to 8 in. (20 cm) tall.

Wild Petunia
Ruellia caroliniensis
(J. F. Gmelin) Steudel

Family: Acanthaceae (acanthus).

Flowers: Corolla funnelform, 5-lobed, pale purple or blue (rarely white). Flowers sessile or nearly so, solitary or in axillary clusters. Style bilobed. Calyx 5-lobed, lobes hairy, linear. Stamens 4.

Leaves: Opposite, entire, ovate or elliptic, stalked, hairy or smooth.

Habitat: Dry woods and open, dry clearings.

Distribution: Throughout the state.

Flowering time: Spring, summer, fall.

Comment: Stem single or branched, hairy or smooth, to 36 in. (90 cm) tall. The blue color in this flower does not photograph well.

Water Willow

Justicia angusta
(Chapman) Small

Family: Acanthaceae (acanthus).

Flowers: Corolla 2-lipped, pale-purple with whitish, purple-spotted centers. Upper lip 2-lobed, lower lip 3-lobed. Flowers axillary, in long-stalked spikes. Styles bifurcated. Sepals 5, glandular, narrow. Stamens 2.

Leaves: Opposite, smooth, sessile or stalked, linear to lanceolate, entire.

Habitat: Wet pinelands and disturbed sites.

Distribution: Throughout the state.

Flowering time: Spring, summer, fall.

Comment: Stem to 12 in. (30 cm) tall. Synonym: *Justicia ovata* var. *angusta*.

Cooley's Justicia

Justicia cooleyi
Monachino and Leonard

Family: Acanthaceae (acanthus).

Flowers: Corolla 2-lipped, purplish-red. Lower lip 3-lobed, with white-purple markings. Flowers axillary or terminal. Sepals 5, linear-lanceolate. Stamens 2, below the corolla lip. Outer surfaces of the bracts, calyx, and corolla hairy.

Leaves: Opposite, lanceolate to nearly ovate, hairy, margins wavy or entire.

Habitat: Rocky woods.

Distribution: Plant localized in Hernando and Lake counties.

Flowering time: All year.

Comment: Stem nearly square, hairy, glandular.

Stenandrium dulce
(Cavanilles) Nees von Esenbeck

Family: Rubiaceae (madder).

Flowers: Corolla 5-lobed, rose-purple. Flowers subtended by ciliate bracts, in terminal spikes. Style 1. Sepals 5, narrow, hairy, pointed. Stamens 4, attached to the inside of flower tube.

Leaves: Basal, ovate or elliptic, dark green, petioles and leaf bases hairy.

Habitat: Wet pinelands.

Distribution: Central and south Florida.

Flowering time: All year.

Comment: Plant gets to 3⅛ in. (8 cm) tall. Flower stem reddish and finely haired. Synonym: *Gerardia floridana*.

Bay Lobelia
Lobelia feayana
Gray

Family: Campanulaceae (bluebell or harebell).

Flowers: Corolla 2-lipped, 5-lobed; 2 upper lobes and 3 lower lobes. Flowers small, bluish-purple, stalked. Calyx 5-lobed; lobes narrow, entire. Stamens 5, united around the style.

Leaves: Alternate, small, ovate to elliptic, stalked, entire or shallowly toothed.

Habitat: Moist areas.

Distribution: Throughout the state.

Flowering time: Late winter, spring, summer, fall.

Comment: Stem creeping, smooth. Endemic to Florida.

Glades Lobelia
Lobelia glandulosa
Walter

Family: Campanulaceae (bluebell or hare-bell).

Flowers: Corolla 2-lipped, 5-lobed; 2 upper lobes and 3 lower lobes. Flowers blue or lavender, in spikelike racemes. Lower lip with whitish center, inner surface hairy. Calyx 5-lobed, hairy; lobes narrow, margins with gland-tipped teeth. Stamens 5, united around the style.

Leaves: Alternate, margins with gland-tipped teeth or entire, linear, lanceolate, smooth, thickish. Lower stem leaves the larger.

Habitat: Low ground.

Distribution: Throughout the state.

Flowering time: All year.

Comment: Stem smooth or nearly so, to 3 ft. (1 m) tall.

Venus' Looking-glass
Triodanis perfoliata
(L.) Nieuwland

Family: Campanulaceae (bluebell or hare-bell).

Flowers: Corolla 5-lobed, bluish-purple. Flowers sessile, in leaf axils of wandlike spikes. Style 3-branched. Sepals lanceolate. Stamens 5, separate.

Leaves: Alternate, toothed, roundish, clasping.

Habitat: Disturbed sites and open fields.

Distribution: Central and north Florida.

Flowering time: Spring, summer, fall.

Comment: Stem square, to 3 ft. (1 m) tall. Synonym: *Specularia perfoliata*.

Florida Bellflower or Florida Bluebell

Campanula floridana
Watson

Family: Campanulaceae (bluebell or harebell).

Flowers: Corolla 5-lobed, star-shaped, purple. Style 3-branched. Flowers stalked. Calyx 5-lobed, lobes narrow. Stamens 5, separate.

Leaves: Alternate, clasping, linear to lanceolate, margins with gland-tipped teeth.

Habitat: Wet areas.

Distribution: Throughout the state.

Flowering time: All year.

Comment: Stem branching, weak, slender, spreading, to 16 in. (40 cm) long. Synonym: *Rotantha floridana.*

Silvery Aster

Aster concolor
L.

Family: Asteraceae (aster or daisy).

Flowers: Heads of violet-purple ray florets and yellowish disk florets. Heads in narrow racemes or spikelike panicles. Bracts hairy, whitish, tips green and pointed.

Leaves: Alternate, grayish, silky, entire, narrow or broadly linear, sessile. Lower stem leaves the larger.

Habitat: Dry pinelands.

Distribution: Throughout the state.

Flowering time: Summer, fall, winter.

Comment: Stem silky, leafy, to 28 in. (70 cm) tall. Synonyms: *Aster simulatus* and *A. plumosus.*

Bushy Aster
Aster dumosus
L.

Family: Asteraceae (aster or daisy).

Flowers: Heads many, stalked, of bluish, lavender, or whitish ray florets and yellowish to reddish disk florets. Inflorescence spreading, branched. Bracts smooth, whitish with green, diamond-shaped tips. Involucre ⅖₅–³⁄₁₆ in. (4–5 mm) long.

Leaves: Alternate, flowering branches with small leaves. Main leaves entire, ciliate, sessile, linear or narrowly elliptic. Lower leaves rough.

Habitat: Pinelands and wet areas.

Distribution: Throughout the state.

Flowering time: Summer, fall, winter.

Comment: Stem slender, branched, to 3 ft. (1 m) tall or more, smooth to sparsely haired. Species variable. The blue color in this flower does not photograph well. Synonyms: *Aster coridifolius* and *A. fontinalis*.

Aster elliottii
Torrey and Gray

Family: Asteraceae (aster or daisy).

Flowers: Heads showy, of 25–50, violet-purple ray florets and yellow-red disk florets. Heads in terminal, leafy branches. Bracts overlapping, smooth or nearly so, tips pointed, margins ciliate. Inner bracts narrow. Involucre ⁵⁄₁₆–⁷⁄₁₆ in. (8–11 mm) long.

Leaves: Alternate, oblanceolate, toothed. Lower leaves the larger to ⅜–1½ in. (1–4 cm) wide, stalked, toothed, elliptic, thickish. Leaf surfaces rough.

Habitat: Wet grounds and swamps.

Distribution: Throughout the state.

Flowering time: Summer, fall, early winter.

Comment: Stem smooth or with hairs arranged in longitudinal lines. Plant gets to 3 ft. (1 m) tall or more. The flower in this photo should be more violet-purple.

Deer-tongue
Carphephorus paniculatus
(Gmelin) Hebert

Family: Asteraceae (aster or daisy).

Flowers: Heads of purple, disk florets in dense, cylindrical, hairy panicles. Ray florets lacking. Lateral stem branches shorter than the terminal ones.

Leaves: Stem leaves alternate, lanceolate, chiefly entire. Basal leaves stalked, elliptic to oblanceolate.

Habitat: Pinelands.

Distribution: Throughout the state.

Flowering time: Fall, winter.

Comment: Stem leafy, hairy, to 3 ft. (1 m) tall or more. Synonym: *Trilisa paniculatus.*

Vanilla Plant
Carphephorus odoratissima
(Gmelin) Hebert

Family: Asteraceae (aster or daisy).

Flowers: Heads of purple disk florets in flattened, terminal corymbs. Ray florets lacking. Lateral stem branches usually overtop the terminals.

Leaves: Stem leaves alternate, toothed, sessile, thick, ovate to elliptic. Lower stem leaves the larger. Basal leaves elliptic to oblanceolate.

Habitat: Moist pinelands.

Distribution: Throughout the state.

Flowering time: Summer, fall, winter.

Comment: Stem to 3 ft. (1 m) tall or more, leafy, smooth. Plant has a vanilla odor, especially when dried. Synonym: *Trilisa odoratissima.*

Carphephorus carnosus
(Small) James

Family: Asteraceae (aster or daisy).

Flowers: Heads of purple, disk florets in compact, terminal inflorescence. Ray flowers lacking. Bracts hairy, spine-tipped.

Leaves: Stem leaves alternate, narrow, clasping, entire. Basal leaves linear to linear-lanceolate.

Habitat: Wet, pine flatwoods.

Distribution: Central Florida.

Flowering time: Summer, fall.

Comment: Stem hairy, to 3 ft. (1 m) tall. Synonym: *Litrisa carnosa*.

Thistle
Cirsium horridulum
Michaux

Family: Asteraceae (aster or daisy).

Flowers: Heads of purple or yellow-whitish disk florets. Ray florets lacking. Heads compact, surrounded by a whorl of spiny, bractlike leaves.

Leaves: Alternate, spiny, deeply lobed.

Habitat: Pinelands, fields, and disturbed sites.

Distribution: Throughout the state.

Flowering time: Spring, summer, fall.

Comment: Plant grows to 3 ft. (1 m) tall or more. Synonym: *Carduus spinosissimus*.

Thistle
Cirsium nuttallii
DC.

Family: Asteraceae (aster or daisy).

Flowers: Heads of pale purple disk florets. Ray florets lacking. Heads compact, lacking a whorl of spiny, bractlike leaves.

Leaves: Alternate, spiny, deeply lobed.

Habitat: Disturbed sites, fields, and open fields.

Distribution: Throughout the state.

Flowering time: Spring, summer, fall.

Comment: Stem smooth, to 3 ft. (1 m) tall or more. Synonym: *Carduus nuttallii*.

Florida Elephant's-foot
Elephantopus elatus
Bertoloni

Family: Asteraceae (aster or daisy).

Flowers: Disk florets 2–5, pale purple. Ray florets lacking. Inflorescence widely branched. Bracts 3, leaflike, triangular-ovate, hairy.

Leaves: Chiefly basal, hairy, broad. Margins toothed or scalloped. Stem leaves alternate, oblong-obovate to ovate, sessile, hairy.

Habitat: Moist and dry pinelands and disturbed sites.

Distribution: Throughout the state.

Flowering time: Summer, fall.

Comment: Stem to 32 in. (80 cm), hairy, branched.

Garberia
Garberia heterophylla
(Bartram) Merrill and Harper

Family: Asteraceae (aster or daisy).

Flowers: Heads squarish, of 3–5 pale purple-pink disk florets. Heads stalked in terminal, sticky clusters. Ray florets lacking. Bracts overlapping, gland-dotted, hairy, narrow apically.

Leaves: Alternate, entire, grayish-green, stalked, broadened upward.

Habitat: Sand pine scrub and oak scrub.

Distribution: Central Florida.

Flowering time: Summer, fall, early winter.

Comment: Shrub woody, hairy, fragrant, to 6 ft. (2 m) tall or more. The flower in this photo should be more purple. Synonym: *Garberia fruticosa.*

Wild Lettuce
Lactuca graminifolia
Michaux

Family: Asteraceae (aster or daisy).

Flowers: Heads of bluish-purple or white ray florets. Disk florets lacking. Heads terminal, cylindric, small, in spreading panicles.

Leaves: Mostly basal, linear to oblanceolate, lobed or entire. Stem leaves narrow, reduced.

Habitat: Dry fields and woods.

Distribution: Throughout the state.

Flowering time: Winter, spring, summer.

Comment: Stem to 3 ft. (1 m) tall or more, smooth, greenish to reddish. Sap milky.

Blazing Star
Liatris tenuifolia
Nuttall

Family: Asteraceae (aster or daisy).

Flowers: Heads many, stalked, of purple, tubular florets in spikelike racemes. Ray florets lacking. Bracts sharp- or blunt-tipped, margins clear or pinkish. Involucre ³⁄₁₆–⁵⁄₁₆ in. (5–7 mm) long.

Leaves: Alternate, linear or filiform, smooth or nearly so, margins entire. Leaves near the base larger than those near the inflorescence.

Habitat: Pinelands and dry, open areas.

Distribution: Throughout the state.

Flowering time: Summer, fall.

Comment: Stem smooth or nearly so, to 3 ft. (1 m) tall or more.

Blazing Star
Liatris pauciflora
Pursh

Family: Asteraceae (aster or daisy).

Flowers: Heads many, stalked, of pink-purple, tubular florets in spikelike racemes. Ray florets lacking. Heads stalked, of about 4 florets located on 1 side of flower stalk. Bracts sharp-tipped. Involucre ⅜–½ in. (10–13 mm) long.

Leaves: Alternate, linear-filiform, margins entire. Lower leaves the larger.

Habitat: Pinelands.

Distribution: Central and north Florida.

Flowering time: Summer, fall.

Comment: Stem smooth or hairy, to 3 ft. (1 m) tall or more.

Blazing Star
Liatris chapmanii
Torrey and Gray

Family: Asteraceae (aster or daisy).

Flowers: Heads many, sessile, of purple, tubular florets in spikelike racemes. Spike dense, heads short-stalked or sessile, overlapping. Ray florets lacking. Bracts sharp-tipped, smooth or nearly so.

Leaves: Alternate, linear-filiform, hairy. Leaves numerous. Lower leaves the larger, decreasing upward.

Habitat: Dry pinelands and scrub.

Distribution: Throughout the state.

Flowering time: Summer, fall.

Comment: Stem to 3 ft. (1 m) tall or more, hairy.

Blazing Star
Liatris spicata
(L.) Willdenow

Family: Asteraceae (aster or daisy).

Flowers: Heads many, sessile, tubular, of purple florets in spikelike racemes. Inflorescence dense. Ray florets lacking. Bracts blunt-tipped, smooth, gland-dotted, greenish-purple. Involucre ⁵⁄₁₆–⁷⁄₁₆ in. (7–11 mm) long.

Leaves: Alternate, linear, smooth or nearly so. Leaf margins at the base nonciliate. Lower stem leaves are the longest and widest.

Habitat: Moist pinelands.

Distribution: Throughout the state.

Flowering time: Summer, fall.

Comment: Stem smooth or nearly so, to 3 ft. (1 m) tall or more.

Scrub Blazing Star
Liatris ohlingerae
(Blake) Robinson

Family: Asteraceae (aster or daisy).

Flowers: Heads rose-purple or lavender, stalked, of tubular florets. Ray florets lacking. Bracts numerous, outer ones roundish, inner ones narrow. Margins of bracts thin, non-green. Involucre ⅝–¾ in. (15–20 mm) long.

Leaves: Alternate, narrow, gland-dotted.

Habitat: Sand pine scrub.

Distribution: Central and south Florida. Localized in Polk and Highlands counties.

Flowering time: Summer, early fall.

Comment: Stem to 3 ft. (1 m) tall or more, minutely haired, branched above.

Blazing Star
Liatris elegans
(Walter) Michaux

Family: Asteraceae (aster or daisy).

Flowers: Heads sessile or stalked, lavender or rose-purple, of about 5 tubular florets. Ray florets lacking. Pedicels hairy. Pappus feathery. Bracts hairy, gland-dotted, tips petal-like and pink-white.

Leaves: Alternate, linear to linear-spatulate, gland-dotted, smooth, pointed. Leaves reduced in size upward. Lower leaves usually absent.

Habitat: Pinelands and sandhills.

Distribution: Throughout the state.

Flowering time: Fall.

Comment: Stem to 3 ft. (1 m) tall or more, hairy.

Blazing Star
Liatris gracilis
Pursh

Family: Asteraceae (aster or daisy).

Flowers: Heads stalked, tubular, of purple florets in spikelike racemes. Pedicels hairy. Ray florets lacking. Bracts blunt-tipped, margins usually ciliated. Involucre ⁵⁄₁₆ or ³⁄₁₆ in. (4 or 5 mm) long.

Leaves: Alternate, upper leaves numerous, linear, reduced, sessile. Lower leaves stalked, spatulate, bases ciliated.

Habitat: Pinelands.

Distribution: Throughout the state.

Flowering time: Summer, fall.

Comment: Stem hairy, leafy, to 3 ft. (1 m) tall or more.

Ironweed
Vernonia angustifolia
Michaux

Family: Asteraceae (aster or daisy).

Flowers: Heads purple, tubular, in wide-spreading, terminal corymbs. Ray florets absent. Bracts overlapping, apices pointed.

Leaves: Alternate, linear to narrowly elliptic, 6 mm wide or less, entire or slightly toothed. Basal leaves lacking.

Habitat: Pinelands and dry woods.

Distribution: Central and north Florida.

Flowering time: Late spring, summer, fall.

Comment: Stem leafy, to 3 ft. (1 m) tall or more.

Ironweed
Vernonia gigantea
(Walter) Trelease

Family: Asteraceae (aster or daisy).

Flowers: Heads purple, tubular, in wide-spreading, terminal corymbs. Ray florets absent. Bracts overlapping, lanceolate, purplish.

Leaves: Alternate, elliptic to lanceolate, 1⅛– 2⅜ in. (3–6 cm) wide, stalked or nearly so, smooth, sharply toothed. Stem leaves reduced.

Habitat: Wet pinelands and margins of woods.

Distribution: Throughout the state.

Flowering time: Late spring, summer, fall.

Comment: Stem to 6 ft. (2 m) tall, leafy, smooth or nearly so.

Ironweed
Vernonia blodgettii
Small

Family: Asteraceae (aster or daisy).

Flowers: Heads purple, tubular, in wide-branched, terminal corymbs. Ray florets absent. Bracts overlapping, lanceolate, purple-green.

Leaves: Alternate, linear to lanceolate, less than ⅝ in. (1.5 cm) wide, reduced upward on stem. Lower leaves entire, smooth, ovate.

Habitat: Pinelands.

Distribution: Central and south Florida.

Flowering time: Spring, summer, fall.

Comment: Stem smooth, to 20 in. (50 cm) tall, base usually branched.

Mistflower or Ageratum
Conoclinium coelestinum
(L.) DC.

Family: Asteraceae (aster or daisy).

Flowers: Heads fuzzy, blue-pinkish (rarely white). Ray florets lacking. Heads clustered in flat corymbs. Bracts pointed.

Leaves: Opposite, stalked, 3-veined, toothed, ovate to somewhat triangular, wrinked.

Habitat: Moist meadows and woodland borders.

Distribution: Throughout the state.

Flowering time: All year.

Comment: Stem to 36 in. (90 cm) tall, hairy, or nearly so, branched usually at the base. Synonym: *Eupatorium coelestinum.* The blue color in this flower does not photograph well.

Roserush
Lygodesmia aphylla
(Nuttall) DC.

Family: Asteraceae (aster or daisy).

Flowers: Heads of pale purple or pink ray florets. Disk florets lacking. Heads usually solitary, large.

Leaves: Alternate, few, chiefly basal, narrow, grasslike.

Habitat: Dry pinelands, scrub, and open, disturbed sites.

Distribution: Throughout the state.

Flowering time: Spring, summer, fall.

Comment: Stem leafless or nearly so, rush-like, to 32 in. (80 cm) tall or more. Sap milky.

Saltmarsh Fleabane or Camphorweed
Pluchea odorata
(L.) Cassini

Family: Asteraceae (aster or daisy).

Flowers: Heads tubular, pale purple. Ray florets lacking. Heads in terminal, dense corymbs. Lateral floral branches overtop or equal the center (oldest) ones. Bracts gland-dotted, hairy or nearly so.

Leaves: Alternate, lanceolate to elliptic-ovate, stalked, toothed, hairy. Leaf blade extends onto the petiole.

Habitat: Wet, disturbed sites and swamps.

Distribution: Throughout the state.

Flowering time: Spring, summer, fall, early winter.

Comment: Stem to 3 ft. (1 m) tall or more, branched. Plant shrubby, odiferous. Synonym: *Pluchea purpurascens.*

Barbara's Button
Marshallia tenuifolia
Rafinesque

Family: Asteraceae (aster or daisy).

Flowers: Heads purplish, of disk florets. Ray florets lacking. Flowers tubular and lobed. Bracts awl-shaped, purple-tipped. A single head terminates a flower stalk.

Leaves: Alternate, smooth. Stem leaves linear, reduced upward. Basal leaves in rosettes.

Habitat: Bogs, flatwoods, and disturbed sites.

Distribution: Central and north Florida.

Flowering time: Summer, fall.

Comment: Stem to 3 ft. (1 m) usually branched, smooth below and hairy above.

Common Cattail
Typha latifolia
L.

Family: Typhaceae (cattail).

Flowers: Male and female spikes usually contiguous. Male flowers, reduced to stamens, are borne on the uppermost, small spike. Female spike lowermost, darker brown, larger.

Leaves: Erect, linear, flat, usually taller than the spikes.

Habitat: Margins of ponds, ditches, and other wet areas.

Distribution: Throughout the state.

Flowering time: Spring, summer.

Comment: Plant gets to 9 ft. (3 m) tall. Rootstocks, young stems, and young flowers can be eaten cooked or raw.

Southern Cattail
Typha domingensis
Persoon

Family: Typhaceae (cattail).

Flowers: Male and female spikes usually separated by a space. Upper, smaller spike bears the male flowers; the lower, large spike bears the female flowers.

Leaves: Erect, linear, equalling or overtopping the spikes. Back surface of leaves weakly convex.

Habitat: Margins of ponds, ditches, and other wet areas.

Distribution: Throughout the state.

Flowering time: Spring, summer.

Comment: Spikes usually narrower than those of the common cattail. Plant gets to 9 ft. (3 m) tall.

Lopsided Indiangrass

Sorghastrum secundum
(Elliott) Nash

Family: Poaceae (grass).

Flowers: Seedhead of many spikelets in terminal, nodding panicles. Spikelets paired, golden-brown, unilaterally or 1-sided arranged. The needlelike awns are ⅝–1¾ in. (1.6–4.3 cm) long.

Leaves: Mostly low-growing, blades flat and elongated, blades and sheaths usually hairy.

Habitat: Pine flatwoods and sandhills.

Distribution: Throughout the state.

Flowering time: Summer, fall, early winter.

Comment: Stem to 3 ft. (1 m) tall or more, stiff, smooth.

Rayless Sunflower

Helianthus radula
(Pursh) Torrey and Gray

Family: Asteraceae (aster or daisy).

Flowers: Heads solitary, mainly of brownish-purplish disk florets. Ray florets short or absent.

Leaves: Hairy, rough. Basal leaves in rosettes. Stem leaves opposite, elliptic to ovate. Upper leaves reduced.

Habitat: Pinelands.

Distribution: Throughout the state.

Flowering time: Summer, fall.

Comment: Stem to 3 ft. (1 m) tall or more, hairy, rough, chiefly leafless.

Catesby's Lily or Pine Lily
Lilium catesbaei
Walter

Family: Liliaceae (lily).

Flowers: Perianth 6-parted, red to red-orange, bases yellow with purplish-brown dots. Flower solitary. Petals and sepals tapered; petals the widest.

Leaves: Alternate, erect, lanceolate. Leaves nearest flower the shortest.

Habitat: Moist pinelands and swamps.

Distribution: Throughout the state.

Flowering time: Summer, fall.

Comment: Stem leafy, to 20 in. (50 cm) tall or more. Species was named for the 18th-century English naturalist, Mark Catesby, who traveled in Florida.

Frost-flowered Neottia or Leafless Beaked Orchid
Sacoila lanceolata
(Aublet) Garay

Family: Orchidaceae (orchid).

Flowers: Perianth reddish (sometimes greenish-yellow). Lateral margins of lip hairy. Lip lanceolate, pale pinkish, not fringed, but pointed. Flowers in terminal spikes.

Leaves: Elliptic or lanceolate. Plant leafless at the time of flowering. Stem leaves scalelike; basal leaves well developed.

Habitat: Wet, pine flatwoods and sandhills.

Distribution: Central Florida.

Flowering time: Spring, summer.

Comment: Stem leafy, 3 ft. (1 m) tall or more. Terrestrial. Only species of genus in Florida. Synonyms: *Stenorrhynchus orchioides, S. lanceolatus,* and *Spiranthes orchioides.*

Butterfly Orchid
Encyclia tampensis
(Lindley) Small

Family: Orchidaceae (orchid).

Flowers: Perianth brownish-green. Lip 3-lobed, lobes erect, terminal lobe white with rose-colored center and lines. Flowers fragrant.

Leaves: Linear-elliptic, thickish.

Habitat: Swamps and wet hammocks.

Distribution: Central and south Florida.

Flowering time: Spring, summer, fall.

Comment: Plant grows on trees from round, bulblike stems. This orchid was first discovered near Tampa, hence the specific name.

Pteroglossapsis ecristata
(Fernald) Rolfe

Family: Orchidaceae (orchid).

Flowers: Flowers occur in a cluster (raceme) at the end of a long stalk. An elongated, narrow bract lies below and surpasses each flower. Lip deeply 3-lobed, light brown to deep purple, base saclike.

Leaves: Linear, grasslike, overlapping, clustered at the base.

Habitat: Dry, sandy sites and pinelands.

Distribution: Throughout the state.

Flowering time: Summer, fall.

Comment: Flower stalk arises at one side of the leaf-cluster. Stem with overlapping leaf-sheaths, smooth 3 ft. (1 m) tall. Terrestrial. Synonyms: *Eulophia ecristata* and *Triorchos ecristatus.*

Coralbean
Erythrina herbacea
L.

Family: Fabaceae (bean or pea).

Flowers: Corolla red, elongated, narrow. Flowers in elongated, terminal racemes. Calyx smooth or nearly so. Stamens 10 (9 united, 1 free). Pod black, 2¾–4 in. (7–10 cm) long, constricted between the seeds. Seeds red, poisonous.

Leaves: Alternate. Leaflets 3, thin, base flared, somewhat 3-lobed.

Habitat: Sandy soils of hammocks and thickets.

Distribution: Throughout the state.

Flowering time: Winter, spring, summer.

Comment: Flowers appear before the leaves. Plant prickly, gets to 3 ft. (1 m) tall or more and may become shrublike.

Hairy Indigo
Indigofera hirsuta
Harvey

Family: Fabaceae (bean or pea).

Flowers: Corolla pea-shaped, reddish. Flowers in axillary, long-stemmed, spikelike racemes. Lower petals (keel) with small, lateral pouches. Calyx 5-lobed, lobes narrow and hairy. Stamens 10 (9 united, 1 free), anther tips pointed. Pods hairy, 4-angled, clustered and pointed downward.

Leaves: Alternate, odd-pinnately compound. Leaflets 5–9, terminal one the largest, oblanceolate, hairy especially below.

Habitat: Disturbed areas.

Flowering time: All year.

Comment: Plant hairy, to 28 in. (70 cm) tall. Branches may be longer than the stem. Naturalized as a cover plant from Africa. Some indigo species were used in making dyes.

Groundnut

Apios americana
Medicus

Family: Fabaceae (bean or pea).

Flowers: Upper petal pale brownish, hooded. Lower and lateral petals reddish-brown. Lower petals (keel) strongly incurved. Flowers fragrant, in compact racemes. Calyx bell-shaped, with 4 short, upper teeth. Pod flattened, many-seeded.

Leaves: Alternate, pinnately compound. Leaflets 5–7, ovate or lanceolate.

Habitat: Wet thickets.

Distribution: Throughout the state.

Flowering time: Spring, summer, fall.

Comment: Vine herbaceous, climbing, nearly smooth. Tuberous enlargements on the roots are edible. Synonym: *Glycine apios.*

Macroptilium lathyroides
(L.) Urban

Family: Fabaceae (bean or pea).

Flowers: Corolla reddish-purple. Lateral petals (wings) the largest and most colorful. Lower petals (keel) coiled. Flowers axillary, long-stalked, in terminal racemes. Flowers open few at a time. Calyx 5-lobed, hairy, tube longer than the lobes. Stamens 10 (9 united, 1 free). Pod elongated, pointed, hairy.

Leaves: Alternate. Leaflets 3, linear-elliptic or ovate, 1½–2⅜ in. (4–6 cm) long, entire, smooth below or nearly so.

Habitat: Disturbed sites.

Distribution: Throughout the state.

Flowering time: All year.

Comment: Stem erect, branched above the base. Native to tropical America. Synonym: *Phaseolus lathyroides.*

Bladderpod

Sesbania vesicaria
(Jacquin) Elliott

Family: Fabaceae (bean or pea).

Flowers: Corolla pea-shaped, red, yellow or blackish, often spotted. Flowers in axillary racemes. Calyx funnel-shaped, bronze-colored, yellow-tipped. Stamens 10 (9 united, 1 free). Pod flattened, usually 1 or 2 seeded.

Leaves: Even-pinnately compound. Leaflets many, paired, elliptic or oblong, entire.

Habitat: Open, disturbed sites and moist thickets.

Distribution: Throughout the state.

Flowering time: Summer, fall.

Comment: Plant sparsely hairy, to 13 ft. (4 m) tall. Cattle have died from eating the poisonous seeds. Synonym: *Glottidium vesicarium.*

Purple Sesban

Sesbania punicea
(Cavanilles) Bentham

Family: Fabaceae (bean or pea).

Flowers: Corolla orange-red. Racemes 2–4 in. (5–10 cm) long. Calyx usually pigmented with red-purple. Stamens 10 (9 united, 1 free). Pod oblong, 4-winged; seeds separated by crosswalls.

Leaves: Alternate, even-pinnately compound. Leaflets 12–40, oblong to linear, entire, spine-tipped.

Habitat: Wet areas, vacant lots, and sandy soils.

Distribution: Central and north Florida.

Flowering time: Spring, summer, fall.

Comment: Shrub deciduous, to 9 ft. (3 m) tall, often cultivated as an ornamental. Native to South America. Synonym: *Daubentonia punicea.*

Bog Batchelor's Button
Polygala lutea
L.

Family: Polygalaceae (milkwort).

Flowers: Heads cloverlike, cylindrical or oblong, of many small, orange-yellow flowers. Flower heads usually solitary.

Leaves: Alternate, entire, spatulate to oblanceolate, somewhat fleshy, clustered at the base. Stem leaves reduced upward.

Habitat: Low grounds.

Distribution: Throughout the state.

Flowering time: All year.

Comment: Roots and lower stem have a wintergreen smell. Stem smooth, often clustered, low-growing. Synonym: *Pilostaxis lutea.*

Rosemary
Ceratiola ericoides
Michaux

Family: Empetraceae (crowberry).

Flowers: Petals absent. Male and female flowers separate, but on the same plant. Flowers minute, red-yellowish; petals 2, sessile, in leaf axils. Sepals 2, fringed, 1 mm long. Stamens 2. Fruit yellowish, small.

Leaves: Needlelike, evergreen.

Habitat: Dry, sandy soils, and sand pine scrub.

Distribution: Throughout the state.

Flowering time: Spring, summer, fall.

Comment: Woody shrub, bushy-branched, to 3 ft. (1 m) tall or more. Only species of its family in the southeast U.S.

Wax Mallow or Turk's-cap Mallow

Malvaviscus arboreus
Cavanilles

Family: Malvaceae (mallow).

Flowers: Petals 5, red. Flowers solitary, drooping, petals remaining close. Styles 10. Sepals 5, united. Bracts linear, 6–10. Stamens many, attached to the pistil.

Leaves: Alternate, elliptic to ovate, stalked, toothed, 3- to 5-lobed.

Habitat: Disturbed sites.

Distribution: Throughout the state.

Flowering time: All year.

Comment: Plant shrubby, to 6 ft. (2 m) tall or more. Often used for ornamental plantings.

Scarlet Hibiscus

Hibiscus coccineus
Walter

Family: Malvaceae (mallow).

Flowers: Petals 5, bright red. Flowers axillary, to 8 in. (20 cm) across. Stigmas 5. Bracts linear, entire, unforked. Calyx 5-lobed, green, cup-shaped. Capsules long as broad or longer, 5-celled, 2 or more seeds/cell.

Leaves: Alternate, palmately divided into 3–5 lobes, long-stalked, toothed, smooth, reddish-green.

Habitat: Swamps and wet areas.

Distribution: Throughout the state.

Flowering time: Spring, summer, fall.

Comment: Plant shrublike, to 3 ft. (1 m) tall or more. Synonym: *Hibiscus semilobatus.*

Ludwigia suffruticosa
Walter

Family: Onagraceae (evening-primrose).

Flowers: Petals lacking. Flowers small, sessile, yellow-green, in dense, terminal spikes that turn reddish. Sepals 4, broadly triangular. Capsule 4-sided.

Leaves: Alternate, smooth, short-stalked, lanceolate to elliptic. Lower leaves the larger.

Habitat: Wet areas.

Distribution: Throughout the state.

Flowering time: Spring, summer, fall.

Comment: Main stem branches alternate, smooth, to 3 ft. (1 m) tall.

Florida Flame Azalea or Orange Azalea
Rhododendron austrinum
(Small) Rehder

Family: Ericaceae (heath).

Flowers: Corolla 5-lobed, funnel-shaped, yellow and orange. Corolla tube on outside glandular and finely haired. Calyx 5-lobed, lobes ciliate. Stamens 5, elongated. Fruit a dry capsule.

Leaves: Alternate, oval, obovate to elliptic, stalked.

Habitat: Moist woods and along streams.

Distribution: Florida Panhandle.

Flowering time: Spring.

Comment: Woody bush to 9 ft. (3 m) tall, twigs hairy and usually glandular. Flowers appear before the leaves. Synonym: *Azalea austrina*.

Butterfly-weed
Asclepias tuberosa
L.

Family: Asclepiadaceae (milkweed).

Flowers: Corolla deeply lobed, petals 5, orange or yellowish. Corolla lobes reflexed. Flowers in terminal umbels. Stamens 5, attached to the stigma.

Leaves: Chiefly alternate, linear, elliptic to oblanceolate or arrowhead-shaped, hairy, sessile or nearly so.

Habitat: Pinelands and sandhills.

Distribution: Throughout the state.

Flowering time: Spring, summer, fall.

Comment: Stem leafy, hairy, to 32 in. (80 cm) tall, lying on or near the ground or erect. Sap not milky. An older name for this plant was pleurisy-root from its former medicinal use.

Asclepias lanceolata
Walter

Family: Asclepiadaceae (milkweed).

Flowers: Corolla deeply lobed, petals 5, red-orange to reddish-purple. Corolla lobes reflexed. Flowers in terminal umbels. Stamens 5, attached to the stigma.

Leaves: Opposite, few in number, linear to lanceolate, smooth petiole short.

Habitat: Wet meadows, swamps, and pinelands.

Distribution: Throughout the state.

Flowering time: Spring, summer, fall.

Comment: Stem smooth, slender, to 3 ft. (1 m) tall or more. Sap milky.

Scarlet Milkweed
Asclepias curassavica
L.

Family: Asclepiadaceae (milkweed).

Flowers: Corolla deeply lobed, petals 5, red-yellow to orangish. Flowers in terminal umbels. Stamens 5, attached to the stigma.

Leaves: Opposite, entire, stalked, nearly smooth, lanceolate to elliptic.

Habitat: Sandy, disturbed soils.

Distribution: Central and south Florida.

Flowering time: All year.

Comment: Stem slender, to 3 ft. (1 m) or more. Sap milky. Naturalized from tropical America.

Scarlet Morning-glory
Ipomoea hederifolia
L.

Family: Convolvulaceae (morning-glory).

Flowers: Corolla scarlet. Corolla tube long, narrow. Flowers solitary or clustered. Flower stalks long, hairy. Stamens and pistil extend beyond the flower tube. Style 1. Sepals 5, separate, overlapping, unequal. Stamens 5.

Leaves: Alternate, entire or toothed, heart-shaped, tips pointed.

Habitat: Thickets, fields, and other disturbed sites.

Distribution: Throughout the state.

Flowering time: Spring, summer, fall.

Comment: Vine smooth, twining. Synonyms: *Ipomoea coccinea* and *Quamoclit coccinea.*

Cypress-vine
Ipomoea quamoclit
L.

Family: Convolvulaceae (morning-glory).

Flowers: Corolla red or white. Corolla tube long, narrow. Flowers long-stalked. Style 1. Sepals 5, separate, overlapping. Stamens 5. Stamens and pistil extend beyond the flower tube.

Leaves: Alternate, dissected into linear segments, feathery.

Habitat: Disturbed sites.

Distribution: Central and north Florida.

Flowering time: Summer, fall, winter.

Comment: Stem twining, smooth. Native to Mexico. Synonym: *Quamoclit quamoclit*.

Standing Cypress or Spanish Larkspur
Ipomopsis rubra
(L.) Wherry

Family: Polemoniaceae (phlox).

Flowers: Corolla tubular, 5-lobed, bright red, whitish inside tube. Flowers in elongated panicles. Style 3-parted. Calyx 5-lobed, lobes lanceolate, hairy. Stamens 5, extending beyond the corolla lobes.

Leaves: Alternate, finely cut, somewhat ferny, succulent, reduced upward.

Habitat: Coastal dunes and dry pinelands

Distribution: Central and north Florida.

Flowering time: Summer, fall.

Comment: Stem leafy, hairy, to 3 ft. (1 m) tall. Synonym: *Gilia rubra*.

Calamintha coccinea
(Nuttall) Bentham

Family: Lamiaceae (mint).

Flowers: Corolla 2-lipped, tubular, red-orangish, over 1 in. (2.5 cm) long. Upper lip 2-lobed, lower lip 3-lobed. Flowers solitary or clustered in the upper leaf axils. Style 2-lobed. Calyx 2-lipped, reddish-tipped, lower lip 3-lobed. Stamens 4.

Leaves: Opposite, small, leathery, entire, evergreen.

Habitat: Dry, sandy soils.

Distribution: Central and north Florida.

Flowering time: All year.

Comment: Plant shrubby, stem loosely branched, base often woody, to 3 ft. (1 m) tall or more. Synonyms: *Clinopodium coccineum* and *C. macrocalyx.*

Tropical Sage
Salvia coccinea
Buchoz

Family: Lamiaceae (mint).

Flowers: Corolla 2-lipped, red. Lower lip bi-lobed. Flowers in terminal, elongated inflorescences. Style 2-branched. Calyx 2-lipped, hairy, glandular, upper lip entire, lower 2-toothed. Fertile stamens 2, arched upward.

Leaves: Opposite, toothed, stalked, ovate. Basal leaves absent.

Habitat: Disturbed sites and thickets.

Distribution: Throughout the state.

Flowering time: All year.

Comment: Stem branched, square, hairy, to 28 in. (70 cm) tall.

Lion's-ear
Leonotis nepetaefolia
(L.) R. Brown

Family: Lamiaceae (mint).

Flowers: Corolla red-orange and purplish, 2-lipped, hairy. Flowers in dense, globular heads that encircle the stem. Style 2-branched. Inflorescence leafless. Calyx hairy, lobes bristle-tipped. Stamens 4, extending beyond the flower.

Leaves: Opposite, stalked, toothed, ovate.

Habitat: Disturbed sites.

Distribution: Throughout the state.

Flowering time: Summer, fall.

Comment: Stem square, branched, hairy, to 3 ft. (1 m) tall or more. Native to tropical America.

Trumpet-vine
Campsis radicans
(L.) Seemann

Family: Bignoniaceae (bignonia).

Flowers: Corolla trumpet-shaped, 5-lobed, red-orange outside, yellowish inside. Calyx 5-lobed, lobes lanceolate. Stamens 4. Fruit an elongated capsule with winged seeds.

Leaves: Opposite, compound; leaflets over 7 in number, ovate, toothed.

Habitat: Moist thickets and woods.

Distribution: Central and north Florida.

Flowering time: All year.

Comment: Vine woody, climbing by aerial roots. Synonym: *Bignonia radicans*.

Coral Honeysuckle or Trumpet Honeysuckle
Lonicera sempervirens
L.

Family: Caprifoliaceae (honeysuckle).

Flowers: Corolla trumpet-shaped, bright red, 5-lobed, lobes shorter than the tube. Flowers usually in sessile whorls. Calyx very small. Stamens 5.

Leaves: Opposite, green above, white below, elliptic, ovate to oblong, entire, smooth or nearly so, sessile or stalked.

Habitat: Thickets.

Distribution: Central and north Florida.

Flowering time: Spring, summer.

Comment: Vinelike shrub. Stem trailing or climbing, smooth.

Cardinal Flower
Lobelia cardinalis
L.

Family: Campanulaceae (bluebell or harebell).

Flowers: Corolla 2-lipped, 5-lobed; 2 upper lobes and 3 lower lobes. Flowers bright red, in terminal, spikelike racemes. Calyx 5-lobed; lobes linear, hairy, entire. Stamens 5, united around the style.

Leaves: Alternate, toothed, stalked, elliptic to lanceolate, reduced upward.

Habitat: Margins of streams and ditches.

Distribution: Central and north Florida.

Flowering time: Summer, fall.

Comment: Stem to 9 ft. (3 m) tall or more.

Tasselflower or Cupid's Shavingbrush
Emilia fosbergii
Nicols

Family: Asteraceae (aster or daisy).

Flowers: Heads of cylindrical, red to pink, disk florets. Ray florets lacking. Heads stalked, terminal, drooping. Bracts linear, equal, sparsely haired, tips pointed.

Leaves: Alternate, mainly low on the stem, lanceolate, clasping; surfaces sparsely haired.

Habitat: Disturbed sites.

Distribution: Central Florida.

Flowering time: All year.

Comment: Lower stem hairy, upper smooth, to 32 in. (80 cm) tall.

Blanket Flower
Gaillardia pulchella
Fougeroux de Bondaroy

Family: Asteraceae (aster or daisy).

Flowers: Heads large, terminal. Ray florets usually reddish-purple, tips yellow, lobed, hairy below. Disk florets reddish-purple. Bracts overlapping, lanceolate, margins ciliate, reflexed.

Leaves: Alternate, narrow, lanceolate to oblanceolate, hairy. Lower leaves toothed, stalked. Upper leaves sessile, entire.

Habitat: Disturbed sites and beaches.

Distribution: Throughout the state.

Flowering time: All year.

Comment: Stem ribbed, branching at the base, hairy, to 24 in. (60 cm) tall.

◆ INDEX ◆